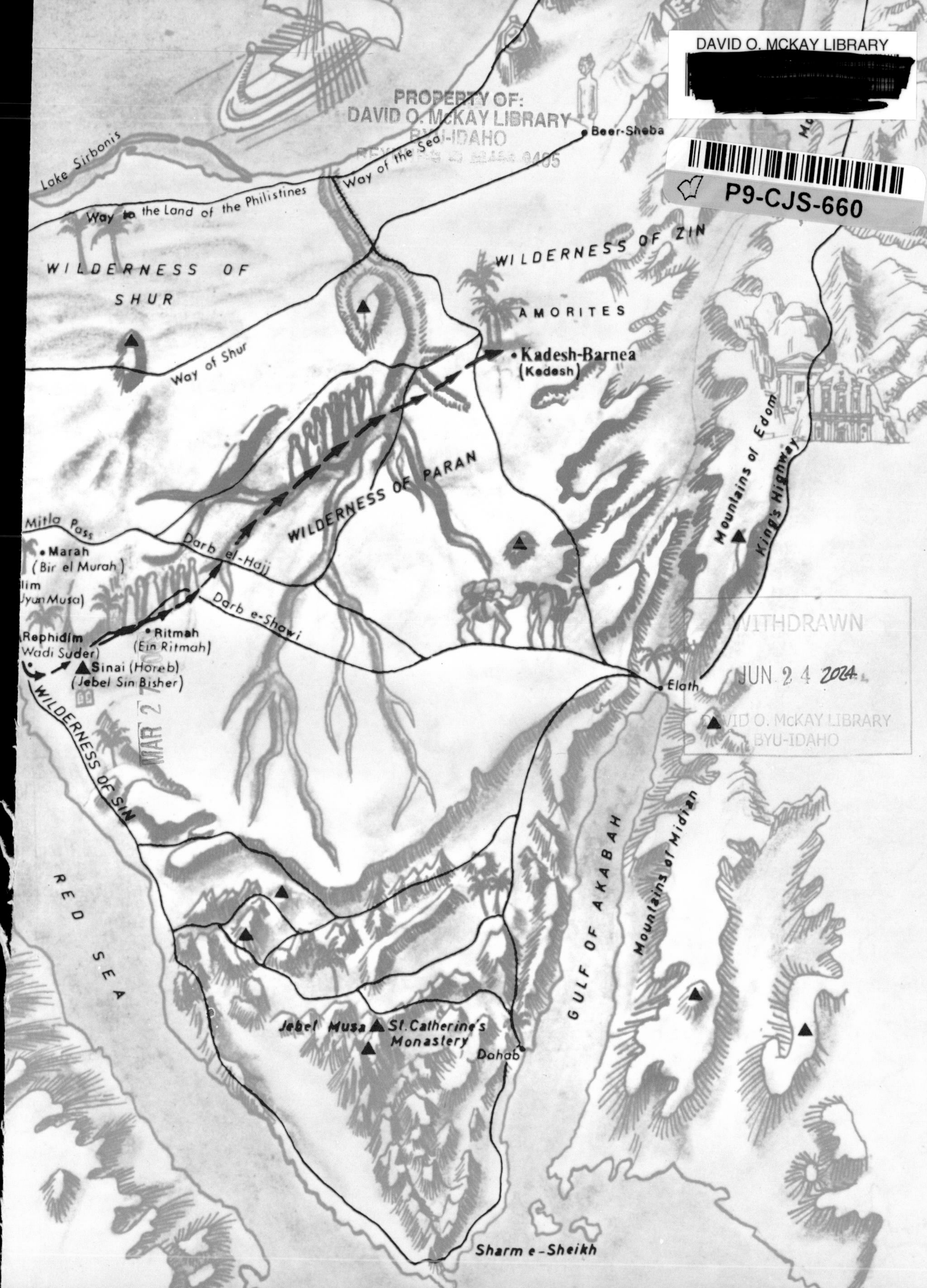
Lake Sirbonis
Way to the Land of the Philistines
Way of the Sea
Beer-Sheba
WILDERNESS OF SHUR
Way of Shur
WILDERNESS OF ZIN
AMORITES
Kadesh-Barnea
(Kedesh)
WILDERNESS OF PARAN
Mitla Pass
Marah
(Bir el Murah)
lim
Uyun Musa)
Darb el-Hajj
Darb e-Shawi
Rephidim
Wadi Suder)
Ritmah
(Ein Ritmah)
Sinai (Horeb)
(Jebel Sin Bisher)
WILDERNESS OF SIN
Mountains of Edom
King's Highway
Elath
RED SEA
GULF OF AKABAH
Mountains of Midian
Jebel Musa
St. Catherine's Monastery
Dahab
Sharm e-Sheikh

A FEAST OF HISTORY

opposite 'The Egyptians pursued them, all Pharaoh's horses and chariots and his horsemen and his army' (*Ex.* IX, 14). An earlier Pharaoh in pursuit of his enemies. Detail of a decorative chest from the Tomb of Tutankhamen (1347–1338 BCE)
overleaf Fragments of a Dead Sea Scroll of Exodus VI–VII describing Moses' struggle with Pharaoh. Dated *ca.* 200–175 BCE, it is written in deliberate imitation of the archaic script used by the Hebrews before the Babylonian exile (586 BCE)

A FEAST OF HISTORY

The drama of Passover through the ages

with a new translation of the Haggadah for use at the Seder

Chaim Raphael

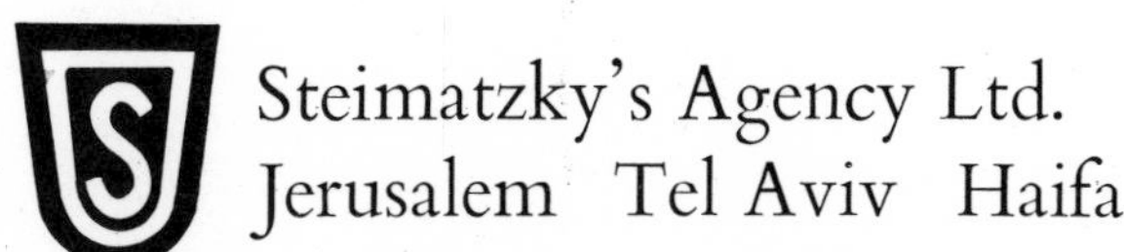

Steimatzky's Agency Ltd.
Jerusalem Tel Aviv Haifa

First published in 1972 by Weidenfeld and Nicolson
Reprinted 1978

Designed by Alex Berlyne
Picture research and selection by Irène Lewitt
Photographs by David Harris

Printed in Great Britain by
Cox & Wyman Ltd,
London, Fakenham and Reading

Contents

1	The Haggadah and Our Times	11
2	The Origins of Passover	35
3	The Development of the Haggadah	67
4	A Seder Roll-call	115
	The Exodus Route	156
	Further Reading	157

One of the most engaging inscriptions from Bible times, carved in the rock wall of Hezekiah's Tunnel towards the end of the eighth century BCE, describes with pride how water was brought into Jerusalem from a spring outside the city. The quarrymen hewed the rock from each end, meeting in the middle:

'And when the tunnel was driven through . . . the water flowed from the spring towards the reservoir . . . '

This book also starts from its two ends: at the Hebrew end, the text of the Passover Haggadah with a new translation; at this end, a discussion of the history and memories that have clustered around these ceremonies for thousands of years.

The two books meet in the middle; and perhaps in this way the meaning will flow, as in Hezekiah's tunnel, from the spring to the reservoir.

ACKNOWLEDGMENTS

The idea for a book that would unfold the Haggadah historically and pictorially, as attempted here, came originally from John Curtis of Weidenfeld and Nicolson, London, and he nursed it to completion with unflagging enthusiasm. The author is profoundly grateful also to Mrs. Irène Lewitt for a display of sheer virtuosity in producing the wealth of illustrations; to Alex Berlyne for his immense skill and imagination in designing the book; and to Asher Weill, Ina Friedman and other members of the staff of Weidenfeld and Nicolson Jerusalem, whose contributions to the book were so important. The teamwork of all these kind and skilful people was a source of great pleasure to the author.

The author and publishers wish to express their gratitude to the following institutions and individuals for their help in providing the illustrations—particularly to the Israel Museum, Jerusalem, for the use of their premises, archives and collections; the Encyclopaedia Judaica for the use of archives; the Museum of the Chief Rabbinate, Hechal Shlomo, Jerusalem, Museum Ha'aretz, Tel Aviv, Rabbi S. Pappenheim, Michael Kaniel and Mr. G. Cornfeld for the use of archives and collections; and those who loaned objects for the Seder table; Cairo Museum, 3, 39; Jewish Museum, Prague, 13 (bottom); Louvre, 15, 48, 88, 123; Dr. A. Kanof, 20; Yad Vashem, Jerusalem, 29; Staalichen Museum, Berlin, 36 (left); British Museum, 36 (right), 45, 104, 107, 126, 136, 221, 227; Schimmel Collection, N. Y., 37; Dr. Roman Vishniac, 41; Jewish Museum, London, 44 (top), 74, 241; Aleppo Museum, 47; Israel Department of Antiquities, 50, 51 (top), 224; James de Rothschild, Hazor Expedition, 51; Goldberg Collection, London, 54; Mr. and Mrs. Joseph Ternbach Collection, N. Y., 57 (right); Hebrew Union College, Cincinnati, 66; Teddy Kollek, 72; Martin von Wagner Museum der Universität Würzburg, 78–9; Hessische Landes und Hochschulbibliothek Darmstadt, 83, 254; Church of St. Pierre, Louvain, 84; National Museum, Naples, 87; National and University Library, Jerusalem, 101; Bibliothèque Nationale, Paris, 103; National Museum, Belgrade, 107; Rijksmuseum, Amsterdam, 119; Johnson Collection, Philadelphia, 125; Brooklyn Museum, N. Y., 126; Shraga Weill, Sifriyat Poalim, 155; Daniel Doron, 172; Armenian Patriarchate, Jerusalem, 178; Maritime Museum, Haifa, 216–7; Sassoon Collection, 218; Sidney J. Lamon Collection, 222; Jewish Theological Seminary, N.Y., 228; Mocatta Library, London, 253; Schocken Library, Jerusalem, 138–40.

We are deeply indebted to Mr. David Harris for photographing most of the pictures in this book, and grateful acknowledgement is made to Meyer Levin for the use of ideas developed for his *Israel Haggadah* and to the following photographer: Hirmer Archive, 3, 38 (right), 39, 88; Tournus, 9; E. Pollitzer, 20; Photo-Emka, 32; Rolf Kneller, 33; Dr. Georg Gerster, 34; Hillel Burger, 37, 48, 50, 61, 91, 112, 140; Ze'ev Radovan, 38 (left), 122; Elly Beintema, 44 (top), 74, 241; Reuven Milon, 49, 107, 108; David Perlmutter, 58–9; David Rubinger, 63, 71; Scala, 64, 124; Skira, 84; Ronald Sheridan, 75, 135; Yale University, 100; Chanan Sadeh, 216–7; Michael Holford, 227. Micha Noy was kind enough to arrange the food for the Seder Table and M. Gabrieli drew the endpapers map.

opposite Building workers in Egypt during the 18th Dynasty (*ca.* 15th century BCE), approximately the time of the slavery of the Hebrews. Detail of a mural from a Tomb of the Nobles at Thebes

1 The Haggadah and Our Times

The Night that is Different

'Haggadah' means, literally, a recital. The Bible says that we should tell (*hagged*) our children the story of the ancient Exodus from Egypt. The Haggadah is, then, the tale that is told at the annual feast—Passover—which celebrates this deliverance.

The word '*haggadah*' is also used in Jewish literature to describe the free-wheeling exposition of scripture by the rabbis, in a style which can include ethics, history, folklore or anecdote, hair-splitting logic or mystical rumination, and indeed any kind of speculation, serious or light hearted, which can be spun out of the verses of Holy Writ. The recital of the Exodus, as we sit round the table at Passover, is presented in this style, ranging far and wide over Jewish history and feeling.

The name 'Seder', which we apply to this gathering round the table on the first night (or first two nights) of Passover means, literally, 'programme', which indicates that the ceremonies accompanying the recital are carefully prescribed. The central feature is a festive meal, around which the recital and ceremonies take place. The Haggadah covers all these activities.

On the surface, then, the Passover Haggadah is merely the libretto for the Seder, but it is, in fact, a book compounded of magic. *Why is this night different?* We know the answers in advance: we were slaves in Egypt, and God set us free; but we await the Seder each year, with mounting excitement as the night comes nearer, to hear history speak again. Ancient as the words of the Haggadah are, we know that we shall hear in them something which has been prepared for us alone. In one sense, time stands still: the ritual of the Seder is set out and followed as it has been, in essentials, for nearly two thousand years. But in another sense, the words have always been charged with fresh meaning for each generation by the situation and drama of the times. And if this

opposite A Yemenite Seder in Israel with the father answering the son's questions. The celebrants are wearing their traditional festive clothes, the men in white '*kittels*' has been true throughout history, how infinitely more personal is the message of the Haggadah for our own times, where the stories it contains—of slavery, exodus, the battles with Egypt, and the triumphs of settlement in the ancestral land—are re-enacted daily before our own eyes.

The Haggadah, with its prayers and songs, can be printed as a small book; but no generation has been content merely to take the ritual words and leave it at that. Artists and writers have reached out beyond the words to try and capture the mysterious associations of the Seder—the dangers, joys, fears, and hopes—that have reverberated throughout Jewish history. In every century the Haggadah has been presented afresh with endless commentary, and with illustrations ranging from the primitive to the most lavish and beautiful. We feel the same need today; yet if we set out in this book to produce a Haggadah for our times, we are impelled to go far beyond the usual commentaries and illustrations.

The reason—obvious enough—is that we are living in an age which has been witness to a revolution in Jewish history and consciousness. The tragedies of our time have shaken Jewish existence to its roots: the achievements have opened up entirely new concepts of what it means to be a Jew. The past has been revealed, through the discoveries of archaeology and epigraphy, in ways that could not have been dreamed of in years gone by; the present is full of a drama that is continuous and compelling. Every element of this excitement finds links and echoes in the Haggadah.

The purpose of this book is to explore and communicate this fresh vision, with an English text in the language of our time, and illustrations that range over the whole of our history. The ancient Haggadah, looked at through the knowledge and experience of our times, becomes the living Haggadah of our own day, an unfinished story, ranging far and wide, in which we, and not only our ancestors, are the protagonists.

Yet if the range of a book that spells out the living Haggadah is boundless, at its heart are the stories and ceremonies which still speak directly to us with all their old simplicity and power. The marvel of Jewish re-birth in our times is that if new dimensions of experience have been added, nothing sacred to the tradition has been taken away. The ancient Haggadah is a supreme example, not only because of the religious faith it enshrines, but through the way it has grown up, in the course of history, to express the character of Jewish life. It emerges each year encrusted with the charm of an ancient ritual, archaic and often bewildering, but much loved, nonetheless, for the memories it evokes of a dream childhood when the world was young. If the Seder ceremonies seem a curious mixture of disparate elements—prayers, questions, Bible readings, affirmations, jokes and songs—this is itself part of the charm. The Haggadah, bringing all this together within the bounds of a single book, expresses what many people feel is a uniquely Jewish attitude to life—a high seriousness that can break into a smile, a reverence that doesn't have to be pompous, a sense of tragedy that never leads to cynicism and despair, a kinship with suffering that transforms itself constantly through courage and hope. Pervasive, too, in a book as old and unchanging as this, is the unbreakable bond of the Jews with history. The Seder is the most universally observed and therefore the most unifying of all Jewish ceremonies. In millions of Jewish homes, the same observance brings Jews together not only with their contemporaries all over the world, but with countless generations of the past. Tradition has turned the Seder into a rock of memory.

We accept, we enjoy nostalgia; but only up to a point. We cannot simply live in the past; and the Haggadah, leading us on to think about our history, makes us aware also, as nothing else can, of the transformation that has come into our lives. For those of us who have lived through the dramas of the last decades, the most powerful feeling emerging from the Haggadah is not that we are following mutely in the steps of our ancestors but that a revolution and a miracle has transformed this kinship.

In the background of this transformation stands the greatest tragedy of our history—surely the most absolutely depraved wickedness in all human history: the deliberate murder of millions —old and young—through Hitler's Germany. Persecution did not start there, nor has it ended since; but the impact of that one period has been decisive for history as nothing else ever could be. From now on, the world has to live with a memory that must root out, for civilized people, any casual acceptance, as in past centuries, that the persecution of Jews, cropping up here and there repeatedly, is so normal that it need not be taken too seriously. The path on which this moves forward has been marked out for all to see.

For Jews themselves, of course, the Holocaust is even more decisive in its impact. No Jew, conscious of history, can sit back any longer and accept what was so often proferred by the rest of the world in the past—a grudging and mixed tolerance—as the price-tag on his race and faith. If we are kin with our ancestors in so many things, we have broken through on this: our watchword is no longer toleration. Whether we are orthodox or free-thinking

above A *moshav* (smallholders' settlement) in Galilee, with Mount Hermon shown in background
below A story never to be forgotten. Detail of the memorial wall in Prague showing names of Holocaust victims

in religion, whether we live in Israel or elsewhere, whether we are inward- or outward-looking in our intellectual and social interests, our freedom as human beings depends henceforth on the character of our pride. We know all too well now that in giving way to evil, it is the first backward step that counts—the first expression of timidity or compromise. In this field, the strongest weapon has to be the will to live, rooted in the self-knowledge that banishes the debility of self-hate.

The transformation is at its clearest in the concept of Israel, where the courage of those who have fought for it and built it up has spread a benediction on all who spring from the same stock. The drama of Israel's re-birth has not merely up-dated, in a fascinating way, so many references in the Haggadah to the ancient land: it has added a new layer of meaning with which we must live. It challenges us, in effect, to deal with reality instead of living with a dream—and this is not always easy.

For almost two thousand years the joy of the Seder evening was, in one sense, unreal—a gathering of often well-settled exiles, a self-satisfying indulgence in psalms, songs and memories endowed with the romantic colouring of dreams. The Jews of an apparently unending Diaspora were at home with this dreaming; they were adjusted to it.

Suddenly this prop of *Galut* sentiment has been knocked away. Israel is re-born; Jerusalem is restored; every Jew can, if he wishes, end his exile. What happens now to the prayers at the Seder? The meaning changes, but far from sounding archaic and outworn, they seem to take on, for the first time, a healthy kind of actuality. Sitting at the Seder table, we know now that we cannot simply go on waiting for the Messiah. The miracle we prayed for has, in some sense, happened. The challenge of the present adds a new dimension to the poetry of the past.

We get this clearly in the vision we now have of Jerusalem. The Haggadah is full of nostalgia: 'and build Jerusalem, Thy holy city, speedily in our days'. We still dream, but the picture that appears is something from our own direct experience. Many of us have now been there. Where once we looked at a crude woodcut in our Haggadah, giving us an imaginary reconstruction of Solomon's Temple, we see now in our mind's eye the golden stone of that eternal city glowing in the sun; we think of the soldiers who won it back—the tears of joy as the *shofar* sounded again at the Western Wall. There are the crowds in the streets on Shabbat evening, the markets and the supermarkets, the chirpy benevolence of the Mayor, the antique echoes of Mea Shearim. To see the word

'Jerusalem' now in the Haggadah brings endless overtones that were unknown to our ancestors.

Something similar is true of all the other references to the past that crowd the pages of the Haggadah. Egypt is not simply the legendary enemy of the old story, re-living the role so tragically today. The Bible story of Egypt, echoing through the Haggadah, comes to us now documented by their own discoveries of their ancient past: what was once our private memory of an involvement with them is immensely broadened. In the same way, the background of all the peoples—Amorites, Moabites, Hittites, Horites, and of course the familiar Philistines and many others with whom the Hebrews dealt constantly in the Old Testament—has been illuminated by discoveries which greatly increase the understanding of our own past. Biblical stories of the patriarchs are paralleled with names, laws, customs and trading conditions in tablets unearthed at ancient cities in their area of origin—Nuzi (excavated in 1925) and Mari (in 1933). The Psalms, which are drawn on so heavily in the Haggadah, convey their poetry and meaning directly; but we see also, from the Ugarit epics (unearthed at Ras Shamra from 1929), how archaic biblical poetry drew on the same language and metaphors and then transformed them. We have a new picture, also, of the rabbis who first structured the Haggadah and are quoted in it so often. They speak to us not only through their writings but through the physical recovery of actual documents of their time. The Dead Sea Scrolls throw light on the world in which Hillel moved, in the last years of the Temple. For the period of Rabbi Akiva, about one hundred years later, we now have the letters of Bar Kokhba, unearthed in the Judaean caves. Not only do they bring the rebel leader to life: they are part of much wider discoveries from that age, reflected so clearly in the rabbinic talk we hear at the Seder.

A Hittite bas-relief from Carchemish (Syria) from the period of King David's reign (*ca.* the beginning of the 1st millenium BCE) showing a mother holding a child on her knees

The new elements in our interpretation of the past do not derive solely from the discoveries of archaeology. The ancient *midrash* (commentary) is reinforced, if we listen, through many pre-echoes of the developments of our time. How interesting it is, from this angle, that the Haggadah talks in one place of the Syrian enemy (Laban) as being more dangerous to the Jews than even the Egyptians—'for Pharaoh decreed death only for the males, while Laban sought to destroy all'. One scholar argues (see page 130) that this *midrash* about Syria must have been composed as early as the third century BCE during the long struggle for control of Palestine between Egypt (the Ptolemies) and Syria (the Seleucids). The Jews felt at the time that the Ptolemies, difficult as they might be, were more tolerant than the fanatical Hellenists of Syria; and so it proved to be a century later, when Antiochus IV of Syria tried to crush the Jewish religion at the time of the Maccabees. Today there are some who might still see Egypt, for all its aggressiveness, as less wicked than the Syrians, whose favourite practice, when they held the Golan Heights, was to rain down shells indiscriminately on the men, women and children of the Jewish settlements below, 'seeking to destroy all'.

Another midrashic pre-echo from the past—a wheel coming full circle—takes us to a small town near Tel Aviv called B'nei B'rak. The Haggadah tells us about a group of distinguished rabbis, including Rabbi Akiva, who were celebrating a Seder there (it must have been around 130 CE) and were so absorbed in discussing the liberation from Egypt that they carried on all through the night and were still at it when their pupils arrived next day for the morning service. B'nei B'rak in Israel today is the centre of an orthodox community, where the rabbinic discussion, we may be sure, is as unbounded as in the past. But is the talk at the Seder solely about the ancient problems? A modern commentator on the Haggadah suggests that when we are told that the old rabbis were talking endlessly about 'the liberation from Egypt', this may be a cryptic reference to their *real* topic—how to secure 'liberation from Rome', which was the burning issue at the time of Akiva. Can we not assume that in modern B'nei B'rak, too, the late-night talk ultimately gets round to the burning subject of contemporary politics? To our own generation, as to Rabbi Akiva's, the biblical story of the struggle for freedom must always carry overtones for the Haggadah of our times.

What is a Jew?

It begins to seem as if one might say of the Haggadah what one of Hillel's disciples (delightfully named Ben Bag-Bag) said of the Bible: 'Turn it over and turn it over again, for everything is in it.' Certainly, as a starting point, the Haggadah can lead a discussion anywhere; and indeed we are told explicitly by the Haggadah itself that the more we can unfold its central theme—the more free-wheeling the discussion—the more we are to be praised.

Fair enough: the challenge is accepted. We hope to range far and wide in this book with comments and illustrations that will stimulate the talk. Nor do we see our aim limited to the Seder night. A book that draws on Jewish experience and history in terms of the age in which we live should have something to offer for any day of the year.

The main purpose will be to see what the scholars can tell us

Unfolding the meaning of the Torah has absorbed Jews continuously, as in the Haggadah story of the all-night talk at B'nei B'rak. A Talmud study group in Jerusalem

about our ancient writings and ceremonies and their historical connections with the Seder. But before we do this we need to consider in this introductory chapter what we can tell ourselves: what are the personal implications of the celebration, impinging on us not through scholarship but through our feeling as Jews? The Haggadah comes to us as a living echo of history. If we feel, as Jews, that history has dealt with us in a special way, we are brought face to face through the Haggadah with the most relentless of all questions: what is the meaning of the Jewish role in history? Put even more simply: what is a Jew?

This is not the place for a technical answer. What we are concerned with here, thinking of the Haggadah, is not to bring someone in or put someone out on 'legal' grounds, but to try to attach some kind of broad meaning to the feeling of being a Jew, linked, perhaps, to the centuries of experience which have led to our sitting round the Seder table year by year.

Any of our ancient ceremonies can stimulate this kind of speculation. The Seder has a unique quality, however, in that it is a ceremony which brings together—and always has throughout history—all kinds of people of Jewish origin, no matter what weight they normally attach to this in terms of belief, practice, political philosophy, social interests or family loyalties. Among our profusion of sceptical Jews (familiar in our literature as *epikorsim* or Epicureans), there are not many who will refuse to attend the Seder 'on principle'—as they might other Jewish observances. On the surface, nothing is committed by attendance. The whole thing is 'rather charming'. It takes one back to childhood. It can be enjoyed without pain. Implicitly, however, there is an unseen meaning to be drawn out.

The history of the Jews in the Diaspora has been the story of a hard core persisting, with an unchanging outlook, side by side with an unending flow of others into various forms of assimilation with the non-Jewish world around them. To Jews themselves, and to the outside world, the Jewish 'character' persists through all these shades of colour. The Seder is one occasion—the recital of the *Kaddish* (prayer for the dead) is another—where the persistence of a Jewish sense of communion clearly springs from the willing participation of all types of Jews in something unchanging. Mostly, the mass of Jews is not caught up willingly in rigid observance, or even in firm theological beliefs. Yet the sense of communion between the 'unbending' and the 'permissive' seems to renew itself, somehow, in every generation. It could not happen, one feels, unless the 'unbending' views were reborn continuously to be the axis around which the 'permissive' could turn, or 'spin off'.

It would be an easy conclusion from this that the ultimate values of Jewish existence lie exclusively in the unchanging rock at the centre, and some, of course, hold this view. The difficulty is, however, that Jews in a less clear-cut position seem equally to have something special to contribute. The orthodox tradition—self-supporting and self-satisfying—is easier, of course, to identify; but the less rooted Jews are not necessarily negative in their approach to their origin. They seem to draw from it more than an occasional indulgence in the nostalgia of family feeling.

Can we identify what it is that they draw? At one level, it seems that they are impelled by the tradition—even when they spin away from it in some respects—into a powerful humanism. In every generation, a proportion of young Jews, starting from the rigid background of the older generation, has turned itself towards the fullest exploitation of the potentialities of man rather than of the particular tribe into which it was born. Out of this has come a story—repeating itself in every century and every culture—of first a slow and then a full and fruitful participation of Jews (using this term broadly) in the secular activities of their time. The whole world, in its civilized moments, pays tribute to the special gifts that these 'emerging' Jews have constantly deployed for the benefit of mankind as a whole—in science and the arts, in social welfare, in political thought, in business, communication and entertainment, and indeed in everything which affects man's well-being. It is not simply that some Jews, as individuals, have played a useful role in society; it is as if there was something specially 'Jewish' in the passion they brought to their search, the daring and imagination which led them into fresh fields, the restlessness which made them push forward tirelessly, as if activity, ambition and exploration were absolutes not to be denied. Yet this barrier-breaking energy and driving universalism are linked—if they are, in fact, Jewish—to a tradition and faith which, on the surface, is exactly the opposite, clinging apparently to beliefs which are ancient and unchanging, and expressing them in a rigid social and intellectual separatism.

It is a paradox which takes us back to history for its resolution—which is why the Seder, so deeply concerned with our history, is a good occasion for considering it. Some may be content to explain the power of 'liberation' in each generation as nothing more than a reaction to the 'confinement' of the tradition; but this is quite inadequate. Certainly young Jews, bottled up in one or another kind of ghetto, grasped eagerly at 'freedom' when allowed out into the world at large; but this explanation covers only part of the ground. For one thing, many Jews deeply committed to a 'narrow' orthodoxy have at the same time made a full contribution to the secular 'progress' of the world at large in all the fields listed above. For another, the so-called 'liberated' Jews have not merely thrown themselves into non-Jewish culture. They have—perhaps unconsciously sometimes—reached back for their humanism into the ancient sources. To understand, then, what being a Jew means, one has to try to derive some meaning from Jewish history itself.

The one inescapable element in Jewish history as a whole is the sense of continuity which has persisted now for nearly four thousand years. One can marvel at this merely for its own sake; but it becomes more significant when one recognizes that this continued existence is, in fact, coterminous with the major part of the history of western civilization. Toynbee's claim that the Jew became a 'fossil' after the days of the Prophets (sixth century BCE) is, of course, ludicrous; but it is equally misleading to believe, as many do, that in terms of western civilization the Jew has been the eternal 'outsider'. In one sense, he is an outsider; in another sense, he has not merely existed throughout western history, but has been, for three thousand years at least, a continuous element in most aspects of its spiritual development. His history is, in fact, to be understood only in terms of the spiritual history of western man. To be everywhere—to be

Cover of a mimeographed Haggadah prepared by American soldiers serving in Korea

at one level unchanging and, at another, completely flexible and adaptive—is bizarre, unique and mysterious. We can record and analyze it in man's terms, but no one should be surprised if some are more satisfied to relinquish rational analysis and turn for an explanation to some unfathomable divine purpose. The Jews themselves have been in the forefront both of those who clung to and those who shied away from the divine hypothesis.

At the centre of the Jewish tradition, expressed in myriad forms, is a respect for the sanctity of life. History is not a pattern of straight development, with a basic idea of this kind receiving a stronger expression in every century, leading to the emergence of the perfect society. It is not even a story of cycles—or of ups and downs in the human condition. Each century makes its own amalgam, full of aspirations and contradictions that refuse to fall into shape. For the individual, too, there is no single outlook: on the one hand, the bounds of existence are the confines of an individual life, fulfilled in the immediate circumstances of family affections and local loyalties; on the other, he is part of the unfolding picture of human existence as a whole. We are all, therefore, both conditioned by our immediate period and timeless; attached to one spot and sharing in the development of man everywhere. The Jews have expressed this perfectly in their infinite adaptiveness throughout history.

The Seder is certainly a symbol of this. Even if the form has always been basically the same everywhere, it is fascinating to think of the variety of social conditions in which it has been celebrated throughout the centuries—in the Roman Palestine of Rabbi Akiva's day, in the Moslem background of tenth-century Spain, at a princely Jewish home in sixteenth-century Turkey, in a humble cottage in nineteenth-century Russia or at a frontier post in Israel today. If, in many cases, the Jews at Passover, with danger around them, were girded for travel like the original Israelites in Egypt, the overwhelming majority, sitting at their tables, had come to terms with the lands in which they lived. In this sense, even outside modern Israel, the celebrant has always been not a wandering Jew but a settled Jew, not an outsider but a native.

Yet this ability to adapt is not the only element in the story, or even the most important one. Behind it is the underlying unity of western life which makes adaptibility possible. It is quite wrong to look on western history as if it were a patchwork of independent, self-contained cultures and governments, with no movement, interaction or transcendent homogeneity. The true picture is that the whole of man's history is a shifting balance between separateness and intercommunion, whether we

Souvenir photograph of a Seder given in 1915 in Franzenbad, for wounded Austrian-Jewish soldiers

are dealing with individuals or nations. The Jew is, in many ways, the symbol and the agent of it.

It is along these lines that our living Haggadah, which is so exclusively Jewish in one sense, merges meaningfully into the living 'Haggadah' of all western man. To think of the Jew this way does not mean that he is a bifurcated being—a Hebrew inside with a thin (or thick) non-Jewish wrapping. The 'inner Jew' is himself, so to speak, part of the wrapping; the wrapping is itself partly Jewish. Western man, as he has developed over the last three thousand years, carries within him a Jewish inheritance as surely as he does a Greek and Roman one. The difference is that whereas the major influence from the classical world is something which springs from one finite period, even if it is perennially strong and flexible in its effects, the influence from Jews has reflected both its source and its continued refreshment. At the source, stretching back to Abraham, Moses and the Prophets, is a recognition of the wonder of life, the God-given power of reason, and an awareness of the moral imperative. Re-living these ideas in the language of different centuries has never been for the Jew something exclusively inward looking. At every stage he has given, borrowed, learnt, adapted to the result and given out afresh in a never-ending process. He is, so to speak, both multiplier and multiplicand. It could never have happened without the wandering, or without the settlement.

To try and list the elements in the Jewish contribution to civi-

lization is as meaningful—or meaningless—as it would be to analyze the contribution of civilization to the Jews. The Jews *are* civilization, not for what they practice separately with all the passionate affections of family tradition, but for what they share, as a founding element in western life, with the whole of the western world.

Every nation has been engaged—Toynbee is right, here—in a constant challenge and response to its history and environment, giving and receiving, and, from time to time, flourishing with a peculiarly communicative power, as in fifth-century Athens or seventeenth-century England. One people—the Jews—by living in so many countries, have had the chance to respond (in a most un-fossil-like manner) to myriad stimuli. Something in their make-up and circumstances gave them—or, more correctly, quite a few of them—opportunities to make considerable and often quite idiosyncratic responses; but the end result is viewed best as a testimony, not so much to the Jews as to the power—or character—of western civilization itself.

Moments of Truth – Old and New

The Haggadah draws us into history in this way not only by the prayers and songs it contains, but through an evocation of the millions of Jews who have sat around the Seder table in countless generations, in infinitely varied circumstances, reciting these same words. But if the roll-call of our ancestors and contemporaries echoes, as it must, the story of man in all his manifold and colourful variety, the ceremony itself, geared to a 'family' recital of our relationship with each other and with 'the God of our fathers', takes us finally back into our personal story. Prayers and memories flowing for thousands of years speak to us, at the Seder table, in terms of Jewish existence at this precise moment of history. We re-live the story of the Exodus as applying to ourselves: we have all come out of 'Egypt'—out of Russia, out of Germany, out of the desperate crises that threatened the newly re-born Israel. We share imaginatively some of the feelings of this kind that must have filled the minds of earlier generations, some turning to the words of the Haggadah to express their relief at salvation from the latest persecution, others, still surrounded by horror, in a ghetto or concentration camp, reaching out in the same words towards a hope which was never to be fulfilled.

Overwhelmingly, the Seder ceremony was an occasion for joy. The 'miracles' outweighed the tragedies. We thanked God—in the famous *She'heheyanu* prayer—that he had 'kept us alive and sustained us and brought us to this moment'. We raised our glasses

opposite A moment of truth. Crowds gather at the Western Wall on Shavuot after the reunification of Jerusalem to the eternal hope: *Next Year in Jerusalem!* Relaxation and happiness; the house transformed with white cloths and special dishes; family and friends; the wine sparkling; the children's eager look. We were free at that moment, whatever the troubles of the daily round.

We can imagine, too, the intense excitement of those Seder gatherings which had to be conducted in secrecy because of the conditions of the time. The most extraordinary were, surely, the secret Passovers of the Marranos of Spain and Portugal. Forced into Catholicism, and rising often to the highest levels of society, many of them nevertheless clung—with an obstinate pride that seems as much Spanish as Jewish—to what they remembered of Jewish ceremonies, risking death if denounced to the Inquisition. Significantly, they observed the traditional fast days more than the feasts; but Passover was an exception: they went to untold effort to keep it. With informers on the lookout, waiting to catch them on the 'official' day, they would postpone their baking of *matzah* until two days later, at which point they would gather in secret for their version of the ceremonies. Many were caught and perished, but many also managed to survive and, ultimately, escape to the freedom of other lands, where they rejoined the faith.

What is it about the Seder that has this extraordinary hold on us? Of the many documents of the Holocaust, none is more moving than the Hebrew diary kept in the Warsaw ghetto by the schoolmaster Chaim Kaplan, discovered after all had been destroyed, and published in 1966 as *Scroll of Agony*. For the first Passover there, 24 April 1940, Kaplan is still able to wonder at the resourcefulness of the Jews in trying desperately to evoke the spirit of the feast:

> 'The synagogues are closed, but in every courtyard there is a holiday service, and cantors sing the prayers and hymns in their sweet voices. In every home the signs of the holiday are manifest . . . The people run around carrying packages of *matzah* as if the sword of sabotage were not hovering over their heads . . .'

A year later, with the Jews now walled up in the ghetto, he writes:

> 'We are faced with a Passover of hunger and poverty, without even "the bread of affliction" . . . For eating and drinking there is neither *matzah* nor wine. For prayer there are no synagogues or houses of study. Their doors are closed, and darkness reigns in the dwelling-places of Israel . . .'

At this point his diary breaks off. How could he know that Passover two years later would signal one of the most heroic episodes in the whole of Jewish history? For Chaim Kaplan the story

opposite A picture from the Birds' Head Haggadah (southern Germany, *ca.* 1320) showing Jews ascending to Jerusalem. This unique Haggadah is discussed on page 109
overleaf A memory of Eastern Europe. A pastel by Abel Pann (1883–1963) of Cossacks expelling Jews from a *shtetl* in Russia

ירושלים

opposite In joyful contrast, a Seder in a Jerusalem kindergarten, 1971. The children prepare and conduct the Seder themselves

right Drawing of a Seder by a child in the Theresienstadt concentration camp. Did it represent a Seder held in the camp, or was it a memory of earlier times?

ended in December 1942 or January 1943, when he was put to death among the thousands of victims at Treblinka. It was on Seder night some three months afterwards—18–19 April—that the Nazis launched their all-out artillery attack on the Jews of the Warsaw ghetto who had finally refused to go like lambs to the slaughter. For three weeks the battle raged until—as at Masada two thousand years earlier—nothing was left but a few survivors to tell the story of heroism.

At one point in his diary, in an entry recording the ordinance of complete ghetto confinement in mid-1941, Kaplan had burst out in anger:

> 'Can the world sit silent? Will evil always be triumphant? O Leader of the world, where are you? But He who sits in Heaven laughs . . .'

It was an authentic cry from the heart; but equally authentic, in a very different voice, is a prayer that was recited in the Belsen concentration camp during Passover of 1944. As there was no *matzah*, the rabbis of the camp had authorized the Jewish prisoners to eat bread. But God had to understand why; and the prayer explained it. The Law had been infringed only to save life, in fulfillment of the verse: 'And ye shall live by the commandments, and not die by them.' One day God's Law would again be observed:

> 'We pray to Thee that Thou mayest keep us alive and preserve us and redeem us speedily so that we observe Thy statutes and do Thy will and serve Thee with a perfect heart. Amen.'

Too often—all too often—the Seder has been the moment of

Da hůb auf der iud Moyses mit samet allen an

A monstrous illustration of a blood libel. The murder of Simon of Trent in the 1470s was ascribed to the Jews and described by a certain 'Tuberinus' in a book translated into German in 1475

truth for the Jews who clung to its celebration. We know of the desperate fears that stirred the medieval Jewish communities of Western Europe—and much more recently those of Russia—when the approach of Passover brought with it the recrudescence of the blood libel—the monstrous assertion that the Jews used human blood at Passover for their ceremonies, for which they would kill, or had actually killed, a Christian child. How, we ask ourselves, did our ancestors—sometimes recently enough to have been our grandfathers—have the courage to hold fast against such atrocities? And how extraordinary it is that after the lapse of only a few short generations, a sense of identity with these same grandparents has stirred many young hearts in Russia itself, so that they look again at Passover and other Jewish festivals for some reunion with their ancient origin. If one tries to draw a meaning from this, it must be that the strength of feeling in the Jewish experience has some objective staying-power, justifying itself ultimately in positive, tangible form where everything seems to be conspiring to smother it.

The way in which this works itself out may be seen, perhaps by recalling three Seders, the first in 1915, the second—just over fifty years later—in 1969, the third in 1971. They take us—as the Seder should—from desperation to hope.

The first of these Seders is mentioned briefly, but poignantly, in the *Autobiography* of Simon Dubnow, the great Jewish historian, whose life was rooted in East European Jewry, and who believed that the type of culture that had developed there—of self-governing, Yiddish-speaking communities—was the true key to fulfillment for the Jewish people wherever they lived. Against the background of the time, and particularly in the last two decades of the nineteenth century when his ideas were germinating, this was by no means as limited and backward looking an approach as it might now appear. To a large extent, it arose out of his feeling that the Jewish community was a unique institution which, through remarkable self-discipline and spiritual steadfastness, had turned the negativeness of exile into a positive and fruitful basis for the good life. Certainly this background was the crucible for much that is powerful and precious to us, but for Dubnow himself it ran into the sand. In July 1941, the German Army entered Riga, where he was living—a revered old scholar of eighty-one. Six months later, he was taken out of the ghetto and shot.

Russian-Jewish soldiers in World War I assembled for the Seder

As with all Russian liberals of the nineteenth century, a key element in Dubnow's optimism had been the longed-for overthrow of the tsarist regime. Despair began to invade him when the outbreak of war in 1914 between Germany and Russia brought untold sufferings to the Jewish people there. At Passover in 1915 he noted in his diary:

> 'We celebrated Seder at the Winawars. We ate our *matzah* in tears and silence. We read the Haggadah and tried to chant its songs, but the mood was lacking. Winawar's question: *Ma nishtana*—"why is this night different?"— remained unanswered. There is no answer. We are just slaves, given to shame and slaughter.'

Were those eighty-one years spent in vain, then? Was his feeling for the internal values of Jewish life futile? In 1969 I spent the Seder at Nir-Am, a small Israeli kibbutz near the Gaza Strip. The members, I found, had come from various parts of Europe and North Africa. The room I was given belonged to a young Algerian Jew, on service with the Army. The bookshelves, rickety as they were, had pride of place, with their bright collection of contemporary French and English novels, and the pile of classical and pop records they somehow managed to support. The kibbutz was not specifically religious; there was no synagogue. But it was 'a Jewish community' in the true sense of Dubnov's idea; and when the members assembled in the dining hall to read the Haggadah, the mood which immediately developed had a solemnity reaching far back into religious memory. There was a palpable reverence in the air. The Haggadah they used had dropped a little of the rabbinic argument but included instead more passages from the Bible itself—the Exodus description and lyrical verses on spring from the Song of Songs. The total understanding of what they were saying elevated the ancient words into an affirmation of the communal will. Dubnow's feeling for Jewish life had been given new form.

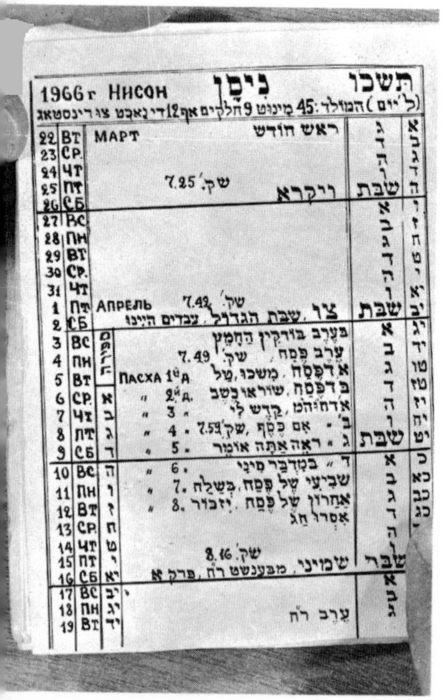

The third Seder, unique in its drama, takes us back in one bound from 1971 to the original flight from Egypt. The new Exodus of Jews from Russia, slow as yet but powerful in its form, has made Vienna the point at which those allowed to leave feel safe at last to breathe freely. After all the uncertainties of travel, they have crossed the Red Sea. Willing hands from Israel are waiting to feed and help them. Ahead they see the Holy Land.

They arrive in Vienna at all hours, clutching their packages, impatient at the inevitable delays in assembling for the final plane. On Passover eve in 1971 there were some 160 waiting. A messenger had arrived from Israel to bring them together for the Seder—a woman journalist who led them in prayer and song like Miriam of old. As they sang, new celebrants arrived, friends and families were re-united, the sense of excitement mounted. One more page in Passover history was being written.

In the immediate aftermath of the Holocaust, Jewish history, for all its previous achievement, seemed to offer a message of bleakness and death. The communities of Eastern Europe, whose vivid feeling had been celebrated by Dubnow and so many other Jewish writers, had run into the sand. In the Holy Land, the remnant faced enmity and restriction. Everywhere in the world there was a pall of sadness among Jews. To look back now and record the transformation is to be witness to a miracle, as dramatic as an earlier miraculous crossing of the Red Sea. Jewish life has not only asserted its living continuity and unity, as in the explosion of feeling at the time of the Six-Day War of 1967, but in the course of this it has become aware of its roots as never before. The past has been uncovered in astounding form and variety. The new generation, hostile or indifferent as it used to be, finds pride and identification.

The symbol of it all is the Passover Haggadah. The story of that far-off liberation, vivid to all of us today, is the Haggadah not only of our time but of all times.

A hand-written Hebrew-Russian *luach* (calendar), symbol of the yearning for identification with Israel. It is open at Nisan, the month of Passover
opposite A kibbutz Seder

2 *The Origins of Passover*

The Name and the Rituals

A Jew can be brought in touch with his ancestral history in two different ways. At one level, it is the story encountered in one's childhood, the handing on by parents and teachers of a tradition which they themselves inherited in this way. The outline of the story has not changed since biblical times, but it is coloured, at each handing-on, by the living circumstances of the time, the personal feelings between parents and children, the social culture into which the child is born, the dramas, often fateful for Jews, in the world 'outside'. At this level, history is not objective but personal. The Seder is a focal point for such feeling. The Haggadah tells a story that rings true because we ourselves have been shaped by it.

At another level, one can explore the past for the excitement of discovery that is outside the range of personal involvement. For Jews this is a rich and, in a sense, daring adventure. No people has had such a long, unbroken concern for its own history, starting with the ancient oral traditions embodied in the Bible and continuing to our own time. But if this preoccupation with the Jewish fate is, in one way, an endless set of variations on inward-looking themes, in another way the themes all deal with Israel's place 'among the nations'. In his own life, every individual Jew expresses a balance between the two; but there is, at the same time, a restless desire, both emotional and intellectual, to understand the 'balance' of the formative times. How far is the tradition based on an exclusive covenant between Abraham and God (or Moses and God), so that everything that followed, in faith and ritual, is to be explained this way? How far, on the contrary, were the ancient Israelites predominantly children of their own time and place, so that nothing of what emerged can be fully understood without some grasp of the character of this ancient world—the movements of peoples, the content of myth and folklore, the emergence of social and ritual

opposite Colossal statue of the Exodus Pharaoh, Rameses II (1290–1224 BCE) from the Great Temple at Abu Simbel

above, left Prisoners being led by Egyptian taskmasters. Relief from the Temple of Sahu-Re, 5th Dynasty (2563–2433 BCE)

above, right Slaying of the Egyptian first-born. Detail from the Golden Haggadah (Barcelona, *ca.* 1320), discussed on page 108

patterns of life which must have put some mark on the ancient Israelites?

The Passover Festival is a perfect jumping-off ground for an enquiry of this kind, for two stimulating reasons. The first is that the variety of the Passover rituals, as described in the Bible, offers rich material for comparative studies. The second reason is equally satisfying. If the tradition is commented on 'from the outside', one hopes that this will not, in some way, dilute or weaken one's living experience, but on the contrary, substantiate and enrich it. Passover yields this bonus. The more the surrounding world of its early days is uncovered, the more mysterious and marvellous is the central fact on which it clearly turns—the creation of a people in its own land, at a moment in time and with a sense of purpose that was to give the Jewish people a character of their own for all time.

As told in the Haggadah, the origin of all the rituals of Passover seems to centre entirely on the events of the Exodus. Our ancestors were slaves in Egypt: God brought us out of this slavery, through many miracles, to be free to settle in the Holy Land. The Haggadah explains that because of this great deliverance—without which we, the descendants, would still be slaves in Egypt—a festival was instituted with three binding ceremonies:

(1) *Pesach*—a special sacrifice at the Temple, as a reminder that God had 'passed over' (*pasach*) our ancestors when He 'plagued' the Egyptians;

(2) *Matzah* (unleavened bread)—eaten for seven days as a reminder that the deliverance was so hurried that the bread being baked that day had not time to rise;

'All the world came to Joseph to buy grain, because the famine was severe over all the earth' (*Gen.* XLI, 57). A field of wheat from a relief at Tel El-Amarna, 14th century BCE, approximately the time of Joseph

(3) *Maror* (bitter herbs)—eaten at the Seder to remind us of the bitterness of the Egyptian slavery.

As a ritual for Seder night this is completely satisfying. But even here we can begin to speculate. Why a sacrifice? Was *matzah* unique to the ancient Israelites? Why is it to be eaten for seven days and not just at the 'sacrifice' or the Seder? Where does the 'spring festival' fit in, since this seems a key part of the story? What indeed does the word *Pesach* really mean? The questions soon begin to multiply.

We turn first to the Bible, and soon find that even there the account is not really as simple as the story we tell aroung the Seder table. It is true, of course, that the Bible narratives have come down to us in a form which organizes everything of Israel's past, and every ritual, around the crucial historic experience of the Exodus; but even so there are many surviving hints in the Bible of a wider background. Loose ends, duplications and even contradictions begin to emerge; they have led scholars into a whole variety of theories.

We might think that at least the Moses story in the Book of Exodus is clear enough, but that is only because the central idea is so forceful. As we read it there, the story emerges, with great literary force, as a 'straight' account of a battle of wills between Moses (encouraged by God) and Pharaoh. The highlight of the drama centres around the events of the last night, which include both the command on the Israelites to carry out a special sacrifice (the *Pesach*) on that night and the coincidental slaying of 'all the first-born of Egypt'. The hurried flight on the next day introduces the origin of *matzah*. All this becomes a historic memory which is repeatedly mentioned in other books of the Bible

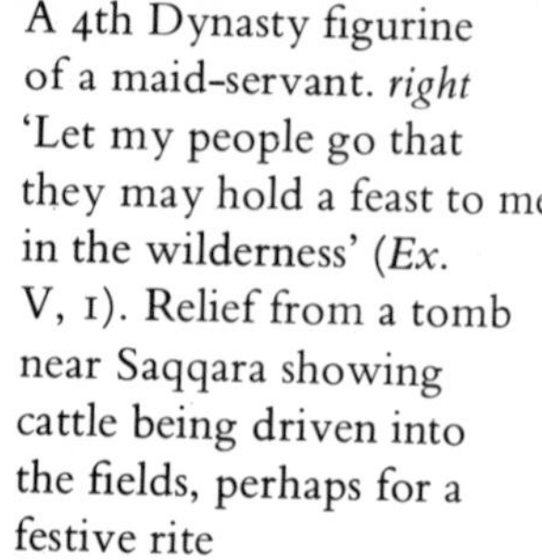

A 4th Dynasty figurine of a maid-servant. *right* 'Let my people go that they may hold a feast to me in the wilderness' (*Ex.* V, 1). Relief from a tomb near Saqqara showing cattle being driven into the fields, perhaps for a festive rite

as the *raison d'être* of a week-long 'Festival of Unleavened Bread', with all its attendant sacrifices and rituals.

One of the problems is that although the whole origin of Passover is built around the special sacrifice in Egypt on that last fateful night, the story in Exodus presents Moses as arguing with Pharaoh, long before this, about the Israelite obligation to hold a festival in the wilderness, for which they must leave Egypt. 'Let us go,' he says, 'three days journey into the wilderness, that we may sacrifice to the Lord our God.' The sacrifice *must* be performed in the wilderness, or God 'will fall upon us with pestilence or with the sword'.

As the argument with Pharaoh continues, Moses indicates that he knows some of the details of this wilderness festival, but not all. He insists to Pharaoh that every single Israelite has to take part ('young and old, sons and daughters'), and to his own followers he says that the women must be bedecked for the festival in fine clothes and jewels, which they must 'borrow' from the Egyptians. But he is not sure (or pretends not to be) what kind of sacrifices will be called for. He tells Pharaoh that they must take all their livestock with them ('not a hoof shall be left behind') for 'we know not with what we must serve the Lord until we come thither.'

This is the kind of material that is meat for the scholars. The ordinary reader of Exodus is probably content to think of Moses as putting forward this 'wilderness festival' quite sincerely as an intention, thought it was never, in fact, celebrated and was replaced by the *Pesach* sacrifice in Egypt itself. But the scholars are more curious. Is it not possible, they ask, that the Bible story of a 'wilderness festival' echoed some existing ancient custom of the Israelites which took them into the wilderness at springtime for a variety of sacrifices, attended by young and old, with the women in their finery? If so, are there parallels to be found with other ancient peoples? Some even dare to suggest that the baking of unleavened bread might be linked to 'camping out' in the wilderness. One can explore these ideas without in the least weakening the historic force of the special *Pesach* sacrifice in Egypt, which became forever linked to the Exodus in the historic memory.

Keeping still to problems raised by the Exodus story, the word *Pesach*—the key to the festival—is itself quite mysterious. It is a very rare word in the Bible apart from its use to signify this all-important sacrifice. What, in fact, does it mean? Before looking at the other rituals which the Bible ultimately brings into the Passover story, it is worth seeing if this basic word, due to become so familiar, can help us through its etymology to understand more of the background.

'Ask every woman of her neighbour, jewelry of silver and of gold' (*Ex.* XI, 2). Necklace of gold, lapis lazuli and other stones from the Tomb of Tutankhamen, 18th Dynasty (1347–1338 BCE)

The word is introduced in connection with God's decision, communicated to Moses, to kill all the first-born of Egypt, human and animal. The Israelites are to be spared. Moses tells them that each household must kill a lamb or kid, smearing some of the blood 'on the lintels and two sideposts' of each house, so that it can be identified. The animal has to be roasted and then eaten 'in haste'; and here is where the word *Pesach* is brought in—for the first time in the Bible. The sacrifice is to be 'a *Pesach* to the Lord' (*Exodus* XII, 2). Explaining this, God says to Moses: 'When I see the blood I will "*pasach*" over you, and there shall be no plague upon to you to destroy you' (*Exodus* XII, 13).

As we all know, the phrase is normally translated as 'I will pass over you': the festival takes its name from this. The image is normally of God (or the Angel of Death) flying over the Israelite house. Can we establish the exact meaning of the word, either through the sense of the rest of the verse, or through some parallel use in the Bible, or perhaps through some other derivation of the root that might throw light on the wider associations of the festival?

Taking the verse alone, the sense might seem to require the words to mean: 'When I see the blood, I will spare you', or 'protect you'. This meaning has traditionally been supported by what seems the only other comparable use of this root in the Bible, in Isaiah XXXI, 5, where it clearly means 'saving'. It is prophesied there that God will protect Jerusalem: 'As birds flying, so will that Lord of Hosts protect Jerusalem: protecting, he will deliver it: saving (*pasoach*) he will spare it.' But of course Isaiah, in using this root *pasoach*, could be turning the now familiar festival name into a verb, saying in effect: 'God will do a *Pesach* act' to save Jerusalem.

Since it is not entirely easy to see from philology how God's 'saving' or 'sparing' act gave its name to the sacrifice, some scholars have suggested that the word might have a more general meaning. There is a root *pasach* in Hebrew which normally means something quite different—'to limp', and from this 'to dance with limping motions'. Among other nations of the Near East, religious ceremonies (connected with fertility rites) included ecstatic dance rituals. Perhaps, say some scholars, this was true for the Israelites too, so that the *Pesach* might mean, in origin, something like 'the limping dance festival'. In support, they argue that this precise word is used of the ritual 'leaping' or 'limping' by the priests of Baal on their altar in the great confrontation with Elijah (*I Kings* XVIII, 26.) But there are two strong arguments against this derivation. The first is that the root *pasach* is never used of any Israelite dancing occasion in the Bible, such as when David 'leaped and danced' before the Ark (*II Samuel* VI, 16.) The second is that there is nothing in the Bible to suggest that an Israelite festal occasion included anything of a ritual 'limping' dance. Indeed 'limping' was an explicit disqualification in Temple ritual. A 'lame man' (*pisseach*) could not take part (*Leviticus* XXI, 18.)

Going further afield, some scholars have tried to derive the name, and its meaning, from other languages. Bearing in mind the ancient Israelite connection with Mesopotamia, one suggestion is that the word *Pesach* might be linked with an Akkadian root *passahu*, meaning 'to placate', which could yield 'a placation sacrifice'; but there are no Mesopotamian festival rituals known that are derived from this root. With still greater ingenuity, it has been suggested that the word might be adapted from an Egyptian root. One such theory would turn *Pesach* into 'the commemoration' another, into 'the blow' (God's decisive blow against Egypt with the Tenth Plague!) another, into 'the harvest'. Passover certainly has harvest connections, as we shall see, but these have more to do with the *matzah* and the *omer* (sheaf of barley) than with the paschal lamb. None of this theorizing is convincing.

We are thrown back to Hebrew, and perhaps to an extended meaning in the original root which was subsequently lost. One scholar, pursuing this line, links the word *Pesach* with similar sounding roots (פשע, פשה) used in the Bible in the sense, respectively, of 'to spread' and 'to march', seeing in all these words a basic sense of 'movement', which might get us back to the most traditional of translations—a literal 'passing over'. But it is fair to warn that this same scholar sees in this derivation a reference not only to passing over the houses, but also to passing over from the old year to the new, one of the ideas about the wider connections of the festival which will be discussed below.

It has seemed worthwhile to pursue the possible meanings of this one word *Pesach* since the sacrifice to which it refers is obviously basic. But the many references in the Bible to other aspects of the festival open up a still wider picture. If we bring these references together, we may be able to hear ancient half-forgotten echoes of rituals that clung, or were grafted on, to the historic festival which came to dominate everything.

To follow the arguments of the scholars on this, we have to recognize that though the Bible can be read very effectively as a straight consecutive story, it was put together with a very flexible time-sense. 'Early' and 'late' have been merged into the text which has come down to us, as the rabbis recognized in a famous dictum: 'There is neither "before" nor "after" in the Torah.' On the biblical ceremonies associated with Passover, it is not at all easy to determine what might have been 'early' (going back to pre-Egyptian folk-memories) and what 'late', being linked to ceremonies developed or transformed by the institution of the Temple.

This, in turn, again raises the question with which we began. What Passover ceremonies of their own did the Israelites bring out of Egypt, reflecting their own earlier nomadic or semi-nomadic existence, and what practices, if any, did they borrow or adapt from other peoples when they had re-settled in Palestine after the Conquest?

There is no need to ask these questions if we think of Passover in outline as simply a paschal sacrifice and *matzah;* but when the details given in the Bible are collected, they offer a formidable set of clues for scholarly investigation.

On the sacrifice itself, there is very great precision. The animal (a male sheep or goat in its first year) had to be selected in advance, on the tenth day of the month of Abib, 'the first month of the year'. When killed, some blood had to be drawn off into a bowl and smeared on the doorposts with a bunch of hyssop. The animal had to be roasted entire and consumed 'in haste', at night, by all the household, the women being dressed in finery, the men with loins girt, 'ready for a journey.' As much as possible of the meat had to be eaten: no bones were to be broken: anything left had to be burnt by the morning. The night of the sacrifice was a 'watch-night'.

Side by side with this concentration on the one night was a Festival of Unleavened Bread (*chag ha'matzot*) lasting for seven days, with its own detailed ritual of sacrifices. The essential element was not merely eating unleavened bread, but even more important-

Woodcut of a 'standing meal' by Hans Sebald Beham (1500–1550), Germany

opposite 'For seven days no leaven shall be found in your houses' (*Ex*. XII, 19). Burning leaven on the day before Passover in Mea Shearim, Jerusalem

ly (as we shall see) removing all leaven from the household for this period. Anyone failing this latter command was to be 'cut off from his people'. This festival was one of three annual occasions for a pilgrimage to Jerusalem.

A harvest element is specifically brought into the story by the command, in connection with Passover, to give an 'offering' of new corn. An *omer* (sheaf) of barley had to be waved by the priest in the ensuing seven weeks, starting 'on the morrow of the Sabbath', taken usually to mean the morrow of the first day of Passover.

Passover as a New Year festival is an aspect which has to be considered too, not only because of the emphasis on the new crop, first-born, and firstlings, but also because of the explicit statement that the month of the festival is 'the first month of the year'.

Emphasis on the first-born, as belonging to God, appears repeatedly as linked in some way to the festival. Not only have the firstling beasts and the first crops to be sacrificed or redeemed, but all first-born males have to be redeemed. Is this significant in connection with the slaying of Egypt's first-born, and the 'redemption' of the first-born of the Israelites during the Tenth Plague?

The special role of males—sometimes including a direct reference to circumcision—is brought out in the more detailed account of the rituals as they developed. No uncircumcised male might eat the paschal sacrifice, but the participation of circumcised aliens or slaves was expressly allowed. It was the males who had to attend the three annual pilgrimages, of which Passover was the first. The week's ritual included a host of sacrifices of animals and food, and any male who failed to participate was to be 'cut off', unless ritually unclean at the time or away on a journey. In that case, he could celebrate the festival one month later.

The rabbis discussed this great complex of ordinances at enormous length in the Talmud. Modern scholars have been no less keen in trying to understand them.

The Israelites among 'the other peoples'

At the heart of any judgment is the question: how 'separate' were the ancient Israelites? We can see a unique conception of God stretching back to Abraham and given undying shape by Moses; but we can also see much evidence of 'mingling' in the Bible itself. The discoveries of archaeology have thrown much light on this.

In the Bible story itself, the two countries which seem to matter most in Israel's ancient past are Mesopotamia (the land of the two rivers) and, at the other end of the Fertile Crescent, Egypt, the mighty empire with which the Israelites are repeatedly involved.

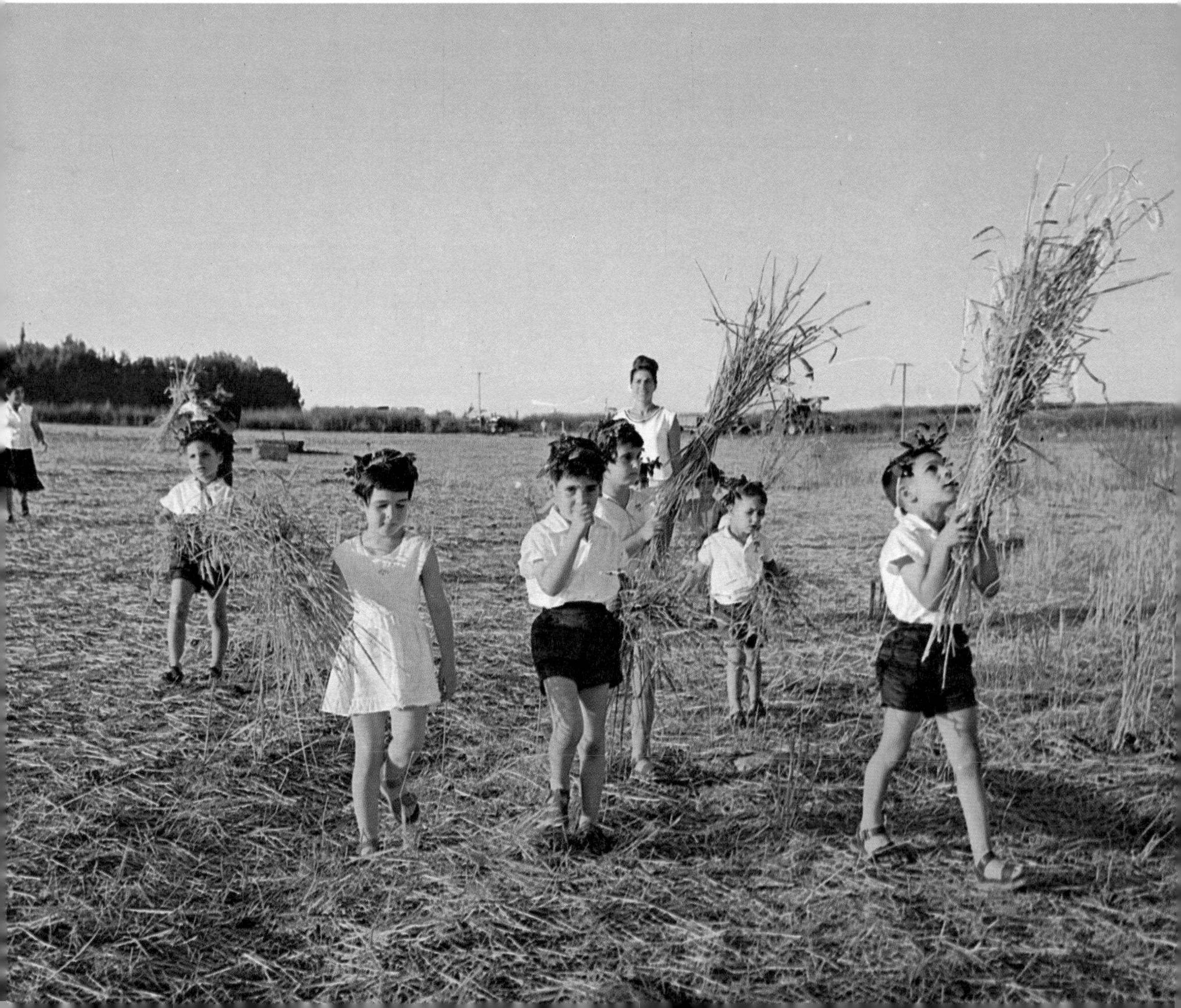

In between there is constant interplay with a vast variety of peoples and tribes living in the Holy Land itself or adjacent to it and impinging on the Israelites. The aim of the Bible story is always to emphasize the religious contrast with the Israelites, but even so we can see how mingled was Israel's history with all these peoples. In the days of Abraham there are stories of his dealing with the 'kings' of the time, his travels (on trade) and his various settlings among them. In the days of the other patriarchs, the interplay continues. In the story of Moses, the importance of his links with Midian, where God appears to him, is clearly crucial. When the Israelites are leaving Egypt, the Bible talks of them having to live among the 'Canaanites, Hittites, Amorites, Hivites and Jebusites' (*Exodus* XIII, 15). The roll-call continues, as they begin the re-settlement, with Amalek, Moab, Edom and many others, among whom the Philistines emerge later to particular dramatic effect.

'Counting the *Omer*', offering (or waving) a sheaf of barley daily on the 49 days from Passover to Shavuot

opposite, above A 18th-century hand-painted parchment *omer* calendar from Holland showing the 49 days of the counting

opposite, below Children in a kibbutz in Israel gathering their sheaves for *omer* celebrations

It is with these peoples who settled in and moved around Palestine itself that the discoveries of modern archaeology have been so revealing for early Israelite history. Much has also emerged, of course, through discoveries in Mesopotamia and Egypt. The former, which had long offered striking evidence of the life and art of Babylon and Assyria, revealed also in recent years the dazzling culture of the Sumerians, immediately linked in our mind (correctly or not) with the patriarch Abraham, who came from 'Ur of the Chaldees'. Egypt has also enriched early Israelite history in our own time through the decipherment of inscriptions which document in a new way her continuous involvement with the neighbouring countries to her north. But the discoveries of particular moment to the Israelite past are in the more central areas of the Fertile Crescent, where we now have an intimate and ever-expanding picture of hitherto very obscure cultures, allowing us to study the writings of these peoples, their ritual and social practices, the successive waxing and waning of their political power, their wanderings and settlements. All of this can be brought to bear on the circumstances which led the ancient Israelites (or some of them) into and out of Egypt, in the course of which a great leader, Moses, harking back to his experience among the Midianites, was inspired to establish an undying religious faith.

below The pre-patriarchal world. Side-panel of 'the Standard of Ur' from the royal graves of Ur (*ca.* 2700–2600 BCE). The pictures of shell and mother of pearl inlaid with lapis lazuli seem to suggest a sacrifice of a ram, as in the Genesis story of Abraham

We start with Father Abraham, moving from Mesopotamia towards Palestine, let us say around 1800 BCE (though some put him later). The Sumerian empire and culture, after a last revival under the Third Dynasty of Ur (ca. 2060–1960 BCE) had begun finally to disintegrate, largely under the pressure of the semitic-speaking Amurru (i.e. western) peoples, whom we meet in the

above 'Execration text' from the 20th–19th century BCE cursing Pharaoh's enemies, written on a pottery figurine *opposite* A man of Abraham's time? An offering bearer from Mari, on the Euphrates, early second millenium BCE

Bible as Amorites. Various city-states of the former Sumerian empire were able to exercise a kind of imperial power successively under Amorite dominance, including, among many others, Ashur/Assyria (on the upper Tigris), Mari (on the middle Euphrates) and ultimately Babylon, under the great Hammurabi (late 18th century BCE). Mari is mentioned here particularly—though its name never even occurs in the Bible—because excavations there just before World War II yielded evidence of a great civilized city, with documents (more than 20,000 tablets and fragments) of vast trading and diplomatic correspondence during the Mari Age (ca. 1750–1697 BCE). It is surely significant that names which echo our own patriarchal names occur in these letters, and that they document the kind of trading journeys that the patriarchs made over the whole of what became Palestine.

Long before this (23rd-20th centuries BCE), nomadic clans of the same Amorite stock had been flooding into Palestine, leaving marks, now discovered, of great disruption. Egypt was normally 'suzerain' of the Fertile Crescent as far north as Byblos, where her wood came from; but she felt the impact of this 'invasion' even at the height of her power under the Twelfth Dynasty. The famous 'Execration Texts'—curses which were written on bowls which were then broken for magic effect—reflect Pharaoh's struggle against his foes there in the twentieth and nineteenth centuries BCE, giving us, incidentally, the name 'Jerusalem' among lists of early Palestine towns. By the eighteenth century BCE—the early patriarchal age—the Amorite invaders had begun to settle down and themselves found towns among the existing Canaanites. These 'invasions' included other peoples too, notably the Hurrians (biblical Horites) from Armenia.

One has a picture from the Book of Genesis of the patriarchs feeling their way carefully in the wake of these migrations. Abraham was himself a chieftain, able to make treaties with his opposite numbers. His clan followed a god of their own, even though in daily customs (and military struggles) they were involved with their neighbours. This involvement has been illustrated dramatically by the discovery at Nuzi, on the Tigris, of many texts dealing with the customary law of that city, with its predominantly Hurrian population. Though dated to the fifteenth century, and therefore a little later than the presumed date of Abraham, they obviously reach back, and the social background they reveal throws light on a number of patriarchal stories, such as Abraham's relationship with his slave Eliezer, and the Laban-Jacob episodes of marriage and trickery.

Fighting in Palestine by Egypt's enemies in the 14th century BCE described in the Amarna Letters, clay tablets with cuneiform inscriptions

The Hurrians come into the story more explicitly because, as they moved southward from Mesopotamia, where they had been exposed to Indo-European influences, they took with them new military techniques—the horse-drawn chariot and the composite bow—which were to be decisive in conquest. Their dominance is shown by the fact that the Egyptians, who were ultimately to learn these new techniques, called Palestine 'the land of the Huru'.

It is in this period, also, that we begin to hear of the Hittites, who were spreading their empire from Asia Minor into the northern, and then the middle part of the Fertile Crescent. It is with the Hittites, of course, that Abraham negotiated (*Genesis* XXIII) for the acquisition of a family burial place at Hebron. The transaction is only properly understood in terms of the feudal character of Hittite law, now attested by the Boghaskoy texts.

Egypt had already been disturbed by the pressure of these various Asiatic invaders to her north. She was now to feel their weight at home. In the seventeenth century BCE, invaders called 'Hyksos'—the word means 'foreign chiefs'—established themselves in the Nile Delta, from which they exercised full power over Egypt itself, as well as over neighbouring countries to the north. The Hyksos seem to have been a mixture of various peoples, including Canaanite and Amorite, from Palestine itself, leading, in some undefined way, a movement southward of the militarily powerful Hurrians. They held sway in Egypt until around 1580 BCE, when native Egyptian rulers came back into power and began to drive them out.

There can be little doubt that the settlement of some Israelite families or clans in Egypt is to be seen in the context of the widespread migration of semitic-speaking peoples and the rule of the alien Hyksos. If Joseph was a power in the land at that time, it is understandable that the Israelites began to suffer, with other alien settlers, when a revived Egyptian dynasty expressed its new strength by launching into grandiose building programmes—culminating in those of the 'Exodus pharaoh', Rameses II—for which hordes of slaves were needed. The Israelites, looking back later to the miracle of their deliverance, naturally saw their settlement and adventures in Egypt as unique to themselves. More objectively, it might have been a less individual story until the sense of purpose which Moses unfolded found form in the 'Law', the Kings and the Prophets.

In trying to assess the Israelite role during these years in Palestine and Egypt, one puzzling element is the repeated mention in Egyptian as well as other documents of a 'people' whose name is usually transliterated as Apiru, but also variously as Khapiru, Abiru, or

Unchanged since long before the Hebrew slavery, a sphinx and pyramids from the 4th Dynasty, as seen in the *Description d'Egypte*, an early 19th-century travel book

even Habiru—a form which obviously tempts identification with the Hebrews. The Apiru are mentioned as slaves in Egypt, which by itself might seem to strengthen the connection. They are also mentioned, however, so much further afield and in such a variety of circumstances as to lead scholars to conclude that 'Apiru' in its various forms is not an ethnic term to be linked to 'Hebrew' but rather a 'class' name, applied in the ancient world to a very widespread type of nomad who lived in any way he could as trader, traveller, servant, adventurer, mercenary or freebooter. The Apiru turn up in this character in documents ranging from twentieth-century Ur and eighteenth-century Mari to twelfth-century Egypt. It is easy to assume that many of the ancient Israelites might well have been described as Apiru at different times because of the circumstances in which they lived; but it is less sure that their Hebrew name established an exclusive identification.

The most tantalizing of the references to the Apiru—because of the possible connection with the Exodus—is that given in the Amarna Letters, found at Tel El Amarna in Egypt in 1887 and subsequently. These letters are from Egyptian vassals in Palestine in the fourteenth century BCE claiming that the Apiru, who are fighting everywhere—stealing chariots and being generally troublesome—are the most difficult problem to cope with. A typical boast/complaint is:

> 'Let the king, my lord, learn that the chief of the Apiru has risen in arms against the lands which the god of the king, my lord, gave me; but I have smitten him. Also let the king, my lord, know that all my brethren have abandoned me, and it is I and Abdu-Heba who fight against the chief of the Apiru . . .'

How interesting if (as some have thought) these fighting Apiru included, in fact, some kin of the Israelites, due later to rejoin the family when Palestine was united under the kingdom of David.

Perhaps these kinsmen had never gone into Egypt, or had managed to escape before the Exodus. These are all questions that come into the speculations of the scholars.

The more we see how turbulent was the background against which the settlement in Egypt and re-settlement in Palestine took place, the more remarkable is the achievement of the Bible in re-structuring the story from the point of view of a single people's covenant with their God, to which the concomitant struggles of kings and peoples are an accompaniment away from the central stage. But even the Bible, giving the story dramatic unity, allows the reader to sense the confusion. Those who emerged in the Exodus included, in the Bible phrase, 'a mixed rabble'. The stories of the Book of Judges also imply a mixed background. Until the full kingdom was established it was a case of the Israelite nucleus building up a nation, absorbing settlers or even kinsmen with a great variety of local cults, and fusing their own cult into a national religion, celebrated ultimately at a national temple. The central element in this process was the increasing identification of all the peoples concerned with an immensely meaningful historical idea. The Hebrews who struggled through the wilderness brought with them a message which can be described as ethical monotheism; but the power behind its acceptance was to lie always (even for the most theological of prophets) in the memory of the historic deliverance, by virtue of which a special covenant had been forged between this people and their God, to last for all time.

Hazor before the Israelite settlement
below Bronze plaque of a Canaanite dignitary found near the temple of Hazor (15th century BCE)

In the Bible books which have come down to us, the Exodus shows up unfailingly as the unique feature of the faith; but the complex of ceremonies and rituals (summarized earlier) which clustered around the Passover festival went far beyond the ritual of the deliverance. It becomes a problem for scholarship to try to determine how much of the fully developed picture—with its treatment of sacrifices, the redemption of the first-born, the blood rituals, the harvest celebrations and the New Year theme—reaches back into a very ancient past, and how much was fashioned, in centuries after the re-settlement, by the Temple 'mandarins', consciously adapting cults, myths and practices that were alive in the whole area.

The echoes and parallels show clearly that much of this must have been worked in. For the Israelite rituals, however, the crucial point is not how much had a common origin but how firmly an absolute difference in principle was asserted. It was not an easy task. The prophets and teachers had a constant struggle to put a special mark on the ideas of people who in so many other respects were absorbed in a common background with their neighbours. Yet the distinction emerged. Rituals, phraseology and poetry were strikingly similar; yet the underlying approach—through which they transformed the old fertility rites and the role of the gods—spoke of something that was new and due to survive all succeeding centuries.

Echo of an early form of *matzah*. Baking dish from the ancient Israelite city of Lachish, excavated in 1932–8

Of all the discoveries in recent years which illustrate both the similarities and the break, two may perhaps be picked out as particularly instructive, though in different ways. The first is at Hazor, in Galilee, where we can now see physical evidence in profusion of the background which the Israelites had to transform; the second is at Ras Sharma, in Syria, where the evidence is literary. A newly discovered literature there—going back several hundred years before King David—seems to talk in a language which often evokes, and even helps to explain, the language of the Psalms; but the difference in religious thought is all the more clear as one examines the parallels.

Hazor, a key fortified city going back to 1800 BCE and with a thousand years of history, was excavated by Prof. Yigael Yadin starting in 1955. It is unique in documenting, through its physical remains the period of transition during which the Israelites were engaged in the re-settlement after the Exodus. The sequence of settlements, in which a major 'sophisticated' city of the fourteenth and thirteenth centuries BCE is seen to have been destroyed, confirms the account given in Joshua. As re-discovered by Yadin, the succession of buildings over the centuries illuminates vividly the Bible background. Of particular interest for Jewish history

The Holy of Holies of a Canaanite temple at Hazor about the time of Joshua (13th century BCE). In the foreground is an incense altar with the emblem of the deity, a weather god

are the fortress and palace buildings of Solomon and Ahab. But here we are concerned with the shrines, for the pre-Israelite echoes.

Taking only one example, a series of four large superimposed temples was discovered to the north of the city. Those going back to the early period (18th–15th centuries) show arrangements for the draining of the blood of the sacrifices, the offering of incense and the inspection of organs for divination. By the fourteenth century, the temple is a major building, 'unique in Palestine', according to Yadin, and the oldest prototype of the Jerusalem Temple—with its halls, porches, holy of holies, etc.—that was to be built more than three hundred years later by Solomon.

The decorations and furnishings of this temple are of particular interest in relation to later Israelite ideas. Among the numerous ritual vessels are an incense altar, a large round basin ('like the sea of Solomon's Temple'), and several libation tables. Inside the temple was a statuette of a seated figure, probably a king; outside were fragments of a statue of a deity which had stood on a base in the form of a bull. The general background is like a running commentary—centuries in advance—on rituals and furnishings due to become familiar at the Temple; at the same time, the broken statue and its bull base (a version of the familiar golden calf) may possibly show the hostility of the invading Israelites in the thirteenth century to image worship—the recurrent theme for centuries to come.

If Hazor (in this special connection) focuses our attention on temple vessels and rituals, the literature discovered at Ras Shamra documents sharply the rich background of myth to which the Israelites were exposed, with special significance for fertility rituals that might be echoed in a spring festival such as Passover.

Hazor has also revealed magnificent buildings constructed under the Israelite kings. *opposite* A general view of the Solomonic casemate wall (foreground) and the pillars of a store-house of Ahab's time. Most dramatic was the 1968 discovery of a shaft and tunnel 190 feet long made by Ahab to assure the fortress a supply of water from springs outside. It is twice as wide as the famous water shaft at Megiddo

The mound at Ras Shamra, on the Syrian coast, was opened up in 1928 by the French archaeologist C.F.A. Schaeffer. It revealed the ancient city of Ugarit, whose culture reached its apogee around the thirteenth century BCE, when it collapsed—like so many coastal cities—before the invading 'Peoples of the Sea', some of whom we know as the Philistines of the Old Testament.

Ugarit, founded by the Amorites at the beginning of the second millenium, was intimately connected in its life with all the surrounding cultures. Diplomatic records found there illustrate every aspect of the history of the area.

But it is the myths revealed in their literature with which we are now concerned, since they help us to define how the ancient Israelites broke through to wholly new ideas in the concepts of nature and providence.

In the Ugarit myths, Baal is the local variation of the dying-and-rising god common to mythology over the whole area—Tammuz (Mesopotamia), Osiris (Egypt), Dionysus (Greece). All the forces of nature were personified engaging in epic struggles—'ritual combats'—for the revival of fertility, which was then celebrated in orgies of abandon. The stories were perhaps not taken too literally. They were great romances: Baal 'dying' and rising again, his enthronement as king, Anat (his sister) cutting down Mot (Death) with a sickle to produce the 'live' corn, Akhat (the magic bowman) whose blood, being spilt, causes sterility, followed by triumph when the new crop emerges: the stories echoed in poetry the rites which had come down over the centuries.

At first it is startling to see how much of the language and imagery of the Ugarit myths are, as it were, familiar to us from the Bible. To quote only one verse from the Epic of Baal:

> 'When Baal gives forth his holy voice . . . his voice convulseth the earth.
> Yea, the very cedars quiver at the touch of his right hand.'

And if one has in mind the specific 'ritual combats' described in these epics (or their Babylonian equivalents)—the victorious god defeating the opposing god 'Storm' or the Sea-god himself—one begins to see in this personification a literary background to many of the metaphors in biblical poetry. Is there an 'annual battle' in Psalm 93: 'The floods have lifted up their voice. The Lord on high is mightier than the noise of many waters'? And as for personification, there is Psalm 114, which we find in the Haggadah:

> 'What aileth thee, O Sea, that thou fleest, O Jordan that thou turnest back.'

The scholars who like this approach have looked to these myths also for the 'real' background to the 'enthronement Psalms', explaining puzzling passages in these Psalms by referring to the rites of enthroning the victorious fertility god annually. They even see a far-off 'ritual combat' origin in Psalms which we are normally satisfied to link directly to our own miracle, the crossing of the Red Sea, such as Psalm 66:

> 'He turneth the sea into dry land: they went through the flood on foot.'

But if it is interesting to pick out striking parallels in individual verses, it is wholly misleading to put so much weight on them, and thus miss the transformation which the ancient Israelites wrought. To the Israelites, nature was not a battle of the gods: it was a witness of the power of one transcendent God, whom they worshipped. Even in those far-off times, the Israelites had rejected the idea of a

opposite 'Destruction of Pharaoh's Host in the Red Sea' by the Flemish painter Peter Paul Rubens (1577–1640)

The gods of ancient times *opposite, left* A Hittite stele from the 2nd millennium BCE showing the god Teshub standing on a bull (a link with the golden calf story) with a lightning fork and an axe in his hand. From Til Barsip, near Aleppo *opposite, right* A bronze statuette of a leonine-headed goddess, Egypt, 7th–6th century BCE

pantheon of 'semi-human' beings whose adventures were related in pornographic myths and then celebrated in debased orgies by those on earth. The joys of fertility were echoed for the biblical writers in happiness, not debauchery. One sees this transformation even where the old myths seem to lurk. In Psalm 65, for example, God is the power 'who stills the noise of the seas . . .', as in a Canaanite myth; but as the Psalm proceeds it becomes sheer poetry:

> 'Thou visitest the earth and waterest it . . .enriching it with the river of God . . .Thou settlest the furrows thereof, making it soft with showers . . . They drop upon the pastures of the wilderness, and the little hills rejoice on every side. The pastures are clothed with flocks: the valleys also are covered over with corn; they shout for joy; they also sing . . .'

This is the criterion, then, for assessing what the ancient Israelites drew from their background. Re-entering Canaan and moving among settled peoples, they adapted themselves to the world they found, and much of the language and metaphor survived in the literature they bequeathed to us—more indeed than they themselves perhaps knew. Later, in setting up an organized system of temple worship, they were particularly receptive to what they saw around them. But they put their own mark on the rituals in relating them to the covenant with their God. Nowhere was this stronger than in the complex of rituals which finally emerged linked to the Passover festival.

The Primitive Festival Transformed

If the reader has never met the work of biblical critics, it might seem at first to be somewhat negative. As celebrants of Passover around the Seder table, we do not have to compare, as they do, one biblical verse with another, putting every divergence and conflict under a microscope. The broad account, as it has come down to us, is all we need to know. But if one is trying to understand more closely the complex of ritual and myth which the Bible itself records, every 'problem' and 'inconsistency' is worth examining to see where it might lead. Some may therefore like to read the following brief account of the great variety of theories about Passover and its rituals which these scholars have put forward. Others may be content to see how a distinguished non-Jewish scholar adds it all up, reinforcing what may be called the 'traditional' view, on page 65.

The ordinary reader of the Bible reads its story consecutively. The critics are anxious to show that even though the Bible was edited to produce a consecutive story, elements in the story come from different areas and periods. They have always put great emphasis on

above The ancient harvest festival revived. A harvest dance celebrating the *omer* in Kibbutz Kfar Menahem

strands emerging from Judah in the south and Israel in the north. They look particularly to the influence which the Temple officials exerted on the story once the Temple was fully established. The ordinances and rituals described in the Book of Deuteronomy are compared with similar passages in earlier books of the Pentateuch as a clue to the processes by which the Temple establishment concentrated power in Jerusalem. This is particularly significant for Passover because of the account given in Kings and Chronicles of how King Josiah re-discovered the 'Book of the Law' (around 622 BCE), cleansed the Temple of heathen priests and cult objects, and ordered Passover to be celebrated on an unprecedented scale. There is also material on Passover 'reforms' in the Book of Ezekiel.

Using all this and other material, some of these scholars have argued that it was only in relatively 'late' times that various ancient springtime festivals celebrated by the Israelites were amalgamated into a national festival to be celebrated in Jerusalem in commemora-

tion of the Exodus. Until the time of Josiah, they say, one of the oldest elements—a springtime sacrifice of firstlings at the new moon—was carried out only by the peoples of Judah (those really concerned with the Exodus) in the south. At this firstlings sacrifice, which these pastoral tribes had actually taken down with them into Egypt, all 'leaven' was avoided because of its 'impurity', and this went much further than the mere eating of unleavened bread. They argue that a separate 'Festival of Unleavened Bread'—lasting seven days—was observed in the northern areas (which were more agricultural) at the full moon before the spring harvest; and at local shrines there, a sheaf of barley was offered when the new crops were sufficiently grown. Josiah's activities (mentioned above) made the Passover sacrifice 'national', as part of his political drive. To achieve this he had to introduce certain detailed changes, which accounts for the differences in the instructions given in Deuteronomy. But this dealt only with the sacrifice. It was through the

The only survival of the original form of paschal sacrifice. A Samaritan Passover on Mt. Gerizim, near Shechem (Nablus), where the paschal lamb is sacrificed and roasted as in biblical times

religious reforms proposed by Ezekiel that the paschal and *matzah* festivals were finally fused and the Bible texts harmonized accordingly (but not thoroughly enough to prevent the critics from spotting surviving differences!).

There are numerous variants of these theories. Some see the full fusion of the tradition taking place in the days of Josiah. Others see the *matzah* festival as celebrated by all (north and south) from early times, but believe that the sacrifice was originally a 'firstling sacrifice' by herdsmen only, on the eighth day after the birth of the animal. This, they say, is why the sacrifice, although broadened later to include all, continued to be linked to the 'redemption' of the first-born.

This comes up from another angle with the scholars who look for the origin not so much in textual criticism but through a study of comparative religion. Some of these see the Passover sacrifice, with its blood being smeared and its flesh eaten by the individual celebrants, as an annual re-enactment, going back to pre-historic times, of a cultic drama, in which the celebrants absorbed some of the divine qualities of the god being worshipped. The smearing of the blood was a prophylactic against misfortune in the ensuing year.

In due course, this ceremony became fused with the historic

memory of the Exodus—the killing of the first-born in Egypt; but in very early times, they believe, the Exodus festival was linked to the autumn New Year ceremonies. Autumn—the end of the sterility of summer—was the season of Creation: the Creation myth—the world being created from water—was echoed in Israel being 'created' from the sea through which they had passed. The linking of the Exodus to autumn survived in the ceremony of going out into the field (or 'the wilderness') to dwell in booths (the Feast of Tabernacles). But gradually the spring became the religious New Year: the ancient New Year sacrifice was connected fully with the story of the Exodus, and its importance was increased by its amalgamation with the agricultural *matzah* festival.

Pidyon Ha'ben (Redemption of the First-born) is still celebrated by the orthodox. *above* Detail from an early 19th-century plate from Galicia, used at the ceremony, shows the *Akedah* (saving of Isaac)

As must be clear already, there is little consensus on conclusions, despite acknowledgement that the evidence, insofar as it is factual, must not be discounted. One of the central arguments is on how much the Israelites adopted from the Canaanites after the resettlement. Some think that the ancient Israelites always had spring as their main festival and were following their neighbours in putting emphasis also on the autumn New Year. We see this in the autumn enthronement of Solomon, which was the nearest thing in ritual to the annual 'enthronement' of the fertility god. But those who lean on comparisons with the nature festivals of the area go further. If the word *Pesach* indicated originally a funereal 'limping dance' (see pages 39–41), does it link up with some primeval sacrifice of human first-born, the faint relics of which had to be stamped out by Israelite teaching? The 'redemption of the first-born' is certainly one of the threads which was woven into the complex of Passover ritual. Theories of this kind are common among those who see different traditions in different verses of the Bible.

Not all the scholars, however, are prepared to see the ceremonies split up in origin this way, depending on whether the celebrants were nomad or settled, pastoral or agricultural. It has been pointed out (notably by Prof. J.B. Segal in his book *The Hebrew Passover*) that the patriarchs were only semi-nomad, so that they could have celebrated harvest festivals—linked with *matzah*—from antiquity. Moreover there were no rigid differences after the resettlement between 'pastoral' Judah in the south and 'agricultural' Israel to the north, so that the *matzah* festival did not have to be 'borrowed' from the north. The basic Passover element (Segal argues) is its fixed timing to the spring equinox. Together with Tabernacles, fixed to the autumn equinox, it set the shape of the year. Both festivals have to be seen ultimately as New Year festivals, with historic factors changing the pre-eminence of one or the other at different times, but ultimately giving the palm to Passover.

In this view, Passover would share, in origin, many of the features common to all New Year festivals in the Near East—'a ritual going-forth from the city to the country . . .rites of purification which include fasting, the wearing of new clothes, processions, sacrifices and feasting'. The sacred procession, culminating in the 'exodus' from the city to the desert, is clearly a very primitive element in the New Year festivals. It can certainly be seen as part of a fertility ritual, the citizens going out into the desert to seek the powers of vegetation. It has even been suggested that the injunction to eat the sacrifice 'in haste' (*b'hippazon*) may reach back to the frenzied running around which used to accompany primitive celebrations, and which had in it an element described by one scholar as 'invigoration'. For males, another element in getting together for the spring festival was, perhaps, to take part in an initiation ceremony. Circumcision, as the Bible emphasizes, is the criterion of participation in the sacrifice.

But if the practices found generally in the Near East lie deep beneath the surface, there are differences in the Israelite Passover which are also marked from early times. A major element of this kind is the contrast between the royal emphasis in the pagan autumn festival—the king, himself a god or demi-god, being reborn and enthroned as the living power of fertility—and the popular element in the Passover, where the sacrifice is by each family, *originally without benefit of priest*, a characteristic that remained paramount and significant.

As a family ceremony, everything in the Israelite ritual acquired a personal significance. By using a bunch of hyssop to smear the sacred blood on his doorposts, the layman-householder could protect his home without being defiled by direct touch of the blood. The removal of all leaven was a way for the individual celebrant to combat 'uncleanliness': fermentation represents decay. Because the sacrifice was to be a good augury for the coming year, it had to be perfect: no bone was to be broken. To guard against any impurity developing from it, anything left over had to be burnt.

There was a strong sense of Passover leading the individual from the old to a new epoch. It has indeed been suggested that we might find in this the real etymology of the word *Pesach*. A Hebrew word that is used for initiation or census-taking of males means literally 'passing over'. It is also used in a sense of sparing. Perhaps the ideas were all combined. It is interesting that Philo, the Jewish philosopher who lived in Alexandria in the first century CE, saw Passover as a 'Crossing Feast', including both the crossing of the Red Sea and a

opposite The desert of northern Sinai, unchanged from the days of the Exodus

symbolic act of purification—'the lover of wisdom occupied in *crossing over* [passing over] from the body and the passions' to virtue.

By the time Philo was writing, many generations before him had already read their own meanings into the traditions emerging from the past. For more than a thousand years, the people of Israel had been living with the festival as a clearly defined historical memory, the visible expression of the Covenant they had made with the God of their faith and the *raison d'être* of their continued existence. From the dim past, they recalled the earliest times in which Abraham's Covenant with God had foreshadowed a special role in history for their tribes, already resisting the pagan rituals of the world they lived in. Out of this past, they had retained primitive feasts and rites which were to fit in with the emergent faith. The Passover, a common enough sacrifice at the spring equinox, had been invested with the full tribal feeling, without which it would never have exerted such a unifying hold on these scattered clans. When history sprang to life at the Exodus from Egypt, everything was re-interpreted around this evident redemption. The Covenant at Sinai, ushering in a new phase of history, seemed to be the motivation of all Passovers, past and future.

The relation of the primitive background to the emergent faith has been summed up in these terms by a Christian scholar (Prof. John Bright in *A History of Israel*, pages 92–9):

'The patriarchal religion was a clan religion, in which the clan was quite really the family of the patron God . . . Yet it resembled neither the official polytheisms of Mesopotamia nor the fertility cult of Canaan, of whose orgies there is no trace in the Genesis narrative . . .

'The cult of the patriarchs is depicted as exceedingly simple, as one would expect it to be. At its centre was animal sacrifice, as among all the Semites; but this was performed without organized clergy, at whatever place, by the hand of the clan father himself.

'As the patriarchs moved into Palestine, they came into contact with various shrines: Shechem, Bethel, Beer-Sheba, etc.: there, no doubt, their cults were practiced and perpetuated in identification with the cults already at home at those places. The patriarchal cult, however, was never a local one, but always the cult of the ancestral deity of the clan . . .

'As the patriarchal clans passed into the blood-stream of Israel . . . we may not doubt that Israel's structure and faith was shaped thereby more profoundly than we know. Her traditions of primeval antiquity, to say nothing of the ancestral migrations themselves . . . became vehicles of her distinctive theology of history. Above all, there was in Israel's heritage a feeling of tribal solidarity between people and God that must have contributed more than we can guess to that intensely strong sense of peoplehood so characteristic of her for all time to come.'

opposite 'Moses Breaks the Tablets of the Law', by the Italian painter Domenico Beccafumi (1486–1551)

3 The Development of the Haggadah

A Family Banquet

History can add a special meaning to quite ordinary words. A thousand years ago, when the exact ritual for Passover Eve was finally established, it was referred to informally as the 'Seder' or 'order' of things, a word that was still quite general. In due course, so popular was the evening that Seder came to mean the ritual for this particular evening only, when we recite the Haggadah and have a good meal, attended by so many familiar customs. This has happened, it should be said, only among Ashkenazi Jews—those coming mainly from Northern and Eastern Europe. Sephardi Jews—those coming mainly from Southern Europe and the East—have never used this term. They call the whole evening, in a general way, 'the Haggadah'. There are other minor differences of this kind in the two traditions, but overwhelmingly the ritual is the same.

The Seder has, in fact, existed for so long, and in such unchanging form and spirit, that it is hard to envisage Jewish life without it. If one asks 'when was the first Seder?', one is almost ready to apply the name symbolically not merely to our current ceremonies but to the original evening more than three thousand years ago when the story began in Egypt. There they were, on that dramatic last night—Jewish families gathered round the table, each in their own house, for a meal which was to symbolize their consciousness as a people and their faith in the future. From that distant night, the same experience, it almost seems, has been repeated year after year without break.

Of course it was not so. The Seder as we practice it now—a family ceremony in memory of the Exodus—began to take its shape only in the last days of the Second Temple, well over a thousand years after the Exodus from Egypt. It was more sharply defined in its present form in the century after the destruction of the Temple—

opposite A Seder scene of the Rococo period from a Haggadah illustrated by Moses Leib ben Wolf of Trebitsch, Moravia (1716–7)

Stone carving from the upper porch of Saint Chapelle, Paris (13th century) showing the *omer* and the Passover sacrifice

say between 100 and 150 CE—when it became, in effect, not merely a celebration of the Exodus but at the same time a nostalgic recall of the period which had followed, when the children of Israel settled in the Land of Promise and built a Temple in Jerusalem to serve their God. Over and over again the prayers and songs of the evening call to mind both the miracles of the past, through which God's promise to Israel was redeemed, and the miracles confidently expected in the future, when Israel would return to its ancient capital: *le-shanah haba'ah bi-yerushalayim*—'Next Year in Jerusalem.'

Yet even if the Seder, as we know it, emerged long after the Egyptian days and adapted itself still further, in subsequent centuries, to meet the conditions of the time, there is a sense in which our celebrations do recreate the spirit of 'the first Seder' in Egypt. The ritual ordered by Moses for that night was basically a family meal, even if it had to be eaten in haste, ready for the journey. In subsequent centuries something of the family aspect of the gathering was lost. When Israel settled down in the Holy Land, the paschal sacrifice took place—certainly after the reforms of King Josiah—at the Temple in Jerusalem, attended ritually by males of 'responsible' age, with the rest of the family not required to participate. The family was brought in much more positively, it is true, in the last years of the Second Temple, when the crowds flocking to Jerusalem for the occasion grew dramatically in number, including wives and children who could join in during the meal in the evening. But it was only after Jerusalem was destroyed (70 CE) that the celebration became once again, as the 'the first Seder' in ancient Egypt, a complete family gathering. It has remained so ever since, linking us across the centuries with the most ancient of our traditions, and illustrating—if it were needed—the power of family affection in Jewish life.

Perhaps one might say—not entirely as a joke—that it also illustrated the power of food in Jewish life, for the Seder, when it began, was planned quite simply as a banquet. We tend to think of it today as a whole series of religious ceremonies in the course of which a meal is eaten, but as soon as we look at it more closely we see that originally things were the other way round: the Seder was a meal, so to speak, from beginning to end, with talk, prayers and songs just breaking in here and there, as they might at any rather formal banquet.

This immediately explains some points in our present ritual that are sometimes rather puzzling. When the Seder was beginning to take shape, a century or so BCE, Palestine was in the Graeco-Roman orbit. A festive meal at that time had the form—as indeed it still has

—of a preliminary drink, some *hors d'oeuvres* leading directly to food, during which there was wine and more talk, continuing after the meal was over. Two points in relation to the Seder become clearer in this context.

A hand holding up the *maror* (bitter herb). Detail from the Livorno Haggadah

The first is the serving of celery—or something similar—at a very early stage. Today, this rather tantalizing mouthful is followed by a very long series of prayers and recitals before the next food arrives; but in ancient times it was recognizably the first course (*hors d'oeuvres*), followed immediately by the rest of the meal. (In Roman times the meal proper often began with eggs, another custom which a Seder tradition maintains.) The other point—a key to the Seder for most of us—is the ritual of the Four Questions. Today these are asked towards the beginning of the evening, yet they imply a knowledge of the food and ceremonies. In early times the Questions didn't assume any advance knowledge but reflected the child's actual observation. The meal was already being served and the child was stimulated: 'How different it all is tonight!' (the correct translation of *ma nishtana*). 'Why this, and why that?' Father started explaining while the food was being served and continued afterwards. But as the child tended to become rather sleepy under this system, the questions and explanations were all moved to the beginning, long before the meal proper. The child stayed awake—first for the food, and later, when they were introduced, for the songs.

It is not surprising that we feel the Seder ceremonies to be very ancient, since the essential ones are described in the Mishnah, the famous code of Jewish law which was edited around 200 CE. This takes the ceremonies still further back in time, for the Mishnah has been described as 'a deposit of four centuries of Jewish religious and cultural activity in Palestine'. On this basis, at least some of the Seder material might go back as far as the second century BC, to the time, say, of the Maccabees or even earlier.

If we reach back to Temple times for some of the Seder material, there is still an essential difference between a ceremony built around the formalities of a Temple sacrifice, and the kind of 'mixed' ritual described in the Mishnah, in which the rabbis, though still recalling the sacrifices vividly, were managing, of course, to live without them. As long as the Temple stood, the sacrifice of Passover was unique. The head of the household himself slaughtered in the Temple the lamb which his family or group were to eat during the evening. This was a great privilege, since all other sacrifices were carried out by the priests. The animal had to be roasted immediately and eaten within 'the Temple area', which was allowed, as the number of celebrants grew, to include the surrounding area of the city of Jerusalem. For those families who lived in Jerusalem, or came together there on pilgrimages, it could be a family meal. For many others, it was a meeting of males, organized in groups with a minimum number of ten participants, but capable of being much larger in number. (One thinks immediately of the exclusively male participants in the Last Supper, if this was indeed a 'Seder' meal—a subject which will be discussed below, page 82).

Gateway of a large synagogue at Bar-Am (Galilee) from Mishnah times (3rd century CE). The ruins of this synagogue were described in travel reports dating back to the Middle Ages

Could these 'sacrifice meals' have had the same character as the Seder? In Temple times, one would think, the emphasis in this Passover celebration, even if it included a certain amount of family jollity, must have centred mainly on the meticulous observance of the innumerable rules concerning the ritual perfection of the animal and the ritual cleanliness of the participants. The Mishnah, looking back to this period over a gap of a hundred years or more, devotes almost the whole of its chapter on Passover to these 'technical' subjects and deals only in the last section of the chapter with the family ceremonies of the meal itself, so familiar to us now. Yet the festive meal even in Temple times must have begun to assume some of its present character. Jewish practice generally was being affected in the last centuries of Temple times by what one might call the 'humanistic rabbinism' of the emerging Pharisees. Their ideas were converting formal archaic ritual into something warm, intelligent and human. We have to understand the Pharisees in order to understand the origin of our present Seder. The Pharisees are usually thought of as having ensured Jewish survival by erecting a fence of ritual distinctiveness; but they also fashioned that attitude of life which allowed the Jews of later generations to enrich their culture with contacts outside. In one form Pharisaism was inward-looking—a search for the full meaning of the Torah (Bible teaching), a reinterpretation of practices and feelings in terms of a lively oral tradition, linked ultimately to the teachings and discussions in synagogues all over the country. In another form it was—more simply—a search for wisdom, not out of tune with the Greek temper of the times. The Pharisees had begun to develop this ultimately flexible or adaptive attitude to the Torah—in argument, law, philosophy, devotion and speculation—when their movement began to take shape at the time of the Maccabees, in the second half of the second century BCE. In this they were in conflict with the Sadducees, who were concerned only with following the Bible ordinances and the Temple rituals literally. The rabbis who put the Mishnah together after the fall of the Temple were, of course, also attached to the minutiae of the Law and

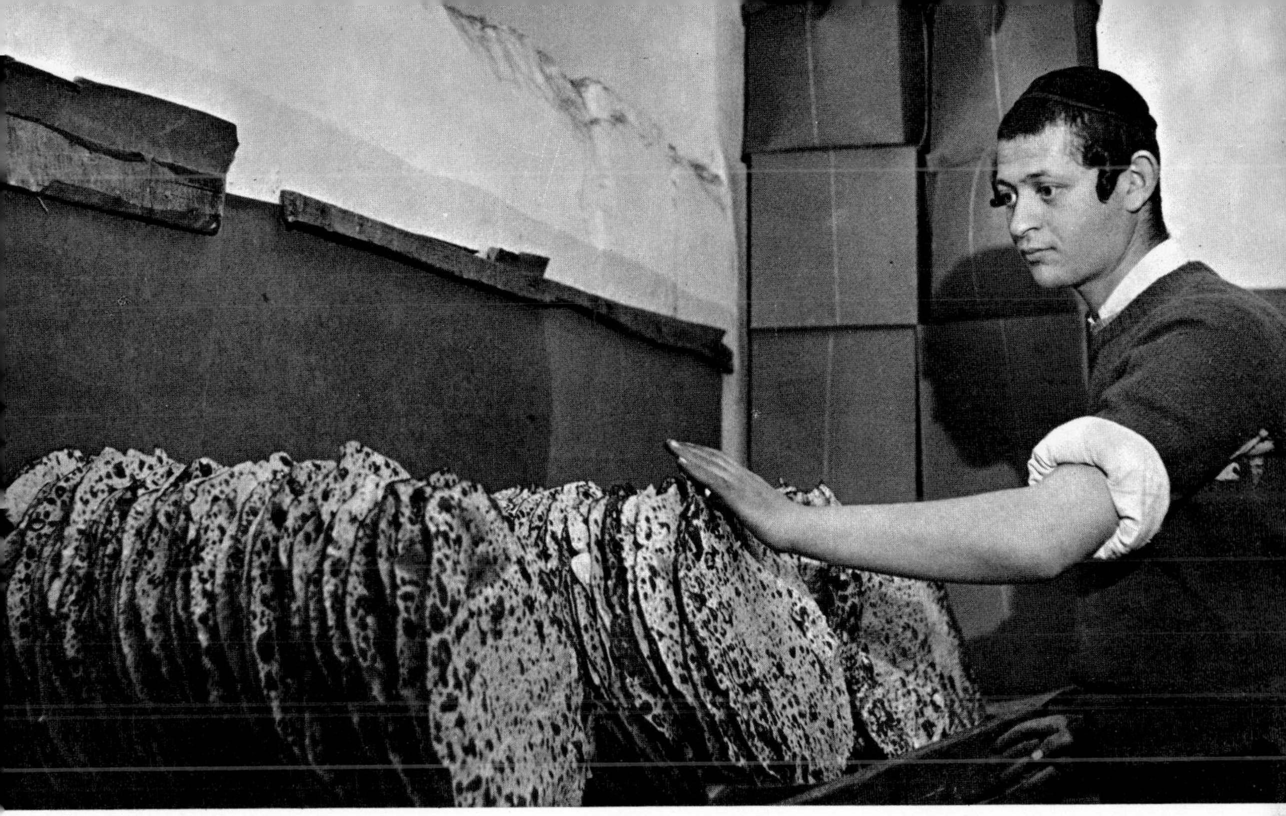

Temple ritual, arguing over every detail meticulously, but at the same time they evoked in their own terms a picture of the Law in practice—the ritual lived out not merely in Temple terms but in the perplexities and vagaries of day-to-day existence. Because the Torah covered every moment of life and not merely fixed ceremonies, it became an expression of the social conditions of the time—an almost anecdotal commentary, in Torah terms, on man in his most secular guise. Looking back from Mishnah days to Temple times, they were ready to assume that this attitude had already existed then, especially with so 'human' a ceremony as the Seder.

Strictly observant Jews prepare *matzah shemurah* ('guarded *matzah*') under the most meticulous conditions (see page 152)
above The baking of *matzah shemurah* in Mea Shearim, Jerusalem

It has never been easy in the course of Jewish history to separate ritualism and humaneness into different watertight compartments. One can see this illustrated frequently in the Mishnah discussion of Passover observance. What could be more ritual, but also more 'social', than some of the detailed instructions in the Mishnah on how to avoid any trace of 'leaven' or fermentation in preparing the Seder:

> 'A man may not chew grains of wheat at Passover to put on his wound, since they will ferment. One may not put meal into the *haroset* or the mustard (because water added later will make it ferment). The following must be removed: Babylonian porridge, Medean beer, Edomite vinegar, and Egyptian barley-beer; also dyers' pulp, cooks' starch-flower, and writers' paste. Rabbi Eliezer says: also women's cosmetics.'

From time immemorial, the Land of Israel has been famous for its wine, and the Four Cups at the Seder symbolize this blessing
above An oil lamp from the 2nd–3rd century CE, found in Israel, bearing symbols familiar in Jewish art, including grapes for the blessing of wine and a *lulav* for Sukkot
opposite A vineyard in Israel today

There is plenty also if one is looking at the other side of the medal—a social aim designed in ritual terms. Here is an example, on dealing with the poor, where a rigorous attention to the Law still left the underlying aim untouched. At the Passover meal, strangers and the poor were all welcome; but one of the rules, as given in the Mishnah, is linked to the more general system under which all towns had to keep a 'charity bowl' full of food for needy travellers. We are told in the Mishnah that from the late afternoon (the time of the sacrifice) on Passover Eve, 'a man must eat naught before nightfall.' This short ritual fast is to apply just as firmly to a needy traveller: he must not be given anything to eat until the formal evening meal, 'even from the charity-bowl'. Very tough; but in the same paragraph, the Mishnah says that at the meal itself 'even the poorest in Israel must be given not less than four cups of wine to drink'.

Here we see the earliest reference to the Four Cups of Wine, so familiar to us at the Seder. The number is sometimes derived in rabbinic argument from the fact that the Bible (*Exodus* VI, 6–7) ascribes four different expressions to God in explaining how he would perform the Exodus: 'I will bring out . . . deliver . . . redeem . . . take. . .'; but in the Mishnah the drinking of four cups is mentioned quite simply as fitting in with the various stages of the meal, as at any other banquet. What is interesting historically, however, is that the Mishnah, in referring to the rota of the Four Cups and other procedures of the Seder, quotes authorities and argumentation from the time of the famous rabbis Hillel and Shamai, who taught at the beginning of the first century, while the Temple was still standing. This confirms the feeling, illustrated also by the Gospels, that even if the full 'family Seder' did not come into its own until after the destruction of the Temple, some of the basic procedures had already clustered around the eating of the sacrifice. The most obvious of these were the benedictions on wine and food, the eating of bitter herbs as well as *matzah*, and the recital of the six 'Psalms of Praise' (*Psalms* 113–118). More important still, the meal in Temple times already included the recital of the story of the Exodus, and to some extent (as we shall see later) the elaboration of this in rabbinic argument. The link of our current Seder with the Temple period itself is therefore, to some extent, assured.

The Formative Years

The Mishnah account—brief as it is—of the early form of the Seder is worth examining in detail because it illustrates vividly how the rabbinic tradition, inflexible as it became, was in its early days much more tentative than it seemed later.

ואלו
הן
דם צפרדע
כנים ערוב
דבר שחין
ברד ארבה
חושך מכות בכורות

opposite The Ten Plagues recorded in decorative script from a Haggadah produced by a London scribe, Abraham Tang, in 1768

right An early 20th-century silver *haroset* dish from Holland, probably a copy of earlier 'wheelbarrow' dishes. It is designed to suggest that the *haroset* is a symbol of the mortar used for building during the slavery in Egypt

The rabbis in the Mishnah are always thought of, correctly, as the founders of the tradition. Everything recorded of them had to be pondered for its authority. Among the devout, nothing of what had been laid down by them could be changed. As a result, a concept arose later in Jewish life that the essentials of rabbinic teaching (as set out in the Mishnah and developed later in the Talmud as a whole) were as immutable as the Ten Commandments. Even in a recital as unforced as the Seder, most participants today want to be told 'the rules'. They would like to observe the Seder 'correctly'.

This is a natural feeling if one belongs to an historic community; yet looking back to early times, one can see that there was nothing pre-ordained in how the things we now observe became fixed. The existing tradition was discussed and written down. At this point, it was fairly flexible in detail. There was room for disagreement. As time went on, the shape of things asserted itself: disagreement fell away to leave an accepted pattern of ceremony which from then on was as 'natural', as if it had existed forever.

To see the Seder rules as described in the Mishnah takes us back, then, to the formative period, when argument was free.

The instructions in the Mishnah specify, first, the drinking of a cup of wine; and two benedictions are mentioned, one for the wine and one for the occasion. (The followers of Hillel and Shammai, respectively, immediately launch into argument about which benediction has to be recited first!) Food is then to be brought, which the celebrant eats 'seasoned with lettuce'. For 'the breaking of bread', they are to bring *matzah*, *hazeret* (lettuce), and *haroset*. This last

A 19th-century East European chopper used to make *haroset*

item—a brown mixture of chopped nuts and wine which is supposed to simulate the mortar of Egyptian building and to sweeten the bitter herbs—also arouses an argument. Most of the rabbis hold that it is not obligatory; one rabbi thinks it is.

The meal is then served (long before the prayers). A second cup of wine follows, after which come the Questions; and these, originally, are set out as three in number and different from those we now use. The earliest Mishnah texts read:

> 'And here the son asks his father—and if the son has not enough understanding his father instructs him how to ask—"Why is this night different from other nights?"
>
> "On other nights we eat seasoned food once, but on this night twice.
>
> "On other nights we eat leavened or unleavened bread, but this night all is unleavened.
>
> "On other nights we eat meat either roasted, stewed or cooked, but on this night all is roast." '

This third question—on why the meat of the sacrifice is roasted—was, of course, dropped after the destruction of the Temple. The fourth question in our current Haggadah—'why do we lean?'—came long later, and was probably an impromptu which stuck. We need not be too surprised. The rabbinical authorities point out in the Talmud that the Questions as set out in the Mishnah were only intended as examples. In the course of time they were elaborated and then became rigid.

With the meal over and the Questions asked, the Mishnah takes us next to the father's answer, which is described in a striking phrase: 'He begins with the shame and ends with the glory.' In our present Haggadah, the shame we begin with is 'we were slaves in Egypt';

Rabbinical discussion after morning prayers, echoing the type of scholastic debate between the rabbis in the Haggadah

but when the form of the Seder was still loose enough to be argued about, some rabbis thought (as we shall see later) that the real shame to start with should be that once we were idolaters ('in the beginning our fathers worshipped idols'.)

Whichever passage is the right one to begin with, we are now launched on 'the story'—the real Haggadah. The Mishnah lays down that the story should be told in the form of an exposition of a passage in Deuteronomy (XXVI, 5–8) beginning: 'My father was a wandering Syrian' and ending: 'God brought us forth . . .with signs and wonders.' In our present Haggadah, a detailed commentary on these verses is actually spelt out—a very elaborate midrashic (homiletical) exposition, with much bandying of scriptural verses, and ending with a 'proof' that the last of the Deuteronomy verses ('with a mighty hand . . .with signs and wonders') has to be understood as a direct reference to the Ten Plagues. Using the same methods, our Haggadah goes on to 'prove', according to one rabbi, that there must have been not ten but sixty plagues. Another rabbi 'proves' two hundred and forty plagues. Rabbi Akiva—implying a *reductio ad absurdum*—raises the total to three hundred. The discussion is typical of the midrashic tradition as it had developed by Mishnah times, capable of light-hearted fun as well as serious exposition. It doesn't sound like the kind of talk we might expect to have encountered around the table as an accompaniment to a sacrifice brought from the Temple. It is too urbane, too 'post-Destruction', too 'Jewish'.

The Mishnah then introduces Rabbi Gamaliel spelling out the reasons for the three basic ceremonies—*pesach, matzah, maror*—leading up, exactly as in our Haggadah, to the recital of the *Hallel*

(*Psalms* 113–118). There is great authority in this dictum of Gamaliel. He was a famous leader, living at the end of the first century CE, who was known in general as a codifier of prayers and ritual. The singing of the *Hallel* is also interesting. An earlier section of the Mishnah had already linked this singing to the Temple sacrifice, by explaining that the Levites sang these Psalms continuously in the Temple while the animal was being ritually slaughtered:

> 'An Israelite slaughtered his own offering and the priest caught the blood . . . The priest nearest to the Altar tossed the blood in one action against the base of the Altar . . . In the meantime the Levites were singing the *Hallel*. If they finished it they sang it anew; and if they finished it a second time, they sang it a third time . . .'

By the time this was being written down in the Mishnah, any detail of this kind recalled from Temple times was mentioned not 'realistically'—in the sense of planning for a resumption—but symbolically, implying that there would always be a holy virtue in trying to understand the form and meaning of Temple ritual, whether it could be resumed or not. The assumption behind this was that the sacrifices themselves were not to be understood as 'automatic' in their effect but always as a way of expressing the interior meaning of Jewish faith. Rabbi Akiva, who died some

The word *afikoman* is thought to have originally meant the dancing and revelry forbidden after the solemnities of the Seder
below Greek dancing from the 'Brygos chalice' (5th century BCE)

sixty-five years after the destruction of the Temple, is explicitly quoted in the Mishnah as turning his thoughts on the sacrifice into a noble expression of the hope of 'redemption'. The prayer he composed is repeated verbatim in our Haggadah:

> 'Bring us in peace to the other set feasts and festivals which are before us . . . May we eat of the sacrifices and Passover offerings whose blood shall reach with acceptance the wall of Thy altar, and let us praise Thee for our redemption and for the ransoming of our soul. Blessed is God who has redeemed Israel.'

Towards the end of the Mishnah instructions, there is a short sentence about the *afikoman* that appears equally bluntly in our Haggadah and has puzzled many celebrants. Literally, it seems to say: 'We don't end the *Pesach* meal *afikoman*'. Most of us know the *afikoman* as the piece of *matzah* which has been hidden by the host early in the proceedings precisely in order to end the meal with it, as a kind of dessert or savoury. It is, of course, 'stolen' by the children and has to be 'ransomed' (by a present) for its ceremonial purpose. The sentence is therefore usually translated loosely as: 'We don't eat anything after the *afikoman* (dessert).' The word is really from the Greek *epikomion*, meaning 'a festival procession', or simply 'revelry', and the instruction is therefore that one should not follow the holy

pleasures of the Seder with some licentious entertainment. We shall discuss this point further below, in relation to parallel non-Jewish 'talk-meals' of the time. The original meaning of *afikoman* is, in a way, less significant than the one it acquired. Within a generation or two of the Mishnah, the word had become obscure to the rabbis, as the Talmud (*Pesahim* 119b) shows. The meaning that has become accepted is that it is simply the final morsel of the meal and an excuse for fun with the children.

Echoes of the Time – Josephus and the Gospels

It is a paradox of Jewish history that in one sense we seem to know so much about the past and in another sense remarkably little. Sometimes the links are documented with absolute clarity; in other cases mere fragments have survived, all the more challenging, of course, for the proliferation of theories as to how they have to be interpreted.

There could hardly be a better example of this than the Seder in its formative period—in the last century of Temple times. On the one hand, as we have seen, we have a full outline written down about eighteen hundred years ago in the Mishnah, which links up directly with the ceremony as we practice it and certainly throws light on the earlier days. On the other hand, very little is available in other writings to tell us of actual celebrations of the time. There are references in the *Book of Jubilees*, the work of an heterodox sect (perhaps Essenes) written around 100 BCE, describing the general excitement of Passover, including the wine-drinking. We also have Philo, a century later, writing from a distance in Alexandria and emphasizing the spiritual character of the feast:

> 'The whole nation performs the sacred rites and acts as priest with pure hands and complete immunity . . .Every dwelling-house is invested with the outward semblance and dignity of a temple.'

But the most interesting passages are perhaps in Josephus and the Gospels.

Woodcut showing the meal of a *chavurah* from a Haggadah printed in Basle, 1815–6. The illustration is reminiscent of representations of the Last Supper

Josephus, himself of priestly descent, went over to the Romans during the Jewish rebellion of 68–70 CE, a fact which colours much of his historical work both in the *Jewish War* (written *ca.* 75–79 CE) and *Antiquities of the Jews* (*ca.* 93–94 CE); but he obviously writes quite factually of the Passover rituals as he knew them before Jerusalem was destroyed in 70 CE.

In the detailed account he gives of the origin and practices of Passover, the explanation of it all (he is writing for non-Jews) is drawn in traditional terms from the Bible. He concentrates on the Temple rituals, giving details of the enormous number of pilgrims, and also describing a special ceremony, the waving of the *omer* (a sheaf of barley from the new crop)—which is recalled now in a prayer on the second night of the Seder. He never discusses what went on at the home meal, but there is one detail he gives—mentioning it almost casually—that is directly relevant and is also important in relation to the Last Supper. It is that the Paschal sacrifice was celebrated by 'groups':

> 'A little fraternity, as it were, gathers round each sacrifice, of not fewer than ten persons (feasting alone not being permitted), while the companies often include as many as twenty.'

He mentions this in connection with the census taken under Cestius (pro-consul 64–66 CE). By counting the number of sacrifices (255,600) and 'allowing an average of ten diners to each sacrifice', a minimum figure of some two and a half million participants emerged. But the 'group' concept is of wider significance.

Towards the end of the second century BCE, some Jews who attached great weight to the scrupulous observance of traditional law had begun to express this by joining a *chavurah* (group), to ensure that they would be dealing with people who observed the proper standard of cleanliness and trust. A basic element in the ritual law was the need to set aside part of the crop, before use, for 'the Priest, the Levite and the poor'. Members of a *chavurah* would pledge themselves to observe these standards and also those of ritual cleanliness. On this basis, they could trustingly do business with each other, knowing, for example, that the food they traded had been properly tithed. The opposite type of person was an *am ha'aretz*—broadly meaning 'one of the common people', but more technically someone careless of religious duty and therefore not to be trusted for business dealings.

It is a striking example of how religious observance, far from being superficial, was carried through into every-day morality. Members of a *chavurah* would tend to be Pharisees, though the terms were not the same. No one could join a *chavurah* without sponsors, and all would have a trial period of membership to ensure that they were *ne'emanim* (trustworthy).

It is clear that a *chavurah* could have the character of a close sacramental fellowship, and this may throw light on the Dead Sea Scroll community at Qumran. Close groups could exist, of course, for less 'orthodox' purpose, such as the group of disciples that gathered around Jesus. Where a *chavurah* existed they might quite naturally share a special occasion, like the Passover sacrifice; and this would be the way to understand the arrangements that the

A jar from Qumran similar to those in which the Dead Sea Scrolls were preserved

disciples had made to eat the Passover meal together with Jesus.

To understand the references in the Gospels to Passover, one must keep in mind the two-fold standard of these writings. At one level the writers, several decades after the death of Jesus, could still draw on folk-memory or tradition for realistic and even vivid detail of his time: at another level, they were concerned quite explicitly with presenting the events of his life in a way which would be in keeping with the Christological faith which had already developed. The Passover references fit in to both these categories.

One natural echo of the time is the brief story in Luke (II, 41–49) about the visit of Jesus to Jerusalem at the age of twelve. It begins with great simplicity:

> 'It was the practice of his parents to go to Jerusalem every year for the Passover festival; and when he was twelve, they made the pilgrimage as usual.'

This is all being told, of course, for what is going to happen at the end of the visit. Jesus, having been lost, is finally found 'sitting in the Temple surrounded by the teachers, listening to them and putting questions; and all who heard him were amazed at his intelligence and the answers he gave'. Strangely enough this too, though probably intended by the writer to show Jesus as 'different', is, in fact, a picture of absolute naturalness in the Jewish tradition. It may have been unusual then, but it certainly became common later to find boy-prodigies of twelve, learned in the Talmud, sitting among the rabbis and amazing all by their knowledge and insight.

We are more directly concerned here, of course, with the Gospel stories of the Last Supper. Was it a Seder, and if so does it throw any light on the celebration of Seder at the time?

There is no doubt, of course, that the Gospel tradition wanted to link this meal with the eve of Passover, and in some ways the near-contemporary account of details is very interesting. Preparations for the meal were numerous: a sacrifice was chosen, and a room to eat it; there was wine, there were hymns (the *Hallel?*) after the food, and there was much discussion. To this extent, a Seder is being evoked: yet the evocation also includes other details which makes it go wrong. Contrary to what one first expects, it does not become clear at all if the meal, as described, should be thought of as an actual Seder. The need of the writers to re-interpret what took place in terms of the Christian faith makes it go wrong.

opposite The 'Pour Out Thy Wrath' page from the Darmstadt Haggadah (Middle Rhine, mid-15th century), one of the most elegant mediaeval Haggadahs. The pictures of young women being instructed by elderly male teachers suggest that this manuscript was executed for a woman

One of the uncertainties arises on timing. According to the Synoptic Gospels (Matthew, Mark and Luke), the meal was actually on the Seder eve; according to John it was, apparently, a day earlier. But it is the character of the meal which is even more per-

פוך חמתך על הגוים
אשר לא ידעוך ועל
הממלכות אשר בשמך

plexing. Nothing is said of the eating of the sacrifice. What we do hear (from the Synoptic Gospels) is that the participants 'dipped into a common bowl' and that at one point a blessing was said on 'bread' (presumably unleavened) and wine was drunk. What we miss, however, is any discussion of the Exodus theme. Instead, the air is full of a more personal drama—Jesus's foreknowledge of imminent betrayal and death, of which the food eaten was to be symbol, so that he can say of the bread, 'Eat, this is my body', and of wine, 'This is my blood, the new covenant, which is shed for many.' The account in John is even less connected with any realistic Seder. It refers to none of the quasi-Seder rituals hinted at in the Synoptic Gospels, and is even more explicit in drawing out the Christological rather than the Exodus message.

If the meal, as described, was not a normal Seder, can we be sure, at least, that the Thursday evening on which it took place was a 'Seder night' (the eve of the feast?). The Synoptic Gospels clearly meant this to be understood, but there are problems. The dramas of the next day—which were to include trial by the Sanhedrin, reference to the Roman authorities and crucifixion—would have had to take place on a festival day, on which a trial was wholly contrary to Jewish practice. The problem is easier in the timing given in John, which seems to envisage the Saturday as the first day of Passover, so that the drama of Friday would be on the day before the festival. But even this is not easy, since 'the day before' a festival was quasi-holy and therefore equally unlikely for a serious trial under Jewish law.

Many suggestions have been made by the scholars to reconcile these difficulties, but the odds seem to be that the meal, as described, was not, in fact, at Seder time. A possible explanation is that the Gospel writers, recognizing the importance of the *Pesach* meal as a symbol of sacrifice, telescoped the events preceding the crucifixion into a period very close to Passover in order to be able to suggest that Jesus was, in effect, the sacrifice of Passover. This suggestion is clear enough even in the Synoptic Gospels, where the official sacrifice is supposed to have already taken place on the day before the crucifixion. It is more explicit still in John, where the symbolism of the crucifixion at the very hour of the Temple sacrifice is stressed and filled out with echoes of appropriate biblical phrases (e.g. 'a bone of him shall not be broken').

In seeking to use to the full the 'idea' of the Passover—even if the account given did not fit in too easily—the Christian writers were trying to use the power of the Passover concept for their new purposes. Even the symbolism of unleavened bread could be trans-

The Old Testament stories never lost their appeal as precursors of a new fulfilment

opposite 'Gathering of the Manna in the Desert' by the Flemish painter Dieric Bouts (1420–1475) formed in this way to meet the new idea, as in I Corinthians (V, 7–8):

> 'Purge out therefore the old leaven that ye may be a new lump, as ye are unleavened . . . Let us keep the feast . . . with the unleavened bread of sincerity and truth.'

But it is the sacrifice idea which is dominant. In its more general form, it is expressed by the Baptist (according to John) when he first sees Jesus: 'Behold the Lamb of God, which taketh away the sin of the world.' In its more intense form, there are the sayings on the bread and wine ascribed to Jesus at the Last Supper. The Gospel writers introduced these concepts—wholly out of keeping with anything that could have entered the mind of a traditional Jew of the time of Jesus—to express a development that had taken the faith of the new sect firmly away from the old tradition.

In a tragic way, this all entered—as we shall see—the Haggadah of later generations.

A Greek Symposium?

We have been taking it for granted that our traditional Seder—in content at least—is wholly Jewish. But if we look into its form, as a 'talk-feast', we find parallels outside which re-open the question asked before: how far are our ancient ceremonies Jewish, in the sense of peculiar to ourselves in concept and style; how far, *per contra*, do they reflect in origin the world in which Jews found themselves while these ceremonies were being shaped for future generations?

Nothing could seem more completely Jewish than the Seder, but for most of us this is because we are not normally very familiar with the symposia—or 'talk-feasts'—that were common in the Graeco-Roman world and which can be shown to have influenced the ritual set out in the Haggadah to a quite remarkable degree. This is not to say that the central theme of the Seder—the desire to talk about the Exodus—is not our own; what bears examination, however, is the precise way in which the biblical command to 'tell' (*ve-higgadta*) our children the ancient story was given its present form.

We can see in other fields how something adopted by Jews from their neighbours in one generation can become almost sacred to Jewish life at a later time. An obvious example is the costume worn by the extremely orthodox—fur cap, long silk coat, brightly coloured stockings—familiar today in Jerusalem's Mea Shearim and other places, but starting as the dress of a nobleman in 16th-century Poland. Something similar happened with the Haggadah in Palestine of the early part of the second century CE. Jewish leaders

The Seder as a Greek symposium?
above Plato teaching in Athens, from a mosaic uncovered in Pompeii (1st century CE)

of the time were quite naturally responsive to the intellectual climate in which they lived, and engaged in symposia like their contemporaries. The social customs of Greek symposia are described in books which show very interesting parallels to the Haggadah style.

One way into this question is to think back to Plato's *Symposium* (and indeed any of the *Dialogues*) in which Socrates and a number of chosen companions—the 'rabbis' of ancient Athens—gather for a relaxed evening of talk, not about trivialities but on a set theme. In the *Symposium*, of course, the theme was personal love and beauty, as keys to a definition of eternal truth. Many parallel types of discussion were written down, exploring set themes in the light of the received traditions of Greek history. At these symposia, food and drink were served lavishly to the privileged participants, but it was the talk which was important.

It was a pattern which grew widely in the 'civilized' world in the centuries which followed, so much so that by the time the Haggadah emerged, books were being written by social historians setting out in great detail the character and 'rules' of these gatherings. They covered not only the type of talk, but also everything a man might find interesting to know about the food and drink themselves—their provenance and preparation, the importance of the dining 'ritual', and above all how the procedures stretched back to the authentic source of 'all history'—Homer himself. Even without direct parallels one would begin to hear echoes of the style of the Haggadah.

But the connections with the actual form of the Haggadah are stronger than this. If we turn to roughly contemporary books explaining the symposia of the time, we find direct parallels for many of the most 'authentic' and accepted phrases and comments of the Haggadah.

The two best-known sources of this kind are Plutarch's light-hearted 'Table Talk' (*Quaestiones Conviviales*), eight books of lively argument and information, and a fifteen-volume work by the second-century writer Athenaeus which might be called in English 'The Sophists at Home' (*Deipnosophists*) or perhaps 'The Gastronomes', concentrating as it does on every aspect of food and drink. The Jewish scholar Siegfried Stein has drawn vividly on these and other symposia writers to throw light on points in the Haggadah which we might otherwise take for granted as of exclusively Jewish origin.

If one thinks in a general way of one of the key phrases of the Haggadah, 'the more one talks, the more praiseworthy one is', the mood of the classical symposium is struck immediately. Even in Athenaeus—ultimately only a cookbook, though the oldest and perhaps the greatest in the world—the form is of an imaginary symposium, reminding us immediately of the rabbis at B'nei B'rak:

> 'Larensis (the host) took pride in gathering about him many men of culture and entertaining them with conversation as well as the things proper to a banquet, now proposing topics worthy of enquiry, now disclosing solutions of his own; for he never put his questions without previous study, or in a haphazard way, but with the utmost critical, even Socratic, acumen, so that all admired the keen observation showed by his questions.'

Another writer, Macrobius, comes even closer to the Seder, explaining that during the Saturnalia a number of distinguished scholars assembled at a certain house 'to celebrate the festive time by discourse'—the host explaining the source of the festival and thus doing homage to religion 'by devoting sacred study to the sacred days.' In the Haggadah, as we remember so well, the rabbis who assembled precisely for this purpose were so absorbed that they talked until their students came next morning to call them to morning service, the time for which was the cock's crow. It was a common experience of the classical world. In Plato's *Symposium*, they talk until the crowing of the cock reminds the guests to go home.

But one gets much closer than this. Jewish scholars (notably Saul Lieberman) have shown us that the Greek language and Greek ideas were far more widespread in early rabbinic Palestine than one might have guessed from what was assumed to be the general hostility to 'non-Jewish' matters. On this basis, the 'Greek ritual' of the meal on Passover Eve must have been natural for any gathering of scholars at a banquet. The odds are that if some of the procedures and talk at one of these gatherings on Passover Eve were put down in writing—say, for example, the meeting which is actually recorded at B'nei B'rak—it could have become a style for Passover Eve and hence the norm or rule for all future celebrations of the Seder in generations to come.

There is no doubt that the rabbis loved banqueting—when they got a chance—as much as their non-Jewish neighbours. Of course they saw these things in proportion. Where a Greek writer like Athenaeus records everything about the food in what we would regard today as a sophisticated, well-ordered style, the rabbinic tradition on this subject is more fragmentary; but it certainly existed. The *midrash* on Lamentations records, for example, that at a banquet before the Day of Atonement a visiting rabbi was offered eighty courses, and wine with each: 'Not one course duplicated another.' There are many stories of this kind. Not much detail is given, however, and perhaps this indicates that for all their pleasure in good food, the ancient Jews of Palestine never elevated cooking to a high art. It is significant of that that whereas Athenaeus gives recipes of Greek, Persian, Sicilian, Roman and a host of other types of cooking, he never provides any Jewish recipes!

But the fragments which have crept into the Haggadah recital are interesting enough. Apart from the obvious parallels in style with Greek banquets—washing the hands, drinking wine throughout the meal, 'reclining' and so on—there are the references to

A Greek banquet showing discussion 'at ease', as at the Seder. Detail from a 6th-century BCE Corinthian *krater* (vase)

specific foods. On the opening *hors d'oeuvres* of lettuce, Stein points out that Athenaeus refers to lettuce repeatedly in his work, describing its role in the meal. Athenaeus also produces recipes for something very similar to *haroset*—ground nuts and fruit laced with spices and wine—quoting a first-century Greek doctor on whether these appetizers were better as *hors d'oeuvres* or dessert. If Hillel—as recorded in the Haggadah—invented the sandwich of *matzah* and bitter herb, we learn from Stein that the meat or lettuce sandwich was already common at the time.

More generally there is the style of the talk. Athenaeus has been quoted above on this. Plutarch—a contemporary of Rabbi Akiva and the other rabbis who met at B'nei B'rak—says something even more applicable to the Seder:

> 'A symposium is a communion of serious and mirthful entertainment, discourse and actions . . .(It furthers) a deeper insight into the points debated at the table, for the remembrance of the pleasures arising from food is short-lived . . .but the subjects of philosophical queries and discussions remain always fresh after they have been imparted.'

There were no hard and fast rules for the talk:

> 'Even Plato did not prepare himself for the contest like a wrestler . . .Questions should be easy, the problems known, the interrogations plain and familiar, not intricate and dark, so that they may neither vex the unlearned nor frighten them from the disquisition . . .The discourse should be like our wine, common to all, of which everyone may equally partake.'

One sees immediately a parallel to the spirit of *ma nishtana*—the Four Questions in the Haggadah. These simple questions about food—'why do we dip? why eat bitter herbs? . . .'—lead to a free-wheeling explanation. In Plutarch similar questions about food also are the natural starting point for general talk: 'Does the sea or the land provide better food? Is it easier to digest a single dish or a variety of food?' There is even a question about the Jews: 'Do they abstain from pork because they worship the pig or because they don't like it?' The answers in the Haggadah are certainly more serious, bringing in, as they do, the whole *raison d'être* of Jewish existence, but the style of questioning is similar. There is common ground in all intelligent discussion.

One scholar has even seen Greek motivation in the emergence of *four* questions. Pointing to the fact that the rabbis adopted 'four types of forensic argument' from Hellenistic rhetoric, he tries to link the four questions to this. But it is hard to force the Four Questions (originally three, it must be remembered) into this kind of straight-jacket. They are much more easily seen as spontaneous

opposite 'The Four Sons' as portrayed in engravings on a late 17th-century silver and gilt Seder goblet from Germany

table-talk which became routinized in the course of time.

What can, possibly, be traced back more directly to a formal Hellenistic source is the section in the Haggadah on the 'Four Sons' —four types of children and how to deal with their questions. A book of Philo that has survived in fragmentary form argues that there are, in fact, four types of children—the 'good one', who follows both father (representing 'perfect reason') and mother (who stands for 'education' and experience); the opposite type ('wicked') who follows neither; and the two who give more weight to either one influence or the other. This kind of analysis sounds like a ready-made formula for an argument which could have been put forward as a talk-gambit at some symposium and repeated later because it stimulated people to good conversation. Certainly the Four Sons—often used later for illustrations in the Haggadah—became favourites.

We have already noted that it was customary for a Greek banquet —however serious the talk—to be followed by some licentious revelry—'epikomion'. In the Haggadah, the wise son is told that the Seder is not to give way to '*afikoman*'; he is intelligent enough to understand why. There may be a similar connection in the reply to the wicked son. The Haggadah says: 'Put his teeth on edge' with your answer. Stein says that in addition to the calm talk at a symposium, there could also be a rather noisy free-for-all type of argument. This is exactly the style of rebuke recommended for the wicked son, which ends very roughly in some versions of the Haggadah: 'If *you* had been in Egypt, you wouldn't have been redeemed.'

There may have been a non-Jewish source or stimulus even in the style of some of the prayers or the selection of the passages for exposition. There is a very beautiful Hebrew prayer, for example, called by its first word *Nishmat* ('the breath of every living thing . . .') which is in the Sabbath morning liturgy and also included in the Haggadah. It is a paean of praise to God in the most mellifluous terms, and is thought to be a striking example of the panegyric style which Greek rhetoric had developed in addressing a royal personage. A high-flown, almost sycophantic exaggeration when applied to a mortal king was clearly thought by the rabbis to be entirely appropriate when addressed to the King of Kings. Another example of Greek rhetoric (it is thought) may lie in the use by the Haggadah of the passage from Deuteronomy (XXVI, 5–8) as a basis for expounding the miracle of the Exodus. As mentioned earlier, the Mishnah instructions on the Seder say that in answering the Four Questions the father 'begins with shame and ends with *opposite* Moses receiving the Torah and descending from Mt Sinai to present it to the Israelites. From the Regensburg Pentateuch (Germany, *ca.* 1300)

glory'. This procedure was the exact style of a Greek eulogy, where the method prescribed was to draw the sharpest contrast between the initial weakness of the character, set against the ultimate triumph. The verses from Deuteronomy were selected for midrashic exposition precisely for this purpose: 'My father was a wandering Syrian . . .They went down to Egypt few in number . . .' and so on, against which God's miracles, including the Plagues, become all the more to be wondered at and praised.

But if these and other parallels from Greek rhetoric and symposia throw light on the literary form of the Haggadah, the most important point to note at the end is how utterly different in spirit was the final product. For one thing, the Seder, unlike the Greek symposium, spread out from a small élite discussion to become something for all to join in. A ready basis for this was the Passover meal which all families ate, without, at first, a stylized ritual. It was natural that, as a pattern of discussion and prayer filtered through from the meetings of the acknowledged teachers, it could spread down to the masses, losing its original flexibility to become a formula used by all.

We have noted other essential contrasts in the motivation and character of these gatherings—above all the concentration of the discussion on history and high purpose. As a book with this aim, the Haggadah is a limited, fragmentary work compared with the elaborate sophisticated books produced by Graeco-Roman culture, which can be read today with profound admiration for the wide-ranging curiosity and intellect which inspired them. The quality which emerged from the Haggadah is very different. It deals not with man as a searcher, but man as a moral being. The moral law, enshrined in the Torah 'given at Sinai', is hailed as the central factor in human existence. As individuals, Jews could and would respond as freely as anybody else to the marvels of free enquiry, of philosophy, of science. As a people, they had come to stand, historically, for the pursuit of a moral millennium. The signal had been their release from bondage in Egypt. If they met as a people at the Seder, it was this that they had come together to serve.

The Haggadah as a Book

Looking back, the social purpose of the Seder—once it had established itself—is clear enough. One has to beware, however, of assuming that it always existed in this clear form. Even in the Diaspora—where the absence of Temple sacrifices might have promoted this type of ceremony, as it did in Palestine after 70 CE —there is no evidence from early times that Passover Eve had produced an established ritual. It is interesting, for example, that

אנכי. לא תרצח
לא יהיה לך לא תנאף
לא תשא לא תגנב
זכור לא תענה
כבד את לא תחמוד

Philo, describing how at Passover 'every house is invested with the dignity of a Temple', talks only in general terms of the 'prayers and hymns' accompanying the banquet. Surprisingly, he records something much closer to a detailed Seder-like ritual being celebrated by an ascetic sect of Jews (the *Therapeutae*) not on Passover Eve but on the Eve of the Feast of Weeks.

opposite The rabbis holding their all-night discussion at B'nei B'rak. From the Erna Michael Haggadah (Germany, *ca.* 1400)

One has to assume a very fluid state of affairs on such matters in the early centuries, even if we see an outline of the Seder emerging in the Mishnah. The background to Jewish social life inside and outside Palestine was very unsettled because of political turmoil, the transition from statehood, the proliferation of sects, and the ambivalent status for a time of the Jewish-Christians. One sees elements in our current Haggadah paralleled in other rabbinic works, but it is very hard to determine which came first. The oral tradition was rich but inchoate, so that sayings within it go back and forth without strict timing.

An example of the confusion in authorship lies in the story already mentioned—of the rabbis meeting at B'nei B'rak. Are we to take it that all the discussion in our Haggadah which follows—including the talk on how many plagues there really were—is being pinned to that 'symposium', or merely the one paragraph about staying up all night? We shall probably never know.

Moving forward from the Mishnah, we might have expected to find historical and illustrative material on the Seder in the Talmud—the voluminous discussions of the rabbis in the learned colleges of Palestine and Babylonia. The basis of their discussions were the rulings of the Mishnah, so that they were called on to expound and expand the basic material on the Seder given there; but their discussions are much more about the long-suspended sacrifices than about the current Seder meals.

There is one way, however, of seeing how strongly the Seder had taken hold, and how old was the tradition which supported it. The first full recording of what is basically our present Haggadah is in a famous Prayer Book, edited by a Babylonian scholar—Rabbi Amram ben Sheshnah—in the ninth century CE. This classical work covering all ceremonies, and usually known as *Seder* (or *Siddur*) Rab Amram—was due to become one of the greatest influences on Jewish religious practice and ceremony for the next thousand years. One reason for its authority was that Amram included with the prayers a running commentary bringing together centuries of 'rulings' by the rabbis of the Talmud and their successors, the *Geonim*. The Haggadah was only a small part of Amram's Prayer Book, but it had been given finite form at last as a complete work, enshrining comments stretching back for centuries, and proving that it had been taking root all the time in Jewish consciousness.

The rabbis of Babylonia were, at this time, much the most dominant influence in the Jewish world. In deciding what was to be the 'correct' Haggadah from then on, Amram was not merely writing down the prayers and rituals that the tradition had guarded; he was also choosing among alternative passages the things he and his colleagues thought should be in it, and in particular he was asserting the view of the establishment—the Rabbanites—against a sect called Karaites who were very active at the time. The Karaites clung to the text of the Bible (*kara*) and had no patience with the rabbinical interpretations that had become 'normative' to the tradition. A predecessor of Amram—the *Gaon* Natronai—had been outspoken in saying that the Haggadah must include the type of *midrash* passages and rabbinical *dicta* we are now used to. Any group which refused to do so (and he meant the Karaites) were to be worthy of excommunication. Here, then, was the stimulus to Amram to put down an approved text of the Haggadah, with its emphasis on the rabbinic approach. It was a final choice. With only small changes, and the addition of a few folk-songs, the Haggadah included by Amram in his Prayer Book is the one we use.

En passant, this moment of literary history enables us to answer a question frequently asked about the Haggadah: 'why isn't Moses mentioned in it?' Moses was surely the hero, in human terms, of the Exodus. Why does his name not appear (except once, incidentally, in a biblical quotation)? Many speculative answers have been offered. The historical answer seems to lie in the Rabbanite-Karaite struggle. The Karaites, restricting themselves to the Bible text, undoubtedly included passages about Moses in their Haggadah, presenting the story simply and literally. The Rabbanites believed that literalism was inadequate. The Bible text needed to be understood in terms of the living oral tradition. To concentrate only on the biblical account of the Exodus, for example, would turn Moses—the Messenger of God—almost into a God himself, and that way lay heresy. Midrashic interpretation of the Bible allowed for philosophic views to be developed and supported allegorically, or symbolically, by Bible verses. It was a view which assumed that man's reasoning faculty had a part to play in establishing his faith. In himself, Moses would certainly have earned a place in the Haggadah. He was taken out, it seems, to assert a principle—to make sure (as we shall also see below, page 118) that he was not too large a figure in the story.

For some time after Amram, the Haggadah ritual remained embedded in the general Prayer Book. This was true of the more

An engraving depicting Karaites from Artamof's *La Russie Historique* (1862)

developed Prayer Book produced in the tenth century by the great *Gaon* Saadya; and even Maimonides, in the twelfth century, simply included the Haggadah as part of his collection of the prayers. The first sign we have of the Haggadah being produced as a separate book emerges from the thirteenth century. Versions may have been extracted from the Prayer Book and copied out for domestic use before this, but it is in the thirteenth century that the practice seems to have begun of not merely copying the specific prayers for Passover Eve but also of adding songs and poems—often poems that were intended for use in synagogue for Sabbath and Festival services connected with Passover.

A book copied out in this way for home use became a precious possession; and it was at this time that increasing attention was given to embroidering the Haggadah manuscripts with decorative letters and a variety of biblical and ritual illustrations. From then on, the Haggadah exists not merely as a domestic Prayer Book but as a medium that was to stimulate the imagination of scribes, printers, commentators, poets, artists and the general public as no other individual book has done in Jewish history.

The reasons for this special passion are diverse, but not difficult to unravel. Behind it all lay the powerful appeal of the Passover festival. There were other holy days of the year which called forth special feelings—the intense confessional of the Day of Atonement, the triumphal mood of Chanukah, the carefree joy of Purim. But Passover was unique because, as it drew near, it confronted every Jew with the history of his people, due to be celebrated in the ambience which had become the most precious of all for Jews—the family unit. During the year, the family might scatter; at Passover—at the Seder—they would surmount every obstacle to be reunited. No preparations would be too great for this momentous celebration. The ritual itself demanded a complete renewal of life—the house to be cleaned out for every stray crumb, dishes and food to be revolutionized, new clothes for parents and children. In this immense recreative act each year, the book which would be produced for reading—the Haggadah—would be a focal point for preparation long in advance. Even before the first printed Haggadahs emerged, at the end of the fifteenth century, every household which could acquire a copy—even an unadorned one—would struggle to do so. But for those with the talent to produce, or the means to acquire, an elaborate version, the happiness of the Seder would find visible expression in a book that was proud to the touch, noble with bold letters and resplendent initials, gay with decorative margins, evocative with illustrations. One imagines these books put away each year and brought out only on Passover Eve to be handled with pride by Father and gazed at with open-mouthed wonder by the children and visitors.

The preparation of a book of this kind was something that could be worked up to for years in advance. But there was an additional drive behind it that leaps to the eye when one sees some of the really magnificent Haggadahs—only a handful, alas—that have survived to our time. Jews living full and rich lives in concert with the world around them grasped instinctively at the opportunity to express the artistic urges that were as natural to them as to their neighbours. The strange thing is that we have learnt through these illustrated

Haggadahs not merely about the Jewish artistic impulses of that time, but about the existence of a highly developed art—half-buried but definitely sustained—from the days of their ancient life in Palestine.

The Illustrated Haggadah – as a Key to History

Until fairly recently it was common to think of mediaeval Jews as cut off completely from any expression of the graphic arts. The Bible, it was thought, had ruled out representational art through the clear statement in the Ten Commandments:

> 'Thou shalt not make unto thee a graven image nor any manner of likeness of anything that is in the heavens above or in the earth beneath or in the water under the earth' (*Exodus* XX, 4).

The prohibition had been spelt out even more clearly in Deuteronomy (IV, 16–17):

> '. . . the likeness of male or female, the likeness of any beast that is on the earth, the likeness of any winged fowl that flieth in the air.'

What was not realized, until the ancient and mediaeval worlds were re-opened to us through the discoveries of modern times, was that this 'commandment' had been read to a considerable degree in its context, as a prohibition against the making of images *for worship*.

The prohibition against idol worship was always linked with the story of the golden calf. An etching of this scene by Jan Van Vianen (1660)

Jewish representational art from the 3rd century CE. This fresco from the synagogue at Dura Europos, on the Euphrates, depicts Pharaoh's daughter finding Moses in the Nile

This attitude was—and is—at the centre of the Jewish religion; but in a social background where representational art was part of the dominant culture, the Jews felt free, we now know, to savour the pleasures it brought, particularly since it could be a medium for strengthening, rather than weakening, the ancestral faith.

This is not to say that the Jews 'kept the flame of art burning,' as it were, through the Dark Ages in response to some deep-seated instinct. The criterion was always—as in so many other things—the social background. In the Moslem world—from the seventh century on —where the prohibition of representation was absolute, the Jews were equally 'geometric' and abstract. During the fanatically iconoclastic period of the Byzantine world, the Jews living there were equally restrictive. But further to the north, the prohibition began to be less pronounced. Although it is usually assumed (and with some reason) that the aesthetic sense was more widely developed among the Sephardi ('Spanish') than among the Ashkenazi ('German') Jews, it was, paradoxically enough, among the Ashkenazim that representational art first re-emerged. We hear of arguments in Germany and northern France from the twelfth century on about how far one was free to go: animals and birds, let us say, but perhaps not the human figure, or if so, not in the round, or not with a realistically painted face. The Sephardi rabbis at this time were still being rigid—though Maimonides, as one might

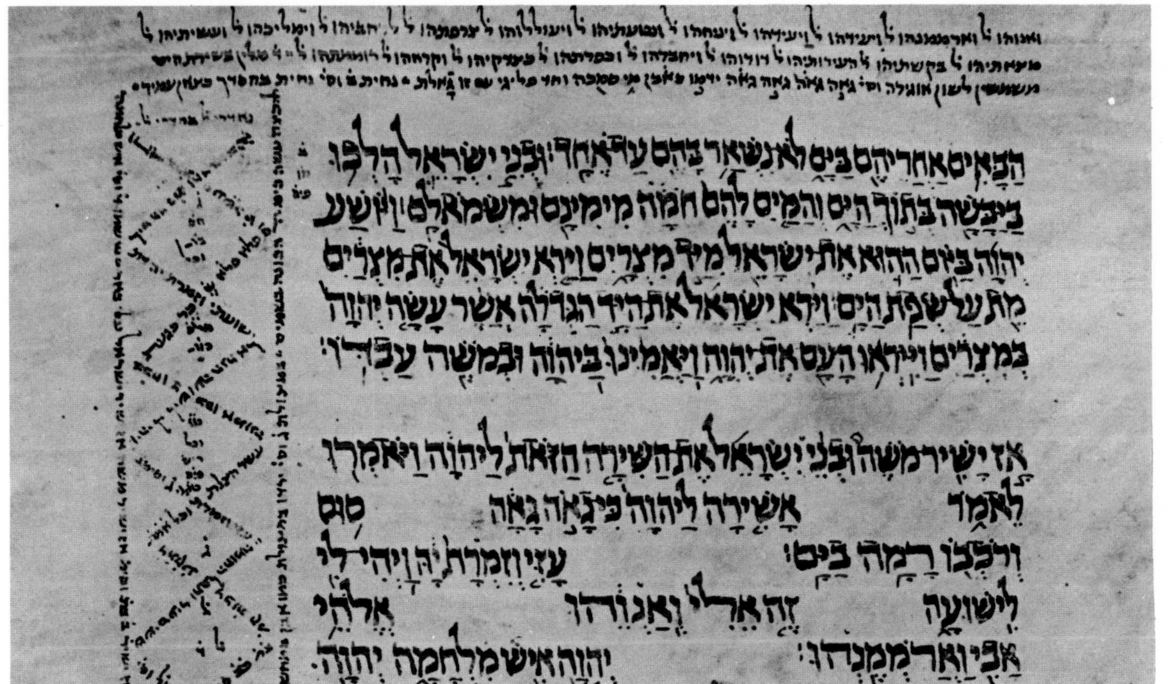
הבאים אחריהם בים לא נשאר בהם עד אחד׃ ובני ישראל הלכו
ביבשה בתוך הים והמים להם חמה מימינם ומשמאלם׃ ויושע
יהוה ביום ההוא את ישראל מיד מצרים וירא ישראל את מצרים
מת על שפת הים׃ וירא ישראל את היד הגדלה אשר עשה יהוה
במצרים וייראו העם את יהוה ויאמינו ביהוה ובמשה עבדו׃

אז ישיר משה ובני ישראל את השירה הזאת ליהוה ויאמרו
לאמר אשירה ליהוה כי גאה גאה סוס
ורכבו רמה בים׃ עזי וזמרת יה ויהי לי
לישועה זה אלי ואנוהו אלהי
אבי וארממנהו׃ יהוה איש מלחמה יהוה

In Moslem countries, Jewish art was strictly non-representational. Page from a Yemenite Pentateuch (1508) with the 'Song of Moses' written in micrographic geometric forms in the margin

have expected, was closer to the more lenient in the Ashkenazi view. By the thirteenth century, representational art must have become widely practised among Jews, at least in 'sophisticated' centres. The proof is that some splendidly illustrated Haggadahs (both Sephardi and Ashkenazi) that have survived come from the early fourteenth century and are clearly dependent on well-established 'schools' or 'workshops' of painting preceding them, in which both general skills and an accepted style had been developed.

It is easy to see why the thirteenth century offered encouragement to the revival of Jewish art, quite apart from the fact that the Moslem anti-represenational influence had waned by then. It was a period—'the first Renaissance'—in which increased interest in learning had stimulated book production generally in Europe. This had led not merely to a growing demand for scribes, but also to an extension of book workshops, with constantly improving techniques in the preparation of parchment, inks and colours needed for illustration. The growth of cities, with an increase in specialized occupations and commerce, offered Jews a better opportunity to hold their own and often rise to considerable wealth. The Jews were, indeed, direct contributors to this increasing urbanization of society. Having been held back from land ownership, and living for preference in larger communities, they had developed the financial and trading skills characteristic of town life. As a result, they were given a certain amount of 'protection' (though it was not always reliable) by the leaders of church and state who needed their expertise. Their position was uncertain and often perilous, but it brought many of them into living contact with the culture around them, leading them to adapt what they admired to their own Jewish interests.

One such influence in the field of art was the existence among the Christians of handsomely illustrated 'picture books' on the Bible. The style that had developed set out Bible stories in the form of miniature paintings (two or four to a page) telling a continuous story. Psalters (books containing the Psalms) were becoming more common, as easier to acquire; and sets of picture-pages would be bound in front of them as pictorial 'supplements'.

Painters around the French court led the way on this, producing schools of illustrators whose influence spread southward to the rich cities of Provence and north-east Spain, where Jewish communities flourished. It is not surprising, then, that the great Haggadahs coming from this area adopted the form of miniature illustration to great effect, as we shall see. What is truly astonishing, however, is to discover that the Jewish illustrators, in following these models, were to a great extent picking up a form of pictorial presentation that their own ancestors had originated nearly a thousand years earlier; for though the style of painting of the French miniaturists was their own, the subjects selected for illustration, and the ways these subjects were handled, are now shown by art historians to flow back in a clear line to specifically Jewish themes as presented pictorially in synagogue mosaics and frescoes as far back as the third century of the present era.

It is only in our own time that this Hellenistic-Jewish art has been revealed, the most striking example being the frescoes of the synagogue at Dura Europos, on the Euphrates, discovered in 1932. The Bible stories—from the Patriarchs on—depicted there in a vivid, realistic style tell us a great deal about the artists themselves and their background. The art historians have shown that where the pictures add detail to the straight biblical account—as happens, for example, where they portray imaginary episodes in the life of Abraham or Joseph--this extra detail is in line with Jewish folklore in the Midrash, which is a fairly strong indication that these Hellenistic-period artists were themselves Jewish and drawing on their own living traditions. Some of the same midrashic episodes show up in early Christian art, and again in the art of the middle Byzantine period. As illustration becomes more sophisticated, the midrashic treatment of biblical subjects continues—in pictures, for example, of Adam 'naming the animals' after Creation, or of David soothing

opposite An example of one of the styles which influenced Jewish illustrators. Four Old Testament scenes from the life of Solomon in a 15th-century French illuminated manuscript

CY COMENCENT · LES · PARABO

Cy commencent les paraboles salomo̅
en francois sur la bible et hystoire.

Es paraboles salomon le filz
de dauid roy disrael a sauoir
sapience et discipline a en
tre parolles et prudence a
receuoir enseignemens
et doctrine et iustice et iu
gement et loyaulte et droiture que sens
soit donnes aux petis cest a dire a humblez
ignorans et que science soit donnee et en
tendement a ceulx qui en ont mestier les
sages seruir plus sages en sera et cellui
qui entent mieulx en saura soy et autrui
gouuerner et apperteura paraboles et i̅

terpretacions et les figures et les parolez
des sages. La parolle de n̅re seigneur est co̅
mencement de sapience les fos despisent
sapience et doctrine mon filz oye la disci
pline de ton pere et ne laisse mie la loy de
ta mere que grace soit adioustee mise
sur ton chief et fermail dor a ton col mo̅
filz se les pecheurs talectent ne les croy mie
Cest a dire se les losengiers te losengent
ne les croy mie que ilz ne te decoiuent se
ilz te dient vien a nous mettons agues
pour occire repomons contre iustice po̅
lui prendre. Engloutissons les comme
enfers tous vis et tous entiers co̅me
descendens en la fosse nous trouuerons

ותתצב אחותו ונערותיה הולכות בתיה מביאה משה לפני פרעה

איש מצרי מכה איש עברי ויך את המצרי ויטמנהו בחול ויקם משה ויושען

the wild-life around him with his lute. The episodes appear in early French biblical cycles of the tenth century and emerge again in twelfth-century Psalters. The wheel comes full circle when parallels appear in illustrations to the Haggadah.

Were the Christian artists drawing on Jewish 'models' carefully preserved during the early Middle Ages? And were the Jewish illustrators of the Haggadah drawing directly on these, or only indirectly? One art historian, Bezalel Narkiss, sums up this highly complicated story as follows:

> 'It seems more and more obvious that an Early Hellenistic Jewish model fashioned not only the Early Christian Western and Eastern Biblical cycles, but also the Middle Byzantine representations.
>
> 'Through Early Christian and Byzantine art, some Jewish elements entered the Biblical representations of Western Europe from Carolingian times onwards. Jewish artists of the Gothic period must have had direct access to an Early Jewish Biblical cycle, which either survived or was continuously copied throughout the Middle Ages.
>
> 'No other explanation can account for the existence of different Jewish elements in Christian art in various places and styles, all of which were accumulated in a late Jewish cycle' (The Golden Haggadah, London, Eugrammia Press, 1970, page 67).

If, in the treatment of biblical stories, the Jewish artists of the fourteenth century were reaching back to their own traditions, in painting techniques they were imitating the most lavish contemporary styles in front of them. Yet the final products were overwhelmingly Jewish, not only because they illustrate Jewish subjects and ceremonies, but for the light they throw on Jewish social life of the times. More broadly, they also reflect the migrations of Jews—forced or voluntary—which made them inevitably catalysts of different cultures. Two famous Haggadahs—the Sarajevo Haggadah and the Golden Haggadah—are of special interest on this.

The Sarajevo Haggadah is so called because, though it originated in north-east Spain or Provence in the mid-fourteenth century, it only surfaced into the public domain in Sarajevo in 1894, when it was sold to the museum there by a Jewish child who had found it among his late father's possessions. Its discovery was sensational, and it is still, perhaps, the most famous and important of Hebrew illuminated manuscripts, if only because of the coverage of the pictures. Where most Haggadah pictures cover the Exodus story and some include also stories from Genesis, the Sarajevo Haggadah covers the whole of the Pentateuch, up to the final drama of Moses. It is a magnificent book, opening with a 'picture supplement' of thirty-four pages devoted to its long cycle of picture-stories (two or

opposite Scenes from the life of Moses in the Golden Haggadah. The pictures depict the finding of Moses, Bithiah bringing him to Pharaoh (not in the Bible but in the Midrash), an Egyptian smiting a Hebrew and Moses saving the daughter of the priest of Midian four miniatures to a page), followed by fifty pages devoted to the Haggadah text, written in a fine, bold script, with marvellously worked initial words, each page surrounded by the most elaborate and imaginative decorations of floral motifs, birds, dragons and drolleries echoing the Gothic art of twelfth- and thirteenth-century France. Included in the text also are pages of illustration related to the Haggadah itself, one devoted to the famous invocation *Ha-Lachma* (the invitation to the hungry), one to Rabbi Gamaliel (who gave the Seder its lasting symbolism, as described above, page 77), two to contemporary scenes connected with the celebration of Passover—a synagogue seen through an open door, and a Seder in action, with the family and guests around the table. Like most other large-scale illustrated Haggadahs, the book also includes many pages of *piyyutim* (poems) drawing on biblical and midrashic themes and intended for use in synagogue at the Passover season.

In this one Haggadah alone, the richness and symbolism of the contents can open up endless speculation not merely on the Seder ceremonies for which it was designed, but on the social and cultural background in which Jews and their neighbours moved and had their being. Some of this emerges in the detail of the miniatures: the procession shown for the burial of Joseph is a contemporary funeral; the Tower of Babel is built with fourteenth-century building methods and materials; Esau goes off hunting with a cross-bow. The figures in the full-scale paintings offer some surprises. Some of the Jews are shown beardless and even hatless in prayer. At the Seder meal, presented very graphically, it is interesting to see a black woman taking part, presumably a slave converted to Judaism. The full-page picture of Gamaliel is particularly significant. It has been argued that the portrayal of a 'sage'—originally Ezra—was prominent not only in the earliest Jewish 'picture-books' (which were used as models for the synagogue frescoes) but also in the earliest Christian art, because the Jewish sage suggested the Evangelist. Another feature spreading its influence from earliest times and given full effect in the Haggadah is the stylized representation of the Temple—a triple-arcaded facade with the 'ark' in the middle—appearing as early as the second century on a Bar Kokhba coin (133 CE), and continuing throughout the centuries with side-effects on Christian artists.

below A coin from the Bar-Kokhba period (132–135 CE) showing the traditional Temple facade *opposite* A page from the Sarajevo Haggadah (Spain, 14th century) showing Rabban Gamaliel with three disciples (see page 209)

The most startling single drawing in the Sarajevo Haggadah is that of a divine hand—of God or an angel—stretching down from Heaven to save Isaac at the *Akedah* (when Abraham might have sacrificed him). The hand appears in the same way in a fresco at the Dura Synagogue, and in a mosaic in the fifth-century Beth Alpha

synagogue. Continuities of this kind led the historian Cecil Roth to say that 'the illustrations to the Sarajevo Haggadah preserve more faithfully than any other document now extant the traditions of the illuminated Jewish Bible codices that existed in antiquity'.

But to explore the biblical tradition in art history is to concentrate on only one aspect of the illuminated Haggadah. The appeal of the Haggadah comes through equally in the variety of illustrations it stimulated, some more personal to the mood of the evening than the scenes from biblical history.

This is true of two types of illustration found in virtually all illuminated Haggadahs—those dealing with items in the text itself, and those with 'preparations' and other rituals connected with the ceremonies. The direct textual illustrations were developed particularly in Haggadahs produced in the Ashkenazi orbit (coming from Germany, northern France and, to some extent, Italy). The characteristic of these Ashkenazi Haggadahs is to introduce illustrations around the text on each page, covering both Bible episodes referred to and Haggadah narrative. An example is that the verse: 'Come out and learn what Laban the Syrian sought to do to Jacob', shows a man dressed for travel, coming out of a mediaeval town gate. Sephardi Haggadahs (from Spain and southern France) have fewer pictures with the text itself; they tend to collect them as 'supplements', usually at the beginning. However, they do include, like the Ashkenazi Haggadahs, some ritual and social illustrations, showing the baking of *matzah*, the cleaning of the house and dishes before the Passover, the emergence from synagogue (with an open door letting us look in), and the family seated around the Seder table. But the Ashkenazi Haggadahs are more prolific in this type of illustration, showing, sometimes, the hiding of the *afikoman*, the eating of different herbs and other scenes giving a lively picture of the daily and festive dress of the Jews, as well as their homes and furnishings.

Page from a hand-written Haggadah with Italian translation (Ferrara, 1769)

If the Sarajevo Haggadah—covering all these subjects—is supreme because of its unique range of Bible illustrations, another of the great Sephardi Haggadahs excels it in other ways, notably in the artistry of its Bible drawings, not to mention its lavish use of gold paint, which has made its name—The Golden Haggadah—inevitable. The Golden Haggadah, now in the British Museum, is one of the earliest, and by far the best in quality, of the fully illuminated Sephardi Haggadahs (about twelve in all) that have survived. Having been produced originally for some princely Jewish patron in northern Spain (probably Barcelona) in the early part of the fourteenth century, it was taken to Italy (presumably after the expulsion of the Jews from Spain) and passed on as a private heirloom for centuries until catalogued in 1864 by a Jewish scholar and then acquired by the British Museum. Bezalel Narkiss has shown in his book on this manuscript how a short series of miniature paintings—fourteen pages of them in all—can reveal more about the underlying elements of Jewish history than a host of 'factual' chroniclers. This Haggadah's biblical paintings, for example, reflect the highly stylized north French influence in its figures (oval, expressionless faces, and so on) but also a distinct awareness of Italian ideas of space and depth. It is clear, therefore, that the artists of this Haggadah had models of both schools available to them; they were working in a period of transition; and the Golden Haggadah, in fact, 'may point to the way in which Italian art influenced Western Europe'.

It is interesting, too, that a Spanish Haggadah should be linked more to Italy and the Byzantine tradition than to Spain. Narkiss shows that the Spanish-Jewish artists did not echo the pictures in tenth- and eleventh-century Spanish illustrated Bibles; their pictures were much closer to Byzantine biblical cycles and Italian church mosaics and frescoes of Byzantine influence. He is led from this to a startling hypothesis: that Jewish artists of the Haggadah 'must have had at their disposal an illuminated manuscript which was modelled upon a Hellenistic-Jewish, illustrated, legendary paraphrase of the Bible'. He even suggests how this might have been brought to Europe. The prototypes may have been preserved in the highly cultured Jewish communities of Babylonia up to the tenth and eleventh centuries and then, when these centres collapsed, been brought by refugees to Asia Minor and Italy. Jewish artists of the period living there drew to some extent on 'native' influences. Their 'reinforced' biblical art spread north to Germany and France (perhaps even as far as England), and then made its way south to Spain when Jews in great number were expelled from France by Phillippe le Bel in 1306. The artists among these Jews brought with them to Spain the art of the French miniature. Later, when the Jews were expelled from Spain, some of them carried the tradition 'back' to Italy.

The ramifications for history are endless; and we cannot leave the subject of hand-illuminated Haggadahs without mentioning, however briefly, one which is, in some ways, the most extraordinary of all—the Birds' Head Haggadah, produced in Germany around 1300 CE.

The Ashkenazi Haggadahs used, in general, the same Bible picture-themes as the Sephardi Haggadahs, showing that they both drew on a common tradition. The *genre* paintings of Haggadah scenes were, of course, different, and so was the gothic fantasy with which the Ashkenazi artists filled the margins of the pages. In the Birds' Head Haggadah something additional was introduced. Representational art was clearly somewhat questionable, still, at that early stage in Germany. In all the pictures, therefore, the human beings—*but only the Jewish ones*—are given the heads of birds. It adds a strange dimension, not of superstition but of a kind of abstract passion to the events depicted.

In all other respects it is a normal Haggadah, and indeed a most beautiful one, with pages devoted to the cycle of biblical stories (from Creation to Joseph) and with interesting *genre* paintings depicting the rituals. It is just in the birds' heads that it is unusual.

Detail from the Birds' Head Haggadah showing a Jewish woman with a hair-net of the period surmounting her bird's head

The use of birds' or animal heads in this way was a device or style found in other Hebrew manuscripts (and, of course, in other cultures), but the Birds' Head Haggadah is unique in carrying through the concept with such single-minded and elaborate thoroughness. Everything about this Haggadah, including its discovery only a few years ago, adds to its symbolism. The manuscript was taken to Israel by an immigrant from Germany in 1946, its existence having been unknown to scholars for all these centuries. It emerged in a period in which a quasi-abstract art of this kind was capable once again of being understood, not as a subterfuge for human representation but rather for the intensely individual feeling it allowed the artist to express. Indeed the infinitely varied ways in which the birds' heads are painted adds to the humanity of the subjects.

Most of the males in these pictures wear—on their birds' heads—the conical 'Jew's Hat' introduced after the Lateran Council of 1215, and the female birds wear the hair nets and jewelled pins which were stylish at the time. The contrast between these 'faces' (full of different expressions) and the other characters in the stories bearing human heads—such as Pharaoh, or even the angels in some pictures—is particularly arresting. The art historian Meyer Schapiro says that even where the scenes are of every-day life, they manage somehow to generate, through the treatment of the birds' heads, a very Jewish quality—reminding him of the feeling of Chagall. There is a kind of built-in humour, at least to modern eyes. At a scene of the Seder, the person pouring the wine—presumably a servant—is shown 'humanly' but with a great bulbous nose. The scene showing the preparation of *haroset* is of a great apparatus, far beyond the practical needs, and suggesting the sense of excitement of the occasion. For the continuity of the tradition, it is interesting to see that the artist here, as in the Sarajevo Haggadah and the ancient Dura frescoes, was not afraid to depict the hands of a divine being—God or an angel—as part of the biblical story. In this case, the hands are throwing down the discs of manna for the Israelites in the wilderness.

Birds' heads were used to illustrate some early Ashkenazi prayer books, but the device soon disappeared. In the famous Darmstadt Haggadah (early fifteenth century), the miniatures have become realistic, gentle and charming. But the themes are still the same; and it is interesting for the continuity of the tradition to note that when the first illustrated *printed* edition of a Haggadah appeared—in Prague, in 1521—the woodcuts used continued the same themes.

The printed Haggadah, especially at the beginning, was still treated as a work of art as well as a book of devotion. The illustrations, it is true, were no longer of the same profusion as had characterized the great Haggadahs we have been discussing. It was inevitable, too, that they soon assumed a much more rigid pattern, starting with a few pictures of 'preparations' (cleaning the house, etc.), followed by some Exodus pictures to accompany the story part of the Seder, and then, after the meal, a few 'messianic' pictures, to accompany the prayers and the mood of hope. Elijah appears; and some vision of Jerusalem—usually ringed in rays of glory—is always brought in to go with the final toast—*Next Year in Jerusalem!* But if these pictures had begun to lose the creativity of the earlier ones, the Haggadah itself could be presented, in print, as a triumph of lettering, engraving, and sheer style. The Prague Haggadah of 1526, which set the tone for all future printed Haggadahs, is so handsome in its ornamental initials, and so imaginative in the profuse decorations which form the borders of its main pages, that it has been described by one authority as 'among the finest productions of the sixteenth century printing press in any language.'

above Detail from the Prague Haggadah. *below* Detail from the Mantua Haggadah showing Abraham 'crossing the river' in a gondola

As printers in different Jewish centres began to produce Haggadahs of their own, they drew on the Prague Haggadah in style, though with changes to meet local conditions. In the Mantua Haggadah of 1560, for example, a picture of Abraham 'crossing the river' to enter the Holy Land shows him in a gondola—since it is Italy—rather than in the ordinary boat of Prague. The Venice Haggadah of 1609 strikes its own individual tone by introducing a whole series of pictures on the Exodus story in terms of seventeenth-century Venetian costumes and battle formations. This Haggadah and its illustrations became the prototype for all Haggadahs printed later, in Italy and the eastern Mediterranean, for Sephardi Jews.

For Ashkenazi Jews, a different prototype emerged in an Amsterdam Haggadah of 1695, which was the first to move from woodcuts to copper-plate engravings. To contemporaries, it seemed a mom-

Then came an ox
And drank the water
That quenched the flame
That burned the stick
That beat the dog
That bit the cat
That ate the kid
My father bought for two zuzim,
An only kid, an only kid.

ואתא תורא·
ושתא למיא· דכבה לנורא·
דשרף לחוטרא· דהכה לכלבא·
דנשך לשונרא· דאכלה לגדיא·
דזבן אבא בתרי זוזי·
חד גדיא חד גדיא:

above Title page of the Amsterdam Haggadah (1695)
below Page from the 20th-century Ben Shahn Haggadah
opposite Opening page of the Book of Exodus from a late 15th-century Hebrew illuminated Bible from Portugal

entous move forward—from what they felt were the 'crudities' of woodcuts to the elegance of engravings. Because the line could be so much more expressive, it had, in their view, 'the same superiority as light has over darkness'. To a modern eye, the change is much less appealing, and basically because this new presentation was being made at a time when the primitive freshness of earlier drawings and the bold confidence of fine layout had given way to a sterile and very limited kind of competence. The title page of this Haggadah is dominated by two large figures of Moses and Aaron—echoed constantly afterwards—with six biblical vignettes arranged in exact balance over their heads and the space between filled with a mass of explanatory but undistinguished Hebrew lettering. It is without taste, and bereft, in its pictures, of the distinctly 'Jewish' quality of earlier illustrations. The engraver was, in fact, a convert to Judaism, and though undoubtedly sincere, drew directly on Christian models—as in a picture of David kneeling in prayer to the 'Holy Spirit'!

Despite this, the Amsterdam Haggadah was reprinted and adapted in numerous German editions. An edition in Metz in 1767 made a conscious effort to eliminate the Christian influence, and the resultant drawings were copied in cheap editions all over Europe and America. Another popular source for illustration was the Vienna Haggadah of 1823. Many of us grew up with crudely printed Haggadahs which included its drawings—notably the strange picture of the Four Sons—the wise son (an aged Rabbi!) being tall and impressive, while the fourth son is presented not only as a moron but also a midget.

The creative impulse had, indeed, run dry. The seventeenth and eighteenth centuries produced, it is true, a whole host of independent easel paintings and engravings on Passover—household scenes, the bustle of preparation, the search for the *afikoman*—and charming they often are; and in modern times fresh attempts were made by Jewish artists—some distinguished and some less than mediocre—to illustrate the Haggadah itself. While some of these drawings (and especially the work of Arthur Szyk and Ben Shahn) have been magnificent, they have one overriding defect for our present age, in that they implicitly take the story of the Haggadah as complete, reflecting an ancient event. Jewish history has, however, been so revolutionized in our own time that the Haggadah itself can be seen as much expanded in meaning. If we respond to this, we can approach the Seder not simply to re-live the ancient Exodus, but to see the whole of Jewish history opened up to our intellect and feeling. The pictures can echo this.

ואלה
שמות בני ישראל
הבאים מצרימה
את יעקב איש וביתו
באו ראובן שמעון
לוי ויהודה יששכר
זבולן ובנימן דן ונפתלי גד ואשר ויהי כל נפש
יצאי ירך יעקב שבעים נפש ויוסף היה
במצרים וימת יוסף וכל אחיו וכל הדור
ההוא ובני ישראל פרו וישרצו וירבו
ויעצמו במאד מאד ותמלא הארץ אתם
ויקם מלך חדש על מצרים אשר לא ידע
את יוסף ויאמר אל עמו הנה עם בני ישראל
רב ועצום ממנו הבה נתחכמה לו פן ירבה

יין
כרמלית

4 A Seder Roll-call

The First Seder–in Sodom?
ca. 1800 BCE

To the rabbis, Passover had existed—somehow—even before the Hebrews had gone into Egypt. Just as they imagined the Patriarch Jacob studying the Torah (unlike his 'good-for-nothing' brother Esau) long before Moses had received it on Mount Sinai, so Abraham was thought of as celebrating *Pesach* centuries in advance. When the three angels visited him (*Genesis* XVIII) and he roasted a young calf for their meal, Sara (say the rabbis) quickly baked some *matzah* to go with it. Why? Because it was *Pesach*. Even the unsavoury Lot was caught up in *Pesach* when he, in turn, was visited by two angels at Sodom. What took place that evening, as described in the nineteenth chapter of Genesis, belongs definitely to *pas devant les enfants*, and therefore, by definition, not to the Seder recital; but for its *timing* there is the Bible text: 'And he made them a feast and did bake unleavened bread and they did eat'. To the rabbis this was a clear indication that it was Passover. We have to con-conclude, reluctantly, that the first recorded Seder night was the one celebrated so primitively at Sodom. Many a young ringletted boy studying this chapter and the Rashi commentary on it in a *cheder* in Eastern Europe will have asked innocently: 'But how could Lot have known about Passover before the Jews even went into Egypt?' The *rebbe*—grimy and smelling of snuff—would probably box his ears. 'What right have you got to ask such questions? Read on: next verse.'

The *rebbe*—bless his weary old piety—was right. Some things can't be spelt out in facts but only in poetry. And so it was that one of the songs sung on the second Seder night—'Let's Talk about the Pesach'—picked up these incidents without a blush. Everything happened on *Pesach*, according to this song, written by the poet Kalir in the eighth or ninth century:

opposite Breaking the *matzah* for *afikoman* at the Seder of a Kurdish family in Israel

overleaf The age-old '*cheder*' (Hebrew school) has taken a variety of national forms throughout history. A French version in a painting by Jacques Emile Edouard Brandon (1831–1897)

'You knocked on Abraham's door in the heat
of the day *on Pesach:*
He fed *matzah* to the shining ones (the angels) *on Pesach:*
To the herd he ran in memory of 'The Ox'
(the Bible reading of the day) *on Pesach:*
Let's talk about the Pesach
'The Sodomites felt your anger and were burnt
in fire *on Pesach:*
Lot baked his *matzah* and escaped from them *on Pesach:*
Let's talk about the Pesach'

Moses Absent but Everywhere *ca.* 1280 BCE

Leaving this aside as pre-history and coming to the Exodus itself, we have already remarked on the absence of Moses from the recital. The rabbis who are said to have excluded him deliberately in order to fight off the Karaite challenge (see page 96) were not engaged merely in sectarian fighting. They seem to have felt that the position of Moses has to be considered very carefully. His story is told with such extraordinary power in the Bible, and embroidered later with such a wealth of legend, that the danger of superstitious reverence has to be fought off, in order not to upset the balance between the divine and the human elements in Israel's fate.

That Moses is not mentioned by name in the Ṣeder recital would seem otherwise to be completely inexplicable—a real case of Hamlet without the Prince of Denmark. The fact is, of course, that even if he is not mentioned in words, he is present at the Seder in everyone's mind: but he is present, as he should be, in human terms. And he is present, not as Freud's Egyptian, but as the archetypal Jew.

Moses is the abiding creator of the Jewish people not merely as the liberator from bondage but because the Jewish character—the Jewish approach to life—seems to have been forged in the style of the narratives which describe him. He is a great man—yet fallible; he has faith in what he is doing—yet he can waver; he has insight and patience—yet his patience can snap; he is beyond anyone in his relationship with God—yet he shows more than a hint of sibling rivalry in his attitude to his brother Aaron.

As a symbol of the centuries which were to follow, everything about Moses was a pre-echo of Jewish existence. For one thing, he was a wanderer, living for years not only (as the Bible tells us) among the Midianites, but also in Ethiopia, where (according to legend) he led the troops of that country to victory against invaders and became, for a time, king. His whole experience had been forged, as it were, among 'non-Jews', starting with his upbringing in the Egyptian court and becoming a man of the world before he turned back to

opposite An echo of 'the first Passover', when Abraham received the angels, in an etching by Rembrandt (1606–1669)
overleaf 'The Song of Miriam' by Lucia Giordano (1632–1705). Miriam's song of triumph at the Red Sea is thought by scholars to be one of the oldest folk-strands in the Bible

opposite 'The Finding of Moses' by Nicolas Poussin (1594–1665)

concentrate his life on the saving of his people. There is a revealing touch about one set of legends: he was thought to have been a very rich man, getting his wealth from Ethiopia when he resigned the crown, or from his father-in-law Jethro as a dowry, or—in the true spirit of folklore—from the Tablets which he smashed in anger at the foot of Sinai, and which turned out to be made of sapphire! How he became wealthy is less important than the concept. Jewish history—so much a story of poverty and suffering—was due also to produce a succession here and there of wealthy men who were not simply princely in their benefactions but princely in their very status, shedding a kind of distinctiveness and pride over the whole people.

Week by week, the story of Moses was read in synagogue in passages from the Pentateuch, and the legends repeated in exposition. He was larger than life, yet ultimately a man like anyone else. He had spoken to God 'face to face', but not in any way which could offend the laws of human existence. If a rabbi sometimes gave Moses an almost divine role—as in one saying that he had atoned for all the sins of humanity down to his time—the consensus was against thinking of Moses in this way, as a kind of foil to Jesus. 'God never descended to earth', the rabbis said, 'nor did Moses ever ascend to Heaven.' As always, they had a biblical verse ready to 'prove' it: 'The heavens are the Lord's: the earth he has given to mankind.' This verse (*Psalm CXV*)—recited at the Seder—is almost the complete expression of the rationalist tradition of Judaism, and the rabbis produced numerous arguments to emphasize the distinction. Moses, the wisest of men, knew the answers to all the mysteries of living, they said, but nothing of what lay beyond the grave. Labouring this point to show—as a novelist might—the buried doubts and weaknesses in the strongest of men, they told stories of how pitifully he pleaded with God, as his death drew near, for a softening of his fate. Could he not, at least, set foot in the Holy Land after all he had done? But he had done wicked things, too, he was told: he had killed a man in anger: an Egyptian, but the sin was the same. Could he then, at least, live a little longer east of Jordan with the Hebrew tribes settled there? No, because if he stayed there, many would want to stay with him: their resolve to settle in the Holy Land would be weakened. Then, could one of his children succeed him instead of Joshua? With each plea, Moses sheds more and more of the shell of his grandeur. In the end, he is an old man dying.

All this has stayed in the historic folk-picture of Moses. Far from weakening his appeal, it is enriching, like the rough surface of a piece of sculpture. We can think of him with the heroism of a Michelangelo or the humanism of a Rembrandt. Here, for our

Moses displays the Tablets of the Law before the people. Title page of a Pentateuch printed in Prague (1801)

personal Haggadah, are the marvellous words which end the book of Deuteronomy:

> 'There, in the land of Moab, Moses the servant of the Lord died . . . To this day no one knows his burial place. Moses was a hundred and twenty years old when he died, his sight was not dimmed nor had his vigour failed . . . There has never yet risen in Israel a prophet like Moses, whom the Lord knew face to face. Remember all the signs and portents which the Lord sent him to show in Egypt to Pharaoh and his servants and the whole land; remember the strong hand of Moses, and the awesome deeds which he did in the sight of all Israel.'

'There was never a Pesach like it.' *ca.* 620 BCE

We were all brought up to read the Bible as a straight narrative, so it comes as no surprise that only a few chapters after the death of Moses, the next book—Joshua—records how the children of Israel celebrated Passover as one of their earliest acts after crossing the Jordan, while they rested in camp preparatory to besieging Jericho (*Joshua* V, 10). We expect this to be a regular strand in the unfolding story and it is a bit of a shock, therefore, to find nothing else in the Bible about Passover that we can get our teeth into for our personal Haggadah until we hear of the great celebrations of Passover more

left 'Moses Striking the Rock' by Jan Steen (1626–1679), a delightful mixture of a Dutch rural scene with the oriental figures of Moses, Aaron and the camels

opposite 'Moses' by Michelangelo (1475–1564)

than five hundred years later in the time of King Hezekiah (ca. 715–687 BCE) and King Josiah (640–609). We get the full story of these celebrations in the Book of Chronicles; and if we read them as they stand, they document a tremendous expression of religious and national sentiment around the festival, setting the tone for the power it exercised in all future generations.

The Hezekiah passages would certainly be included in any 'new' Haggadah that was setting out to tell the continuous story of this joyous feast in relation to Jewish history. Of course, one sees immediately that politics are involved. The northern kingdom, following Assyrian conquest, is virtually at an end, and King Hezekiah is trying to bring the hapless Israelites of the north under the suzerainty of Jerusalem; but the description of his Passover has, nonetheless, an excitement that was to cling to the festival throughout the centuries (II *Chron.* XXX):

Papyrus from Elephantine closed with clay seal

> 'And Hezekiah sent word to all Israel and Judah, and wrote letters also to Ephraim and Manasseh, inviting them to come to the house of the Lord at Jerusalem, to keep the Passover unto the Lord, the God of Israel . . . Never before had so many kept it according to the prescribed form. Couriers went throughout all Israel and Judah with letters from the king and his offers, proclaiming the royal command: "Turn back, men of Israel, to the Lord the God of Abraham, Isaac and Israel, so that He may turn back to those of you who escaped capture by the kings of Assyria . . . Submit yourselves to the Lord and enter his sanctuary which he has sanctified forever . . ."
>
> 'So the couriers passed from city to city through the land of Ephraim and Manasseh, and as far as Zebulun, but they were treated with scorn and ridicule. However, a few men of Asher, Manasseh and Zebulun submitted and came to Jerusalem . . . Many people, a very great assembly, came together in Jerusalem to keep the pilgrim feast of unleavened bread . . .'

The Chronicler then describes the frenzy of excitement as the Levites destroyed all the pagan altars in the city and plunged everyone into an immense act of re-dedication, conducting all the sacrifices according to 'the law of Moses, the man of God'. The joy was so great that they all decided to prolong the feast for another seven days: 'There was great rejoicing in Jerusalem, the like of which had not been known since the days of Solomon son of David, king of Israel.'

Within two or three generations, Chronicles tells us, history repeated itself in a massive celebration of Passover by King Josiah. Once again details are given of the immensely long round of sacrifices, and the total enthusiasm of the people. We have to allow, of course, for a little exaggeration. The Chroniclers were writing history in the ample style of court historians. We get a sharper picture of Josiah's Passover from the less polished story-teller in the Book of Kings. We read there of the drama which sparked it—the discovery in the sanctuary of 'the Book of the Law', perhaps Deuteronomy. There is a ring of truth in the story told of its effects on the king. Calling all the people together—'high and low'—he read the book to them: 'And then, standing on the dais, he made a covenant before the Lord to obey him and keep his commandments, his testimonies and his statutes, with all his heart and soul . . .'

It was in this spirit that Passover was then revived. It was a feast that exceeded even that of Hezekiah: 'No such Passover had been kept either when the Judges were ruling Israel or during the times of the Kings of Israel and Judah' (*II Kings* XXIII, 22).

There is great joy in celebrating Passover after something momentous—like Josiah's discovery—has happened. What did the people of Israel feel at the Seder of 1949—the first Seder after the restoration of an independent State? And what did they feel after 1967? 'No such Passover had been kept even in the days of Josiah and Hezekiah . . .'

Seder Instructions by Mail
419 BCE

We follow history mostly on the big highways: but the byways can offer more intriguing questions.

We are not surprised that when the Jews returned to the Holy Land after their momentous exile in Babylon, they plunged eagerly—as the Book of Ezra tells us (VI 18, 22)—into a joyful celebration of Passover. What is less expected is a story from this time of a Passover kept in much stranger circumstances by a colony of Jews living in Egypt, at a military outpost on the Upper Nile called Elephantine.

The post itself is thought to have been established around 588–569 BCE. How and when the Jews came there is quite unknown. The most natural assumption is that they were among the many Jews who escaped exile in Babylon after the fall of Jerusalem (587 BCE) by taking refuge in neighbouring countries, setting the first pattern of the world-wide *Galut* that was to come.

The evidence that has survived of this early scattering to lands other than Babylonia is, in general, fragmentary; but the strange little community at Elephantine has become known through a wealth of Aramaic texts from there that began to come to light in the early years of this century. The Jews, carrying on their religion there had to deal both with local Egyptian officials and (after 525 BCE) with Persian overlords. Their faith had taken a somewhat unorthodox form: they had built a Temple, contrary to the rule that sacrifices could take place only in Jerusalem, and their worship linked other divine names to the 'one God' of Jewish tradition.

There are some fragmentary mentions of *Pesach*—including

something about 'examining the pots'—in writing on two potsherds from there that have survived from the fifth century; but their most interesting Passover document is a letter on papyrus which, defective as it is, records an historical event. The letter was written in 419 BCE—'fifth year of Darius [II]'—by a certain 'Hananiah' to the Jewish garrison at Elephantine, telling them of an edict, or ruling, given by Darius to Arsham, the Persian governor of Egypt, on how the Passover was to be celebrated there. The fragments of writing, for all their gaps, have a familiar ring:

> 'To my brethren Yadoniah and his colleagues the Jewish soldiers from your brother Hananiah. The peace of my brethren, may the gods . . .
>
> 'And now this year, the year five of Darius the king: from the king there was sent to Arsham . . .
>
> 'And as for you, thus shall ye count: fourteen . . .and from the fifteenth day to the twenty first day . . . be ye clean and take heed. Work not . . . ye shall not drink and eat anything at all of leaven . . .from the setting of the sun to the twenty first day of Nisan . . .ye shall not bring into your chambers and ye shall seal during the days . . .'

What does it mean? The scholars have discussed it endlessly. Some have seen it as an attempt by the Jewish authorities, with Persian backing, to limit the celebration to what was proper outside Palestine, in particular that at their Seder they were not to have a sacrifice. Others think the opposite: that it was to prevent the Egyptian priests, who were jealous of Jewish privileges, from interfering with the sacrifices. More simply it might be conveying permission for Jewish soldiers to be free of duty during Passover week, with a reminder of the rules of ritual observance.

The most interesting aspect of the Elephantine texts, historically, is how they reflect on the ties between Palestine and the *Galut.* The Elephantine Temple was destroyed nine years later (410 BCE) in the course of a riot against the Jews. Pleas were immediately made to the priestly authorities at Jerusalem for permission to rebuild, but in vain. The Elephantine Jews then wrote to the civil governors at Jerusalem and Samaria, offering to give up animal sacrifices and restrict themselves to incense and meal offerings. Their request was finally granted, and their Temple, rebuilt, was in existence until at least 402 BCE.

But it was a special case. We have to remember that it was at this period that the Books of Chronicles were being written, asserting firmly that Jerusalem had been established, under Hezekiah and Josiah, as the focal point for all sacrifices, with pilgrims coming from all over the Mediterranean lands. The Chroniclers were giving an historical basis to what was obviously an ever-growing religious and social custom. Jews in the *Galut* were henceforth to accept this completely, as they showed when they fought and sent financial aid in support of Jerusalem against alien domination.

A Haggadah Detective Story *ca.* 165 BCE

If there is one gap in the evolution of the Haggadah that one would like to fill it is the period of the Maccabees, and especially the decades before Judas Maccabeus won his victory in 166 BCE. Here, in the second century BCE is one of the most dramatic times of Jewish history, yet as far as literature is concerned it seems to come unheralded out of the blue.

The contrast with earlier centuries is quite startling. From the primitive days of the Patriarchs, the Bible unfolds Jewish history as a continuing story, but now its distinctiveness seems lost. The Jews are back in the Holy Land but live in the shadows of other civilizations, first the authentic Greeks and then the Hellenistic Ptolemy and Seleucid dynasties. What was going on in the hearts and minds of the Jews at this time to produce the revolt of the Maccabees and the distinctive view of life that was to emerge later under the rabbis?

Could the Haggadah, perhaps, offer a clue? We have seen that when the form of the Seder was established in broad terms in the Mishnah (second century CE) it included elements that went back to Temple times. Questions by the children, blessings on bread and wine and the chanting of Psalms went back that far, some of which is confirmed in the Seder-like ceremony described in the Gospels. And some of the prayers—notably the basic elements of the Grace after Meals—were also pre-Destruction. Yet this, after all, is only the skeleton of the Seder. The real flavour of the Haggadah seems to lie in joyful story-telling, and in the rabbinic arguments and songs that emerged later. On the surface we have nothing to to indicate what kind of discussion and ritual preoccupied the Jews of Palestine in the centuries before 'normative' Judaism established itself.

The scholars have re-created some of the spirit of these 'unknown' centuries by considering the Wisdom Literature (Proverbs, Job, Ecclesiastes) and some other parts of the Bible which might be equally 'late'—Jonah, Ruth and some of the Psalms. In relatively recent times, they have been able to draw also—with increasing confidence—on some apocalyptic books which are echoed to some extent in the Dead Sea Scrolls. But these works are largely sectarian. One would like to know what kind of talk went on more generally in the schools and synagogues. What kind of issues concerned them, for example, as they gathered round the table on Passover Eve?

Can we work our way back to the oral basis for what we now have in our Haggadah?

Most scholars would be hesitant on this; but one distinguished American scholar, Louis Finkelstein, has put forward the startling theory that we know precisely what was in 'the Haggadah' of pre-Maccabean times for the very good reason that much of it has come through *verbatim* into our own Haggadah. Far from being a rabbinic *pot-pourri* of the second century CE, our Haggadah (on this view) is only explicable in terms of the political, social and theological conditions of three centuries earlier. Because of the 'fortunate chance' which preserved the Haggadah, we can see now what was really going on in pre-Maccabean Israel.

According to Rabbi Finkelstein, the clue to understanding the various statements and arguments of our Haggadah lies in something usually ignored yet absolutely vital: the tug of war between Syria and Egypt to rule the Jews of Israel, and its obverse: the extreme care which the Jews had to exercise not to offend whichever of these two powers was dominant at the time.

The dates have to be borne in mind. The Ptolemaic dynasty of Egypt was in broad control of Palestine from about 301 to 198 BCE, though in constant battle with the Seleucids of Syria. In the second century Syria took over, until the Maccabees led their revolt against the profanation of the Temple in 168 BCE, founding the Hasmonean dynasty, which was to give the Jews independence of a sort for more than two hundred years.

Jewish life under the Ptolemies was dominated in formal terms by the High Priest and the patrician class, but the 'Scribes' had already begun to emerge, working closely in political terms with the authorities but laying the groundwork at the same time, as midrashic teachers, for the distinctive view of life which was to emerge later. What sort of things were they teaching? According to Finkelstein a full picture can be built up, partly from what is included in our Haggadah but also from alternative passages that survived in the rabbinic literature or have come to light through the discovery of fragmentary manuscripts (as in the *Genizah*). He goes even further by putting weight on apparently slight differences in Haggadah texts found in different versions all over the world. Putting all this together is like writing a detective story.

Here is one example of what emerges. The Haggadah says: 'Go forth and learn what Laban the Syrian sought to do to Jacob our father.' It is a midrashic commentary on a verse from the twenty-sixth chapter of Deuteronomy. But why would the rabbis of the second century CE work out this particular comment? The answer is (says Finkelstein) that they didn't. It goes back to pre-Maccabean times. The biblical passage from Deuteronomy is the 'confessional' recited by Jews when they brought their offerings of first-fruits to the Temple. Every Jew of Temple times would know it by heart. The *midrash* on that verse is also directly related to that period—some time before the second century BCE, when Egypt was in control. The Jewish leaders felt it politic to be on good terms with their Egyptian rulers and hostile to Syria. The interpretation therefore criticizes the 'Syrian' Laban and softens the tale of 'oppression' in Egypt. The theology of the passage also stamps it as pre-Maccabean, since the views it expresses on angels, and on the 'visibility' of God, indicate that it must have been written before the Pharisees, who had different views, emerged. We are being taken directly back, as it were, to a Seder at the end of the third century BCE!

'Our ancestors worshipped strange gods . . .' A view of such worship in a woodcut from a Haggadah printed in Livorno (1867)

Here is another example. The present 'answer' to the child's Four Questions begins: 'We were slaves to Pharaoh in Egypt. . .'; but there is a clue in a passage once considered as an alternative introduction: 'In the beginning our ancestors worshipped strange gods. . .' Using this verse would show how ancient was their revolt against paganism. The aim (says Finkelstein) is to combat the argument of Egyptian propagandists of the second century BCE that they—and not the Greeks or the Jews—were the 'mothers of wisdom'. But the passage also stresses the old connection of the Jews with Mesopotamia. This Mesopotamian/Syrian connection was also 'anti-Egyptian'. This passage must therefore have been written under Syrian rule, i.e. after the beginning of the second century BCE. It continued to be used as an 'introduction' until the Syrians offended the Jews irremediably at the time of the Maccabees. There are many other detailed points in this elaborate 'who-dunnit', including an analysis of the way in which economic issues of the time would have affected the form of Jewish self-expression. The commercial leaders of Jerusalem had an immense trade not only with Egypt but also with the rich 'Greek cities' of Palestine. The struggle for power within the Jewish community reflected these rivalries. In connection with this, and what emerges about the social structure of Israel just before the Maccabean uprising, we are offered a truly startling suggestion: that the man labelled usually as the Jewish 'traitor' in the Maccabean drama—the Hellenizing High Priest Jason—played, in fact, a moderate and constructive role, and even, as we shall see, contributed directly to our Haggadah.

Pursuing this approach, we get even more shocks. The four types of sons who have to be answered in the Haggadah were, in pre-Maccabean times, only three. Finkelstein shows how the fourth

פַּארֵי גּוֹשְׁטִיסְיָיה ייו אִי נו מֵינְשַׁאגֵ֗ירו · ייו יְיָ ייו אֵיל אִי נו אוטְרו :

כיד קוֹן פוֹדִיר פוּאֵירְטֵי אֵיסְטָה לָה מוֹרְטַאלְדַאר · קוֹמוֹ דִיזֵי אֵיל פָּסוק אֵינ פוֹדֵיר דֵי יְיָ

קִיבְרַאנְטַאן אֵין טו נַאנַאדו קֵי אֵינֵיל קַאמְפּו אֵין לוס קָאבַאלְיֵיוש אֵין לוש אַזְנוש

דיסטרוסייון די לוס אידולוס · אי די טודוס פרימו׳גיניטוס די א׳גיפטו

Jews expelled from Spain in 1492 continued to speak Spanish, which they wrote in Hebrew characters, and the language survived as Ladino. Page from a Haggadah with Spanish commentary in Hebrew characters which reads: '*Destruction di los idolos, di todos primoginitos di Egypto*' ('Destruction of the idols and all the first-born of Egypt')

son (confusing the argument) was added much later. There is an equal surprise over the Four Cups of wine. There was a great discussion, for a long time, if there shouldn't really be five! Indeed this is said to be one reason why we put a cup on the table for Elijah. Whenever the rabbis couldn't agree on the answer to a problem they used a formula: Elijah will solve all problems. The fifth cup was therefore put out for him to decide on.

But the theory that really startles is on the date and authorship of one of the most popular features of the Haggadah—the song *Dayyenu*. On the surface it seems hard to give a date to what is just a jolly recital of benefits by God, to each of which alone we would have been prepared to shout (as we do) *Dayyenu*—'We're satisfied!' But let Sherlock Holmes get to work. The first thing we note is that in the list of benefits, the climax is the building of the Temple. Nothing is said about 'may it be rebuilt speedily . . .' so we conclude that it was still standing. The next thing we note is that there is no mention in the song of Jerusalem the capital. Surely that was a benefit. We learn however from detective Finkelstein that, until the freeing of Jerusalem by Judas Maccabeus, the priestly authorities played down the importance of Jerusalem as a capital and put all their emphasis on the Temple. Only after the Maccabean victory does Jerusalem appear in all prayers and blessings, so we are taken back to 168 BCE, before Judas Maccabeus captured the holy city.

Another indication of the song's priestly origin is that nothing is said of Moses in the list. The priests were always playing down the role of Moses, who was a mere Levite! All this, plus some theological analysis, pins the author of the song down to a priest—probably the High Priest—shortly before the Maccabean rising. Whoever wrote the song was heavily anti-Egyptian and, by implication, pro-Syrian. Can you name him? Finkelstein can: the High Priest Jason, whom he has already rescued from obloquy.

How much of all this rings true? Each person will make up his own mind. But no one can deny that it is just this kind of talk that we are entitled to pursue at the Seder.

A Break from the Rabbis

ca. 30 CE

We have been discussing Passover and the Haggadah in terms of what became the rabbinic tradition. As a diversion, let us look briefly at how Passover was interpreted in roughly the same period by a philosopher we have already mentioned—Philo, who lived in the first century CE in a background open to many other influences, the city of Alexandria.

Alexandria—a great port, a city of commerce and wealth, with a mixed, lively and even fiery population—was the New York of the day. Like New York, it included a large Jewish population, attached to their ancestral faith yet drawing at the same time, in a natural and fulfilling way, on the non-Jewish (in this case, Hellenistic) traditions expressed in the city's culture.

To all Alexandrian Jews, Jerusalem was the central shrine, yet their local Greek culture affected them profoundly; and at the numerous synagogues all over the city, the Bible was read, and sermons delivered, in Greek. In the hands of Philo, this synthesis of backgrounds received a unique expression. As a philosopher he pursued Greek ideas, formulating an abstract, half-mystical view of God and his relation to man which was to be a powerful influence on the emerging Christian Church. But he remained 'Philo Judaeus', expounding his philosophy in terms that fitted in with his ancestral religion. Anything odd or primitive in 'the sacred writings' or the age-old ceremonies could be explained symbolically or allegorically. This was not to explain them away: there was virtue in ancestral observance—if properly 'philosophized'.

In this spirit he wrote about Passover. There was something distinctly midrashic in his tone, though his exposition was far from the legalism of the rabbis, or the carefree mood of *Dayyenu*. Passover to him, as he explained the symbolism of the rules, was basically a spiritual experience of a poetic kind:

> 'In the spring equinox we have a kind of likeness and portraiture of that first epoch in which this world was created. The elements were then separated and placed in harmonious order with reference to themselves and each other . . .Every year God reminds us of the creation of the world by setting before our eyes the spring, when everything blooms and flowers . . .
>
> 'The feast begins at the middle of the month, on the fifteenth day, when the moon is full, a day purposely chosen because then there is no darkness, but everything is continuously lighted up . . .
>
> 'The food consumed is of a different and unfamiliar kind, namely unleavened bread . . .Food, when unleavened, is a gift of nature: when leavened, a work of art . . .Since the springtime feast is a reminder of the creation of the world, and its original inhabitants must have used the gifts of the universe in their unperverted state before pleasure got the master, God ordained for use on this occasion the food most fully in accord with the season. He wished every year to rekindle the embers of the serious and ascetic mode of faring . . . and as far as possible to assimilate our present-day life to that of the distant past . . .'

It is all very high-flown, yet something is missing in this ascetic approach. 'The guests,' he says, 'are not there to indulge the belly with wine and viands, but to fulfill with prayers and hymns the customs handed down by their fathers.' To most of us, this doesn't tell the whole story. Yet what Philo wrote—addressing himself mainly to the non-Jewish world around him—is still part of the unseen Haggadah. Jews have spoken with many voices in different ages.

'Can one make Kiddush on Beer?'
ca. 300 CE

We have already noted that the Talmud, which we might have expected to tell us most about the Seder, tells us least. There is plenty about the sacrifices, but virtually nothing about the current celebrations in the home. Presumably the Seder, being so well established by then, was taken for granted.

There is not even much of the incidental detail about Passover that we get in the Gospels or Josephus. The Talmud tractate on Passover does include, it is true, some arguments on whether this or that prayer should be recited, but there is not much in the way of anecdote to add to what comes through in our Haggadah. The vagueness is illustrated by the fact that the one firm anecdote in our Haggadah—the story of a group of rabbis talking all night at B'nei B'rak—is told in the Talmud about some different rabbis who sat talking through the night at Lydda!

What we do get from the Talmud, however, is a living picture of the kind of men who sat down to the Seder in those far-off days—their warmth, their humanity, the quizzical mixture of learning and wit which was to be (we like to think) typical of the Jewish spirit. Much of this has come through in the legends of the Midrash, where fantasy and reverence are equally mixed; but there is plenty of human comment even in a book as legalistic as the Talmud tractate on Passover.

One rabbi wants to know, for example, what happens if you rent your house to another Jew from the fourteenth day of Nisan—the day before Passover. Every householder has a bounden duty to get rid of anything 'leaven'—the merest crumb—by that morning; but who is the householder in this case? Whose job is it? There is a lively argument, and then someone produces the clincher: when you rent your house to another Jew, he asks, whose duty is it to make sure that a *mezuzah* (the amulet on the door) is fixed? The tenant's. All right: let the same reasoning apply.

There is a legal discussion on the problem of beer at Passover—because it is a fermented drink—and someone asks more generally: 'Can one ever recite the *Kiddush* (blessing on wine) on beer?' One rabbi, it seems, visiting a town which only offered beer, always refused to; but once, wanting to have a proper meal at the close of the Sabbath, which requires, first, the formal blessing on wine, said: 'Oh well: it's the wine of the country,' and gave in. Someone then tells a story of how 'Rabbi' (the editor of the Mishnah) was once sent some very strong beer, and on tasting it said: 'On beer like this, it is fitting to recite *Kiddush* and to utter all the psalms and praises in the world.' He seems to have drunk his fill, for during the night he woke up with tremendous stomach-ache. 'The question has to be re-phrased', he groaned. 'Not can you make *Kiddush* on beer, but can you bless anything which gives you such pains?'

A silver *mezuzah* from Russia, 1873

It seems rather a long way from the spirit of Philo, and so, indeed, is another of the stories on drinking. The Mishnah says that one should fast during the afternoon on Passover Eve so as to be able to eat more *matzah* at the Seder. Raba—another rabbi—had a better system. He used to drink wine all day: 'It whets my appetite for the evening,' he said.

The wine of the time was fairly rough, and needed to be mixed with water to be properly acceptable. This is turned into a rabbinic 'rule': if a man drinks the four cups neat, he has discharged the duty of celebrating the Passover, but not the duty of symbolizing his freedom, (for that, he has to *enjoy* the wine).

The aim of it all—*pace* Philo—is pleasure, for we have to fulfill the verse: 'And thou shalt rejoice in the feast, thou and thy son and thy daughter' (*Deuteronomy* XVI, 14). What then, they ask, really makes people happy. For men, the answer is wine; for women, clothes. In Babylon, we are told, the fashion was for coloured dresses; in Palestine, ironed linen dresses.

opposite Scene from the Golden Haggadah showing the Egyptian pursuers as mediaeval knights carrying lances
overleaf The crossing of the Red Sea from the Second Nuremberg Haggadah (Southern Germany, mid-15th century) with the pursuing Egyptians depicted as knights

They start with Passover, and wander off anywhere. One of the rules, for example, covers the feeding of poor visitors 'from the charity bowl', as we saw earlier. Rabbi Akiva, to show how highly he prizes the symbolism of the Seder, says: 'Normally, I'd rather profane the Sabbath than take help from the charity bowl, but I'd accept it at Passover—'to advertise the miracle'. Having mentioned Akiva, they go on to quote a whole host of his sayings, including a rather pungent one: 'Don't cook in a pot that your neighbour has cooked in,' which is interpreted as 'Don't marry a divorced woman during her husband's lifetime, for when a divorced man marries a divorced woman, there are four minds in the bed.'

They were full of practical advice of this kind. 'When your daughter attains puberty, free your slave and let him marry her'—one way of getting over the problem of having a tempting teenager in the house. In the same style: 'Watch out for your wife with her first son-in-law.' But the nicest story is one told to illustrate the dictum: 'God himself is filled with wonder at a bachelor who lives in a big city without sinning.' It appears that this saying was originally applied to two bachelor rabbis, R. Hanan and R. Oshaiah, who earned their living as cobblers. The Talmud says that they lived in a harlots' street and cobbled shoes for them. When they took the shoes in, the girls looked at *them*, but *they* lowered their eyes. 'My goodness' (or the equivalent in Aramaic), said the girls, 'those rabbis are really holy.'

'Pour out Thy wrath...' 1189 CE

There is a moment at the Seder that no one is quite sure about. The banquet is over, but before resuming the ceremonies, with the songs in the offing, there is a break. The front door of the house is opened 'for Elijah', and with the door standing open, a 'prayer' is recited, entirely out of keeping with everything else at the Seder. The rest of the Seder is joy and thankfulness, but these three sentences—all from the Bible—are like a burst of anger: ''Pour out Thy wrath upon the nations that have never known Thee...'

It is generally thought that the custom of reciting these verses was introduced in the Middle Ages—perhaps during the slaughters that accompanied the Crusades. It is easy to rationalize the link with the prophet Elijah. According to Malachi IV, 5 (read on the 'great' pre-Passover Sabbath), the Messiah will be preceded by Elijah. If there is a moment, at the centre of a joyous celebration, when the slaughter of the innocents is to be recalled, it leads to the hope of a messianic age of peace, heralded by the arrival of Elijah. The door is, therefore, opened for him. It is opened, too, because Passover has always been a 'watch night' (as described in Exodus), when the

מצה
זו שאנו אוכלין על שום
מה על שום שלא הספיק
בצקת של אבותינו להחמיץ
עד שנגלה עליהם מלך
מלכי המלכים הקב"ה וגאלם
שנ' ויאפו את הבצק אשר
הוציאו ממצרים עוגות

הן פסח מצה ומרור

פסח שהיו אבותינו
אוכלין בזמן
שבית המקדש קיים על
שום מה על שום שפסח
המקום על בתי אבותינו
במצרים שנ' ואמרתם זבח
פסח הוא לה' אשר פסח על
בתי בני ישראל בנגפו את
מצרים ואת בתינו הציל
ויקד העם וישתחוו

חרון אפו עברה וזעם וצרה
משלחת מלאכי רעים עברה
אחת וזעם שתים וצרה
שלש משלחת מלאכי רעים
ארבע אמור מעתה במצרים
לקו מאתים מכות
לקו ארבעים מכות ועל הים
ר' עקיבא אומ' מנין
שכל מכה
ומכה שהביא הקב"ה על
המצרים במצרים היתה של
חמש מכות שנ' ישלח בם
חרון אפו עברה וזעם וצרה
משלחת מלאכי רעים אחו

ancient Israelites, waiting for the departure from Egypt, were on the lookout for what might be happening.

How all these various elements were brought together in this precise ceremony is quite unknown; but that the Seder should become an occasion for focusing the minds of the Jews—however briefly—on the persecutions that had become so widespread from the time of the Crusades is not surprising. The Crusade massacres —starting in 1096—did not have a special Passover connotation; but all too soon, tragedy was linked to this season directly through the spread of the blood libel. The first accusation of ritual murder at Passover (or Easter) was made after the death of a boy called William in Norwich in 1144. From then on, it was to reappear with desperate results in many parts of Europe, and throughout the centuries.

The idea that Jews somehow needed human blood in connection with the celebration of the Passover—to 'mock at the Passion', to smear on the doorposts, or, in the most fantastic of all forms, to use in baking the *matzah*—is so unspeakable to the Jewish mind that words literally fail. Insofar as Christian mobs were stirred into violence by demagogues at Easter (which inevitably fell close to Passover), the idea of 'vengeance' for the crucifixion was clearly dominant. More specifically, the prominent place given to the ritual 'pouring' of animal blood in the ancient sacrifices of the Bible, with its 'explanation' that this blood was linked to atonement for sin—*ideas that vanished for Jews with the Temple*—had assumed a vivid form in Christian theology, with Jesus as 'the sacrifice'. To Jews, blood as a symbol of life was so precious that the slightest trace of it made any food prohibited for eating. To Christians, the saying of Jesus—'This is my blood'—as the wine was drunk had established a sacrament of central importance. Church authorities tried for centuries to stamp out the idea that Jews, too, had some ritual involving blood, but all in vain.

In looking for other elements in the violence at Passover, some have thought that Christians were puzzled, and fearful, because of the 'mysterious' activities of Jews at this time—their concentration on baking the *matzah*, their gathering at night on Passover Eve for strange ceremonies. But if this created—as it might have done—an aura of mystery, it could surely have been only a small element in these outbreaks. The Middle Ages are full of sad Passover stories. For the modern period, it is enough to recall that it was on the last day of Passover in 1903 that the Kishinev massacre took place, with many pogroms following.

If we are to attach 'Pour out Thy wrath' to one of the early mediaeval tragedies, we can think of York in 1189. Riots had broken

opposite The last night in Egypt, from the Second Nuremberg Haggadah, depicting the sacrifice of the paschal lamb, the collecting of blood and the smearing of blood on the door-posts (*Ex.* XII, 6–7)

Woodcut from Hartmann Schedel's *Weltchronik* (Nuremberg, 1493) showing the burning of Jews

out against the Jews at the coronation in London that year of Richard I. They spread through the country. At York, the Jews, shut up in the castle, decided to anticipate massacre by mass suicide, as had happened—certainly unknown to them—at Masada 1100 years earlier. The day was the Sabbath before Passover—a day normally celebrated as 'the Great Sabbath', when thoughts turn to the approaching festival of freedom.

Can one wonder that around this time some rabbi put down these three verses from the Bible to express the utter despair at being unable to move men from such evil? It is not a direct prayer, but a recall of the words of the Psalmist. It talks of the 'destruction' of 'the heathen'—a conscious archaism.

But is one free to call for *anyone's* destruction? To some rabbis, it was extremely important to define who, in fact, was the target for these ill wishes. In Bible times, the 'heathens' were literally idolaters, and therefore 'deserving' of destruction, not because of what they had done to the Jews but through their offense to God. But could one be sure that the Christians fell into this category? They might seem to get close to paganism through the 'worship' of images, or through the doctrine of the Trinity; but despite these 'errors', they did, after all, believe basically in a single God, 'the creator of heaven

A disputation between Christians and Jews, from Kohut *Geschichte der Deutchen Juden*

and earth'. If, then, they had a common basis of belief with Jews, one could not apply the words 'Pour out Thy wrath' to them. The Jews might have problems with their non-Jewish neighbours, but the underlying basis of society was just and had to be maintained.

This idea was first expressed by a famous rabbi, Eliezer Ashkenazi, in a commentary he wrote on the Haggadah in 1583. It was picked up in very positive terms in the writings of a Lithuanian rabbi of the mid-seventeenth century called Moses Rivkes; and it is perhaps apt at the Seder—having dwelt on the troubles of the Middle Ages—to savour the gentleness of his words:

> 'King David prayed to God to pour out His wrath on the heathen, who did not believe in the wonders which God performed for us in Egypt and at the giving of the Torah. But the Gentiles in whose shade we, the people of Israel, are exiled and among whom we are dispersed, do in fact believe in *creatio ex nihilo* and in the Exodus and in the main principles of religion. Hence we stand on guard to pray continually for the welfare and success of the kingdom and the ministers, and for all the States and places over which they rule. As Maimonides has said, in concurrence with Rabbi Joshua (of the Talmud): 'the pious of the Gentile nations, too, have a portion in the world to come.'

Which might well be described, if we remember the background, as an exercise in turning the other cheek.

The Portuguese Diplomat 1652 CE

We are coming closer to our own time. If, to end this Seder roll-call, we allow ourselves a last look at Jewish history, there are two moments that we can perhaps light on, so startlingly different in their relation to the Seder that they might be taken as symbols in themselves of the extraordinary range of Jewish life.

The first is the rich, resplendent and ultimately tragic period of the 'Marranos' of Spain and Portugal in the sixteenth and seventeenth centuries, where Passover was a secret—potent, and often decisive to their fate. The second was the crude and largely poverty-stricken Jewish world of Eastern Europe in the nineteenth century, where it was the greatest of public celebrations—the axis around which the world of social life turned—the symbol of affirmation.

The Marranos—Christians of Jewish origin who somehow clung to what they knew (or thought they knew) of their ancestral faith—were beneficiaries, at one level, of one of the richest and most sophisticated cultures of Europe. The Jews had lived in Spain since Roman times, and after a 'golden period' of life with the Moslems there—ending in ruthless persecution from the twelfth century on—had found an even greater opportunity for a settled and fulfilled existence under the Christian rulers, who were to take over the whole peninsula. Deeply acculturated, and playing an ever-increasing role in public life as statesmen, civil servants, soldiers, scientists and philosophers, many of them had surrendered in time to the advantages of adopting the dominant faith. To the other Spaniards—who continued for generations to think of these converts as 'New Christians'—they were never entirely trusted, and many in fact found it hard to let go of all Jewish loyalties, keeping up tenuous links with the more steadfast Jews.

The broad story of what happened is well-known; the details, as modern research has brought them to light, are strangely pathetic, with Passover always, for some reason, in the background of the play of forces. The zeal of some of the fanatical church leaders, bolstered by sporadic hatreds and riots of the populace, began to be applied in the fifteenth century towards rooting out any imagined heresies among the New Christians. The Inquisition—which was to torture and burn alive thousands for the greater glory of God—was introduced for this purpose in 1481. In 1492, those Jews who had never apostatized were expelled from Spain to avoid 'tempting' the New Christians. When many of these 'real' Jews fled to neighbouring Portugal, they were exposed there, within a short time, to a series of mass conversions by force, so that from the sixteenth century on there were New Christians in both countries—but with a difference: in Spain, they had drifted into the new faith 'voluntarily'

A pre-expulsion Seder plate from Spain (probably *ca.* 1490). The errors in the Hebrew words suggest that it may have been made by Marranos whose knowledge of Judaism was growing weak

and were increasingly vague, as time went on, about their older traditions; in Portugal, those converted had a much stronger background to draw on, and seized any opportunity to give it full expression.

The Inquisition was introduced into Portugal in 1531 and was rampant over the whole peninsula (and in the colonies overseas) for two hundred years or more. It is astonishing to read, on the one hand, of the extraordinary vitality and power of the Marrano families, increasingly and indissolubly mixed through marriage with the Church, the aristocracy and even the royal families; and, on the other hand, to follow the relentless persecutions, where the 'proof' of secret Judaizing—unless atoned—could lead to the stake. In many cases the Jewish practices they were supposed to be engaged in were family customs whose origin they hardly knew. There were just a few that they understood and would not give up: one of the most important of these was Passover.

It was a Passover quite remote in some ways from our present

An Inquisition scene from *The Ceremonial and Religious Customs of the Various Nations* (London, 1733) by Bernhard Picart (1673–1733)

Seder. They had no Hebrew books, no Haggadah, and little or no instruction. But they had the Bible—in Latin—and tried to apply its instructions literally, without benefit of the rabbinical formulas to which we have become used. The Bible said that a lamb was to be roasted whole—so they did this, and ate it, like the ancient Jews in Egypt, standing, booted, and staff in hand, ready for the journey. They had no idea when the month of Nisan came exactly, so they took the fourteenth day of the first full moon in March and hoped for the best. The general baking of *matzah* in advance might have given them away, so they baked it a few days *later* than the fourteenth, and the eating of it then was their Seder.

There were a few other occasions that remained vestigially in their family memory. Yom Kippur—the Day of Atonement—had

The 'Inquisition' of our time. Detail from 'The Warsaw Ghetto' by the American painter Jack Levine

survived as *dia pura*. It, too, was celebrated for safety on the wrong day: some would go off into the country to avoid drawing attention to their fasting. Most poignantly of all, perhaps, they remembered 'the Fast of Esther' at Purim—so joyous an occasion for 'ordinary' Jews—since Esther, like them, had had to conceal her Jewish origins when she married the Persian king.

But the most extraordinary aspect of Passover—for the mystique of Jewish history—was the way it somehow became the moment for unexpected drama, as in the songs we now chant at the Seder, when everything in the past was supposed to have happened at this feast. Cecil Roth, historian of the Marranos, tells the story of how the Inquisition itself was finally set up—after much hesitation by the Pope—through the accident of a fateful Seder in 1477.

A man in a *sanbenito*, the costume worn before being burnt by the Inquisition, from Picart

For some time before, a campaign against the New Christians had been mounted by a Dominican monk, Fra Alonso de Hojeda, prior of the Convent of S. Pablo in Seville, who outdid even Torquemada in virulence. It was a time of civil war, however, and Isabella, who was being greatly helped by her New Christian citizens, resisted any diversion. In 1477 the civil war came to an end and Isabella moved to Seville, remaining there for over a year:

> 'The sight of the *conversos* who thronged the Court, monopolising many of the highest offices, stimulated Hojeda to fresh efforts. For a long time he had no success; but a chance episode strengthened his case.
>
> 'On the night of Wednesday, 18 March 1478, a number of Jews and *conversos* were surprised together, at some mysterious celebration, by a young cavalier who had penetrated into the *Juderia* for the purpose of carrying on an intrigue with a fair Jewess who had taken his fancy. As a matter of fact, it was the eve of Passover, and it is obvious that they had come together for the purpose of the Seder celebration. By an unfortunate, but by no means uncommon coincidence, it happened to be Holy Week. Under the circumstances, no explanation commended itself to the general mind except that these miscreants had assembled, at the season of the Passion of Jesus, in order to blaspheme the Christian religion.
>
> 'When the news reached the ears of the prior of S. Pablo, he immediately hastened to Court and laid the evidence before the sovereigns. This, according to report, finally decided them. The Spanish ambassadors to the Holy See were immediately instructed to obtain a Bull authorizing the establishment of an Inquisition. Sixtus hesitated . . .but ultimately complied. On November first, 1478, a Bull was issued empowering the Spanish sovereigns to appoint three bishops . . .with complete jurisdiction over heretics and their accomplices. In this simple unostentatious way, the Spanish Inquisition was launched on its career of blood' (*A History of the Marranos*, pages 40–1).

It was on a Seder evening—21 March 1497—that the forced baptism of all the Jewish children in Portugal between the ages of four and fourteen took place, amid scenes of family poignancy that were enshrined in Hebrew elegies and lived long in the memory. It was a Seder also, in 1506, that signalled the first fury of a Portugese mob that turned into murder. For a time, until then, the Jews who had fled to Portugal had been trying to come to terms with their position as forced converts. The Portuguese had given them a certain freedom to adjust slowly to their new faith. Bringing with them the high culture of Spain, their talents had earned them a strong and useful role in public life. But it was an uneasy status: jealousy and suspicion had led to attacks and riots.

On the night of 7 April 1506, a number of New Christians were surprised celebrating the Seder. They were arrested, but released after only two days' imprisonment. The mob still raged, however, led by two Dominican friars who paraded the streets with uplifted crucifix, crying *Heresia.* A terrible massacre began. According to contemporary accounts, more than five hundred New Christians were murdered on the first day. A Christian eye-witness, appalled at what he saw, wrote of thousands being killed in all:

> 'Women with child were flung from the windows and caught on spears by those standing underneath, their offspring being hurled away. Many women and girls were ravished in the fanatical pursuit.'

Historians are always reminding us that violence, rape and massacre—linked to religious passions—were very widely spread all through the Middle Ages. If Jews had their fill of it, they were by no means the only victims. One has to keep remembering, also, how resilient human nature is. Against a background of many episodes like the 1506 massacre, the Marranos of Portugal—amazingly—continued to build up an extraordinarily creative life, participating fully, unless denounced, in the most important achievements of the country which, as their native land, they continued to regard with love.

The ironies and tragedies were, however, endless. Some deeply embedded family custom could nullify generations of thorough identification—as happened to one of the most eminent men of Portugal, Manuel Fernandes Villareal, with Passover again as the link. Villareal, a prominent soldier and writer, had been one of the foremost champions of the restoration of the royal house of Braganza, and had been rewarded by being sent as Consul-General to Paris, where he became a friend of Cardinal Richelieu. Returning to Lisbon on a visit in 1650, he was denounced by a fanatical friar as a secret Jew who had been trying to improve the position in Portugal of the New Christians, and evidence was produced that while in Paris he had been in the habit of going to Rouen with his wife to celebrate the Seder. What followed is not a pretty story. He confessed, professed repentance, and gave information about others. But nothing helped. 'As a member of the nobility,' Roth writes, 'he was spared the indignity of being burned; but on 1 December 1652, he was garrotted.'

One has to take a long view to come to terms with all this. Courage and cowardice, love and betrayal, intelligence and fear have all been mingled in Jewish history—as in the history of all peoples.

Mechel and Sara-Leah *ca.* 1900 CE

At the other end of Europe, where Jews had been settling increasingly in self-contained communities—almost completely cut-off socially from their neighbours—Passover and the Seder were as open and fulfilling as Thanksgiving Day in the United States. It was, like Thanksgiving, a great, 'national', annual festival—but with a difference. For Americans, the Pilgrim harvest of 1621 had been the first sign of the enormous bounty to come. For the Jews of Eastern Europe, Passover, the festival of freedom, was the recreation of an ancient triumph in a background that superficially, at least, spelt alienation, poverty, sterility and defeat.

Yet nothing would be more misleading than to think this way of the Passover spirit among the Jews of Eastern Europe. Surrounded by hostility, with the danger of murderous attack particularly prevalent at Easter, they threw themselves into Passover nevertheless with a joy and abandon that transformed their whole existence. They were celebrating an ancient miracle, and they saw it being repeated, in some degree, each year as they gathered round the Seder table, free at last from the drudgery and despair of the daily bondage.

To some extent—as in its most ancient form—*Pesach* was the symbol of release from the winter. We tend sometimes to think of East European Jews—the inhabitants of the *shtetl* (small town)—as somehow boxed-in ghetto-dwellers, cut off from natural life; but they were often much more like country folk, intensely responsive to the beauties of nature, as their secular writings—prose and poetry—show. The blooming of spring had its counterpart in the slow burgeoning of Passover, with memories stirring and preparations being made long before the full delights were to be enjoyed. Some of the preparations had started, indeed, in winter itself, with special wine being brewed, and goose-fat for cooking being carefully husbanded—all put aside under 'top security' conditions to avoid any mixing-up with 'non-Passover' food.

Purim, however, was the turning point. This carnival festival comes exactly one month before Passover. The moment it was over, the real work for Passover could start. There was *borsht* (beetroot soup) to be prepared and left, as it were, to mature. There were clothes and shoes to be made or ordered. Charity collections had to be organised, so as to ensure that the poorest of the community would not lack for *matzah*, potatoes and wine. Passover pans and crockery had to be thought of. Letters were to be written to members of the family checking that all would manage to be present at the great reunion.

opposite 'The Goose Market in Cracow' (1837) by Wilhelm Unger, a vivid evocation of the Jewish scene in Eastern Europe

The cleaning of the house itself was a month-long operation. This was no half-hearted washing and sweeping, but a scouring—or, as someone has put it, a 'purging'—of the house to make it worthy of the great feast that was to come. And in the midst of the bustle

top Three festive Delft plates for Passover and other holy days. The words appearing are '*Pesach*', '*Yontefdik*' (for holidays) and '*Gut Yontef*' (happy holiday)

below, left Scouring the dishes before Passover
below, right Baking the *matzah*. From Johanne Leusden's *Philologus Hebraeo-Mixtus* (Amsterdam, 1682)

at home and in the market, there was the all-consuming activity centred on the communal baking of the *matzah* itself. Even for 'ordinary' purposes, the baking had to be conducted under careful supervision, to make certain that there was not the slightest contact with 'non-Passover' implements or dishes, and no trace of *chametz* (leaven); and for this purpose the flour had to be watched from the time it was ground, so that no dampness could enter and lead to fermentation. For the most devout, however, this was not enough. The wheat that was used for *matzah shemurah* ('guarded *matzah*')

'The Seder' by Picart

had to be watched over from the beginning of the harvest.

The children would be carefully preparing for their great moment at the Seder when they would ask the Four Questions. The men, keeping an eye on the practical work, would also be deeply involved in the study side of the festival. From Purim on, they would have been studying the *Shulhan Arukh* (code of practices) to enjoy the rehearsing of all the technicalities. On the Sabbath before Passover ('the Great Sabbath'), the rabbi would bring all this together in a synagogue discourse in the afternoon lasting perhaps several hours

—a performance that would be his annual exhibition of knowledge, acumen and oratorical skill. At this advanced level of 'learning', the men would have been working, under the guidance of the rabbi, at finishing a tractate of the Talmud, all carefully timed to be brought to completion on the morning before Passover, which would entitle them to stage a *Siyyum* ('Completion Feast')—and incidentally to secure exemption, if they were first-born, from 'the Fast of the First-born,' a minor fast that was otherwise enjoined, in memory of the Jewish first-born having been spared in Egypt.

That same morning would also see the ritual of 'burning the *chametz*'—a ceremony in which the father threw into a fire, often a communal bonfire, the crumbs of leaven that he and his family had first carefully planted and then collected in the spring-cleaned house. At the rabbi's house there were the complicated formalities of 'selling' Jewish-owned 'non-Passover' property to a non-Jew, to be 'bought back' in a week's time when the festival was over. The excitement would be mounting in every home as the Passover dishes, stored each year, were brought out, cleaned and polished for the evening feast. And at long last, with Father clothed in a resplendent white *kittel*, and Mother in her new fine dress, the family and all the visitors would sit down to the Seder.

The joy of the Seder itself has communicated itself to all successive generations; but perhaps none of us in our more sophisticated lives will ever recapture the simple folk-happiness of that strange period of Jewish life. To understand it we have to look at the paintings of Chagall, or read the mysterious dream-like novels of Agnon.

There is a story in Agnon's book *The Bridal Canopy* which evokes this feeling.

Mechel the *shamash* (beadle) has finished all his work at the synagogue and is on his way home to a lonely Seder. He is a widower, and has refused all invitations to join in other Seders, out of some obscure need to live out his aloneness.

On his way home he sees the gaiety of the preparations everywhere, and passes the house of the rich widow Sara-Leah, who stands alone at her window and gives him the festal greeting. They talk, and after a while he enters her house and once again sits at the head of a Seder table, while Sara-Leah speaks the Four Questions.

A dialogue between them has started. It moves on through the beauty of the prayers and the happiness of the blessings into the poetry of the Song of Songs. As Sara-Leah prepares their food the next morning, the sound of a man's voice can be heard singing in her house. Mechel has rejoined life, in the act of rejoining his people.

opposite Illustration to the Song of Songs by Shraga Weill

The Route of the Exodus (see endpapers)

The scholars who put forward many differing theories about the route of the Exodus and the location of Mount Sinai are agreed only on one point: that while the biblical stories reflect a powerful historic memory, the placing of the events described must remain conjectural. The Bible account is full of 'precise' names, but these offer few reliable clues; surviving place-names can be linked with biblical ones, by scholarly ingenuity, to suit any theory. The description of various places and the timing of journeys between them can also be used malleably. Centuries of study—up to the latest researches by Israeli scholars in the Sinai Peninsula—still leave all the questions open.

The crossing of the 'Red Sea' has been located at three lakes along the Mediterranean coast, at other lakes all the way down to Suez, and even across the Gulf of Akabah. Mount Sinai could be a mountain in the north, the centre or the south of the peninsula or even at a volcanic site east of Akabah, where some believe that the wanderings really took place, emphasizing the religious connection of Moses with Midian. Most scholars, it is true, assume that the Sinai Peninsula, being close at hand, is more likely to be the area, and look for physical clues. The geographer Dr. Menashe Harel has developed this approach in recent work. At the opposite extreme, the Sinai archaeologist Beno Rothenberg prefers to emphasize the fact that in all his explorations of ancient roads and settlements in the peninsula, no physical signs of any connection with the biblical period were found, though there was also much material for earlier and later periods.

The map here—taking the Israelites through the centre of the peninsula—follows the analysis given by Dr. Harel in a study in *The Jerusalem Post*, 20 April 1970. Some key points in his arguments are:

1. '*Pi-Hahiroth*' (*Exodus* XIV, 2), where, before the crossing, the Israelites were hemmed in between the mountains and the sea, can be identified as the narrow area between Jebel Geneife and the Bitter Lakes.

2. *The Crossing* was entirely possible at the narrow juncture of the Great and Small Bitter Lakes. Pre-Suez Canal data show how shallow the water was there in ancient times.

3. '*Marah*' (*Exodus* XV, 23), so-called because the water was bitter (*marah*), could be Bir el-Murah.

4. '*Elim*' (*Exodus* XV, 27) could be Uyum Mussa (12 kms. from Marah) where there are twelve springs and palms as at 'Elim'.

5. '*Rephidim*' (*Exodus* XVII, 1). The Amalekites suddenly appear here, fighting the Israelites (*Exodus* XVII, 8). This is understandable if Rephidim is put at the mouth of the Wadi Suder, about fifty kilometres south of Suez. This wadi was a junction of all the main routes across the peninsula (see map). Rothenberg has shown, in the *Palestine Exploration Quarterly* for Jan.–June 1970, that the ancient main road of central Sinai, the *Darb e-Shawi*, which had served as a major thoroughfare since the fourth millenium BCE, had its western terminal in this wadi. The Amalekites—far from home—were engaged in what Harel calls 'a life and death' struggle with the Israelites for the water and arable land of the area and control of the routes.

6. *Mount Sinai* (or *Mt. Horeb*) could be 'Jebel Sin Bisher', a mountain close by. It is not very high, but is a landmark, and near enough to Egypt to correspond to the timing of the wanderings. The Israelites stayed at Sinai for a year, which would be plausible with the pasture and water of the Wadi Suder.

Against locating Sinai as one of a number of mountains in the south, it is argued that the Israelites could not have lived in that rocky area for a year. In addition there would be dangers from Egyptian troops guarding the turquoise (and some copper) mines. Against the northern route, there is the flat statement in Exodus XIII, 17 that this was too 'dangerous'. It was, in fact, a main military route for the Egyptians. It was also accessible to water and fish, which would have ruled out Israelite 'murmuring'. But none of these arguments would convince scholars urging one of these routes.

7. *The Wanderings.* The 'great and terrible wilderness' (*Deuteronomy* I, 19) before Kadesh-Barnea is the mountainous desert of the central Negev. Defeated there by an alliance of Amalekites, Canaanites and Amorites, and subsequently opposed also by the King of Arad, the Israelites had to wander for thirty-eight years through the deserts of Paran and Zin. With direct access to the Holy Land barred, they ultimately moved eastwards, circumventing Edom, forcing their way (by defeating the Amorites) around Moab, to enter the Land from 'the other side of the Jordan'.

Further Reading

The text of the Haggadah presented here is the familiar Ashkenazi version as it has been printed in hundreds of editions in recent centuries. Many commentaries have brought out textual variations in manuscript and printed editions from many countries and periods, but by and large the text is remarkably uniform, stretching back to the authoritative formulations by *Gaon* Amram and *Gaon* Saadya in Babylonia in the ninth and tenth centuries.

A note on the translation appears in the introduction at the other end of the book.

In the chapters on the history and background, footnotes have been completely eschewed. Books referred to in the text and a few others that bear on the issues—almost all easily available—are listed briefly here.

Bright, J.: *A History of Israel*, 1960.

Cowley, A.E.: *Aramaic Papyri of the Fifth Century BC*, 1923.

Danby, H.: *The Mishnah*, 1933.

Daube, D.: *The New Testament and Rabbinic Judaism*, 1956.

Finkelstein, L.: 'The Oldest Midrash: Pre-Rabbinic Ideals and Teachings in the Passover Haggadah' (*Harvard Theol. Rev.*, xxxi 1938, page 291ff.); 'Pre-Maccabean Documents in the Passover Haggadah' (*Harvard Theol. Rev.*, xxxv 1942, page 291ff., xxxvi 1943, page 1ff.).

Gaster, T.H.: *Passover. Its History and Traditions*, 1958.

Goldschmidt, E.D.: *The Passover Haggadah: Its Sources and History* (Hebrew), 1960.

Goodenough, E.R.: *Jewish Symbolism in the Greek and Roman Period*, 1954.

Goodman, P.: *The Passover Haggadah*, 1961.

Gordon, C.H.: *Before the Bible*, 1962.

Grant, F.C.: *Ancient Judaism and the New Testament*, 1960.

Hooke, S.H. ed.: *Myth, Ritual and Kingship*, 1958.

Italiener, B.: *Die Darmstadter Pessach-Haggadah*, 1927.

Katz, J.: *Exclusiveness and Tolerance*, 1962.

Kraeling, C.H.: *Excavations at Dura Europos: The Synagogue*, 1956.

Meek, T.J.: *Hebrew Origins*, 1950.

Narkiss, B.: *The Golden Haggadah*, 1970.

Roth, C. ed.: *Jewish Art*, 1961.

—— ed.: *The Sarajevo Haggadah*, 1963.

Rowley, H.H.: *Worship in Ancient Israel*, 1967.

Segal, J.B.: *The Hebrew Passover*, 1963.

Spitzer, M.: *The Birds' Head Haggadah*, 1969.

Stein, S.: 'The Influence of Symposia Literature on the Literary Form of the Pesah Haggadah' (*Journal of Jewish Studies*, viii 1957).

Thomas, D.W. ed.: *Archaeology and Old Testament Study*, 1967.

Yadin, Y.: *Hazor*, 1958.

——: *Bar-Kokhba*, 1971.

Zeitlin, S.: 'The Liturgy of the First Night of Passover' (*Jewish Quarterly Review*, xviii 1948 No. 4, April).

For the Seder itself, turn now to the 'Hebrew end' of the book. The page numbers of this part of the book are printed in red.

Only One Kid

This is the kid
That DAD bought.
  Two *zuz* at most
  Was all it cost.
Poor little kid!
Poor little kid!

This is the cat
That ate the kid
  That DAD bought.

This is the dog
That bit the cat
That ate the kid
  That DAD bought.

This is the stick
That beat the dog
That bit the cat
That ate the kid
  That DAD bought.

This is the fire
That burnt the stick
That beat the dog
That bit the cat
That ate the kid
  That DAD bought.

This is the rain
That quenched the fire
That burnt the stick
That beat the dog
That bit the cat
That ate the kid
  That Dad bought.

This is the ox (*with crumpled horn*)
That drank the rain (*the very next morn*)
That quenched the fire
That burnt the stick
That beat the dog
That bit the cat
That ate the kid
  That DAD bought.

Then came a butcher (*all forlorn*)
Who slew the ox (*with crumpled horn*)
That drank the rain
That quenched the fire
That burnt the stick
That beat the dog
That bit the cat
That ate the kid
  That DAD bought.

Beelzebub—that so-and-so—
Now laid the mournful butcher low.
He'd killed the ox
That drank the rain
That quenched the fire
That burnt the stick
That beat the dog
That bit the cat
That ate the kid
  That DAD bought.

Now God spoke up, in Whom we trust:
'Beelzebub must bite the dust:
He's slain the butcher
Who killed the ox
That drank the rain
That quenched the fire
That burnt the stick
That beat the dog
That bit the cat
That ate the kid
  That DAD bought.'

Two *zuz* at most
Was all it cost.
  Poor little kid! Poor little kid!

Chad Gadya

חַד גַּדְיָא
חַד גַּדְיָא.
דִּזְבַן אַבָּא
בִּתְרֵי זוּזֵי.
חַד גַּדְיָא
חַד גַּדְיָא:

וַאֲתָא שׁוּנְרָא.
וְאָכַל לְגַדְיָא.
דִּזְבַן אַבָּא
בִּתְרֵי זוּזֵי.
חַד גַּדְיָא
חַד גַּדְיָא:

וַאֲתָא כַלְבָּא.
וְנָשַׁךְ לְשׁוּנְרָא.
דְּאָכַל לְגַדְיָא.
דִּזְבַן אַבָּא
בִּתְרֵי זוּזֵי.
חַד גַּדְיָא
חַד גַּדְיָא:

וַאֲתָא חוּטְרָא.
וְהִכָּה לְכַלְבָּא.
דְּנָשַׁךְ לְשׁוּנְרָא.
דְּאָכַל לְגַדְיָא.
דִּזְבַן אַבָּא
בִּתְרֵי זוּזֵי.
חַד גַּדְיָא
חַד גַּדְיָא:

וַאֲתָא נוּרָא.
וְשָׂרַף לְחוּטְרָא.
דְּהִכָּה לְכַלְבָּא.
דְּנָשַׁךְ לְשׁוּנְרָא.
דְּאָכַל לְגַדְיָא
דִּזְבַן אַבָּא
בִּתְרֵי זוּזֵי.
חַד גַּדְיָא
חַד גַּדְיָא:

וַאֲתָא מַיָּא.
וְכָבָה לְנוּרָא.
דְּשָׂרַף לְחוּטְרָא.
דְּהִכָּה לְכַלְבָּא.
דְּנָשַׁךְ לְשׁוּנְרָא.
דְּאָכַל לְגַדְיָא.
דִּזְבַן אַבָּא
בִּתְרֵי זוּזֵי.
חַד גַּדְיָא
חַד גַּדְיָא:

וַאֲתָא תוֹרָא.
וְשָׁתָא לְמַיָּא.
דְּכָבָה לְנוּרָא.
דְּשָׂרַף לְחוּטְרָא.
דְּהִכָּה לְכַלְבָּא.
דְּנָשַׁךְ לְשׁוּנְרָא.
דְּאָכַל לְגַדְיָא.
דִּזְבַן אַבָּא
בִּתְרֵי זוּזֵי.
חַד גַּדְיָא
חַד גַּדְיָא:

וַאֲתָא הַשּׁוֹחֵט.
וְשָׁחַט לְתוֹרָא.
דְּשָׁתָא לְמַיָּא.
דְּכָבָה לְנוּרָא.
דְּשָׂרַף לְחוּטְרָא.
דְּהִכָּה לְכַלְבָּא.
דְּנָשַׁךְ לְשׁוּנְרָא.
דְּאָכַל לְגַדְיָא.
דִּזְבַן אַבָּא
בִּתְרֵי זוּזֵי.
חַד גַּדְיָא
חַד גַּדְיָא.

וַאֲתָא מַלְאַךְ הַמָּוֶת.
וְשָׁחַט לְשׁוֹחֵט.
דְּשָׁחַט לְתוֹרָא.
דְּשָׁתָא לְמַיָּא.
דְּכָבָה לְנוּרָא.
דְּשָׂרַף לְחוּטְרָא.
דְּהִכָּה לְכַלְבָּא.
דְּנָשַׁךְ לְשׁוּנְרָא.
דְּאָכַל לְגַדְיָא.
דִּזְבַן אַבָּא
בִּתְרֵי זוּזֵי.
חַד גַּדְיָא חַד גַּדְיָא:

וַאֲתָא הַקָּדוֹשׁ בָּרוּךְ הוּא.
וְשָׁחַט לְמַלְאַךְ הַמָּוֶת.
דְּשָׁחַט לְשׁוֹחֵט.
דְּשָׁחַט לְתוֹרָא.
דְּשָׁתָא לְמַיָּא.
דְּכָבָה לְנוּרָא.
דְּשָׂרַף לְחוּטְרָא.
דְּהִכָּה לְכַלְבָּא.
דְּנָשַׁךְ לְשׁוּנְרָא.
דְּאָכַל לְגַדְיָא.
דִּזְבַן אַבָּא
בִּתְרֵי זוּזֵי.
חַד גַּדְיָא חַד גַּדְיָא:

Who knows Six? I know Six: Six books of Mishnah, Five books of Torah, Four the Fathers, Three the Mothers, Two the Tablets, One is God in Heaven and Earth.

Who knows Seven? I know Seven: Seventh day for Sabbath, Six books of Mishnah, Five books of Torah, Four the Mothers, Three the Fathers, Two the Tablets, One is God in Heaven and Earth.

Who knows Eight? I know Eight: Eighth day to circumcise, Seventh day for Sabbath, Six books of Mishnah, Five books of Torah, Four the Mothers, Three the Fathers, Two the Tablets, One is God in Heaven and Earth.

Who knows Nine? I know Nine: Nine months to bear, Eighth day to circumcise, Seventh day for Sabbath, Six books of Mishnah, Five books of Torah, Four the Mothers, Three the Fathers, Two the Tablets, One is God in Heaven and Earth.

Who knows Ten? I know Ten: Ten Commandments, Nine months to bear, Eighth day to circumcise, Seventh day for Sabbath, Six books of Mishnah, Five books of Torah, Four the Mothers, Three the Fathers, Two the Tablets, One is God in Heaven and Earth.

Who knows Eleven? I know Eleven: Eleven stars *(for Joseph)*, Ten Commandments, Nine months to bear, Eighth day to circumcise, Seventh day for Sabbath, Six books of Mishnah, Five books of Torah, Four the Mothers, Three the Fathers, Two the Tablets, One is God in Heaven and Earth.

Who knows Twelve? I know Twelve: Twelve the Tribes, Eleven stars *(for Joseph)*, Ten Commandments, Nine months to bear, Eighth day to circumcise, Seventh day for Sabbath, Six books of Mishnah, Five books of Torah, Four the Mothers, Three the Fathers, Two the Tablets, One is God in Heaven and Earth.

Who knows Thirteen? I know Thirteen: Thirteen God's attributes, Twelve the Tribes, Eleven stars *(for Joseph)*, Ten Commandments, Nine months to bear, Eighth day to circumcise, Seventh day for Sabbath, Six books of Mishnah, Five books of Torah, Four the Mothers, Three the Fathers, Two the Tablets, One is God in Heaven and Earth.

opposite A 19th-century, Hungarian *matzah* cover of velvet with gold threads and real fish-scales

עֲשָׂרָה מִי יוֹדֵעַ. עֲשָׂרָה אֲנִי יוֹדֵעַ. עֲשָׂרָה דִבְּרַיָּא. תִּשְׁעָה יַרְחֵי לֵידָה. שְׁמוֹנָה יְמֵי מִילָה. שִׁבְעָה יְמֵי שַׁבְּתָא. שִׁשָּׁה סִדְרֵי מִשְׁנָה. חֲמִשָּׁה חֻמְשֵׁי תוֹרָה. אַרְבַּע אִמָּהוֹת. שְׁלֹשָׁה אָבוֹת. שְׁנֵי לֻחוֹת הַבְּרִית. אֶחָד אֱלֹהֵינוּ שֶׁבַּשָּׁמַיִם וּבָאָרֶץ:

אַחַד עָשָׂר מִי יוֹדֵעַ. אַחַד עָשָׂר אֲנִי יוֹדֵעַ. אַחַד עָשָׂר כּוֹכְבַיָּא. עֲשָׂרָה דִבְּרַיָּא. תִּשְׁעָה יַרְחֵי לֵידָה. שְׁמוֹנָה יְמֵי מִילָה. שִׁבְעָה יְמֵי שַׁבְּתָא. שִׁשָּׁה סִדְרֵי מִשְׁנָה. חֲמִשָּׁה חֻמְשֵׁי תוֹרָה. אַרְבַּע אִמָּהוֹת. שְׁלֹשָׁה אָבוֹת. שְׁנֵי לֻחוֹת הַבְּרִית. אֶחָד אֱלֹהֵינוּ שֶׁבַּשָּׁמַיִם וּבָאָרֶץ:

שְׁנֵים עָשָׂר מִי יוֹדֵעַ. שְׁנֵים עָשָׂר אֲנִי יוֹדֵעַ. שְׁנֵים עָשָׂר שִׁבְטַיָּא. אַחַד עָשָׂר כּוֹכְבַיָּא. עֲשָׂרָה דִבְּרַיָּא. תִּשְׁעָה יַרְחֵי לֵידָה. שְׁמוֹנָה יְמֵי מִילָה. שִׁבְעָה יְמֵי שַׁבְּתָא. שִׁשָּׁה סִדְרֵי מִשְׁנָה. חֲמִשָּׁה חֻמְשֵׁי תוֹרָה. אַרְבַּע אִמָּהוֹת. שְׁלֹשָׁה אָבוֹת. שְׁנֵי לֻחוֹת הַבְּרִית. אֶחָד אֱלֹהֵינוּ שֶׁבַּשָּׁמַיִם וּבָאָרֶץ:

שְׁלֹשָׁה עָשָׂר מִי יוֹדֵעַ. שְׁלֹשָׁה עָשָׂר אֲנִי יוֹדֵעַ. שְׁלֹשָׁה עָשָׂר מִדַּיָּא. שְׁנֵים עָשָׂר שִׁבְטַיָּא. אַחַד עָשָׂר כּוֹכְבַיָּא. עֲשָׂרָה דִבְּרַיָּא. תִּשְׁעָה יַרְחֵי לֵידָה. שְׁמוֹנָה יְמֵי מִילָה. שִׁבְעָה יְמֵי שַׁבְּתָא. שִׁשָּׁה סִדְרֵי מִשְׁנָה. חֲמִשָּׁה חֻמְשֵׁי תוֹרָה. אַרְבַּע אִמָּהוֹת. שְׁלֹשָׁה אָבוֹת. שְׁנֵי לֻחוֹת הַבְּרִית. אֶחָד אֱלֹהֵינוּ שֶׁבַּשָּׁמַיִם וּבָאָרֶץ:

Who knows One? I know One: One is God in Heaven and Earth.

Who knows Two? I know Two: Two the Tablets, One is God in Heaven and Earth.

Who knows Three? I know Three: Three the Fathers, Two the Tablets, One is God in Heaven and Earth.

Who knows Four? I know Four: Four the Mothers, Three the Fathers, Two the Tablets, One is God in Heaven and Earth.

Who knows Five? I know Five: Five books of Torah, Four the Mothers, Three the Fathers, Two the Tablets, One is God in Heaven and Earth.

Who Knows One?

אֶחָד מִי יוֹדֵעַ. אֶחָד אֲנִי יוֹדֵעַ. אֶחָד אֱלֹהֵינוּ שֶׁבַּשָּׁמַיִם וּבָאָרֶץ:

שְׁנַיִם מִי יוֹדֵעַ. שְׁנַיִם אֲנִי יוֹדֵעַ. שְׁנֵי לֻחוֹת הַבְּרִית. אֶחָד אֱלֹהֵינוּ שֶׁבַּשָּׁמַיִם וּבָאָרֶץ:

שְׁלֹשָׁה מִי יוֹדֵעַ. שְׁלֹשָׁה אֲנִי יוֹדֵעַ. שְׁלֹשָׁה אָבוֹת. שְׁנֵי לֻחוֹת הַבְּרִית. אֶחָד אֱלֹהֵינוּ שֶׁבַּשָּׁמַיִם וּבָאָרֶץ:

אַרְבַּע מִי יוֹדֵעַ. אַרְבַּע אֲנִי יוֹדֵעַ. אַרְבַּע אִמָּהוֹת. שְׁלֹשָׁה אָבוֹת. שְׁנֵי לֻחוֹת הַבְּרִית. אֶחָד אֱלֹהֵינוּ שֶׁבַּשָּׁמַיִם וּבָאָרֶץ:

חֲמִשָּׁה מִי יוֹדֵעַ. חֲמִשָּׁה אֲנִי יוֹדֵעַ. חֲמִשָּׁה חֻמְשֵׁי תוֹרָה. אַרְבַּע אִמָּהוֹת. שְׁלֹשָׁה אָבוֹת. שְׁנֵי לֻחוֹת הַבְּרִית. אֶחָד אֱלֹהֵינוּ שֶׁבַּשָּׁמַיִם וּבָאָרֶץ:

שִׁשָּׁה מִי יוֹדֵעַ. שִׁשָּׁה אֲנִי יוֹדֵעַ. שִׁשָּׁה סִדְרֵי מִשְׁנָה. חֲמִשָּׁה חֻמְשֵׁי תוֹרָה. אַרְבַּע אִמָּהוֹת. שְׁלֹשָׁה אָבוֹת. שְׁנֵי לֻחוֹת הַבְּרִית. אֶחָד אֱלֹהֵינוּ שֶׁבַּשָּׁמַיִם וּבָאָרֶץ:

שִׁבְעָה מִי יוֹדֵעַ. שִׁבְעָה אֲנִי יוֹדֵעַ. שִׁבְעָה יְמֵי שַׁבַּתָּא. שִׁשָּׁה סִדְרֵי מִשְׁנָה. חֲמִשָּׁה חֻמְשֵׁי תוֹרָה. אַרְבַּע אִמָּהוֹת. שְׁלֹשָׁה אָבוֹת. שְׁנֵי לֻחוֹת הַבְּרִית. אֶחָד אֱלֹהֵינוּ שֶׁבַּשָּׁמַיִם וּבָאָרֶץ:

שְׁמוֹנָה מִי יוֹדֵעַ. שְׁמוֹנָה אֲנִי יוֹדֵעַ. שְׁמוֹנָה יְמֵי מִילָה. שִׁבְעָה יְמֵי שַׁבַּתָּא. שִׁשָּׁה סִדְרֵי מִשְׁנָה. חֲמִשָּׁה חֻמְשֵׁי תוֹרָה. אַרְבַּע אִמָּהוֹת. שְׁלֹשָׁה אָבוֹת. שְׁנֵי לֻחוֹת הַבְּרִית. אֶחָד אֱלֹהֵינוּ שֶׁבַּשָּׁמַיִם וּבָאָרֶץ:

תִּשְׁעָה מִי יוֹדֵעַ. תִּשְׁעָה אֲנִי יוֹדֵעַ. תִּשְׁעָה יַרְחֵי לֵידָה. שְׁמוֹנָה יְמֵי מִילָה. שִׁבְעָה יְמֵי שַׁבַּתָּא. שִׁשָּׁה סִדְרֵי מִשְׁנָה. חֲמִשָּׁה חֻמְשֵׁי תוֹרָה. אַרְבַּע אִמָּהוֹת. שְׁלֹשָׁה אָבוֹת. שְׁנֵי לֻחוֹת הַבְּרִית. אֶחָד אֱלֹהֵינוּ שֶׁבַּשָּׁמַיִם וּבָאָרֶץ:

(A free version)

'Mighty, He...'

Mighty, He; Right is He,
  Build the Temple in our days.
  Speedily, O speedily,
  Build that all may sing Thy praise.

Blest is He, the Best is He,
Awesome in his mystery,
Famed is He, Acclaimed is He,
Glorious in history.
  Build the Temple in our days,
  Speedily, O speedily,
  Build that all may sing Thy praise.

Strong and Never Wrong is He,
Worthy of our Song is He,
Never failing,
All prevailing.
  Build the Temple in our days.
  Speedily, O speedily,
  Build that all may sing Thy praise.

(A literal translation would run:)

Mighty, He: He will build his Temple soon, speedily, speedily, in our days, soon. O God build—O God build thy Temple soon.
Chosen, He, Great is He, Distinguished, He, He will build, etc.
Glorious, He, Ancient, He, Just is He, He will build, etc.
Gracious, He, Pure is He, Unique is He, He will build, etc.
Powerful, He, Learned, He, King is He, He will build, etc.
Splendid, He, Overpowering, He, Heroic, He, He will build, etc.
Redeemer, He, Righteous, He, Holy, He, He will build, etc.
Merciful, He, Almighty, He, Strong is He, He will build, etc.

אַדִּיר הוּא. יִבְנֶה בֵיתוֹ בְּקָרוֹב. בִּמְהֵרָה. בִּמְהֵרָה. בְּיָמֵינוּ בְּקָרוֹב. אֵל בְּנֵה. אֵל בְּנֵה. בְּנֵה בֵיתְךָ בְּקָרוֹב:

בָּחוּר הוּא. גָּדוֹל הוּא. דָּגוּל הוּא.
יִבְנֶה בֵיתוֹ בְּקָרוֹב. בִּמְהֵרָה. בִּמְהֵרָה. בְּיָמֵינוּ בְּקָרוֹב. אֵל בְּנֵה. אֵל בְּנֵה בְּנֵה בֵיתְךָ בְּקָרוֹב:

הָדוּר הוּא. וָתִיק הוּא. זַכַּאי הוּא.
יִבְנֶה בֵיתוֹ בְּקָרוֹב. בִּמְהֵרָה. בִּמְהֵרָה. בְּיָמֵינוּ בְּקָרוֹב. אֵל בְּנֵה. אֵל בְּנֵה. בְּנֵה בֵיתְךָ בְּקָרוֹב:

חָסִיד הוּא. טָהוֹר הוּא. יָחִיד הוּא.
יִבְנֶה בֵיתוֹ בְּקָרוֹב. בִּמְהֵרָה. בִּמְהֵרָה. בְּיָמֵינוּ בְּקָרוֹב. אֵל בְּנֵה. אֵל בְּנֵה. בְּנֵה בֵיתְךָ בְּקָרוֹב:

כַּבִּיר הוּא. לָמוּד הוּא. מֶלֶךְ הוּא.
יִבְנֶה בֵיתוֹ בְּקָרוֹב. בִּמְהֵרָה. בִּמְהֵרָה. בְּיָמֵינוּ בְּקָרוֹב. אֵל בְּנֵה. אֵל בְּנֵה. בְּנֵה בֵיתְךָ בְּקָרוֹב:

נָאוֹר הוּא. סַגִּיב הוּא. עִזּוּז הוּא.
יִבְנֶה בֵיתוֹ בְּקָרוֹב. בִּמְהֵרָה. בִּמְהֵרָה. בְּיָמֵינוּ בְּקָרוֹב. אֵל בְּנֵה. אֵל בְּנֵה. בְּנֵה בֵיתְךָ בְּקָרוֹב:

פּוֹדֶה הוּא. צַדִּיק הוּא. קָדוֹשׁ הוּא.
יִבְנֶה בֵיתוֹ בְּקָרוֹב. בִּמְהֵרָה. בִּמְהֵרָה. בְּיָמֵינוּ בְּקָרוֹב. אֵל בְּנֵה. אֵל בְּנֵה. בְּנֵה בֵיתְךָ בְּקָרוֹב:

רַחוּם הוּא. שַׁדַּי הוּא. תַּקִּיף הוּא.
יִבְנֶה בֵיתוֹ בְּקָרוֹב. בִּמְהֵרָה. בִּמְהֵרָה. בְּיָמֵינוּ בְּקָרוֹב. אֵל בְּנֵה. אֵל בְּנֵה. בְּנֵה בֵיתְךָ בְּקָרוֹב:

'Right and Proper...'

(A free version leaning on the alphabet in the original)

Ancient of days,
Blessed in praise
His **C**hosen cry: 'To Thee! To Thee!
Right and proper, all acclaim,
Blessings on His Holy Name!

Dear is our King,
Ever we sing,
Father ours
Great His powers
High above,
Infinite love
Judge us then,
King of men
Oh **L**ord, we cry: 'To Thee! To Thee!
Right and proper, all acclaim,
Blessings on His Holy Name!

Make us strong
Now in song;
O'er the world
Peace unfurled,
Question fails,
Right prevails
His **S**oldiers sing: 'To Thee! To Thee!
Right and proper, all acclaim,
Blessings on His Holy Name!

Trust will call
Unto us all
Venerate and
Wonder great
'**X**-tra! sing

The **Y**oung in spring
The **Z**ealous cry: 'To Thee! To Thee!
Right and proper, all acclaim
Blessings on His Holy Name!

(A literal translation of the first verses would run:)

For to Him (praise) is proper: for to Him it is due.
Mighty in dominion, chosen as by law, his troops say to Him: To Thee, and to Thee, to Thee but to Thee, to Thee especially to Thee, to Thee O God is the kingship. For to Him (praise) is proper, to Him it is due.
Distinguished in dominion, glorious as by law, his faithful say to Him: To Thee and to Thee, etc.

אַדִּיר בִּמְלוּכָה

בָּחוּר כַּהֲלָכָה.

גְּדוּדָיו יֹאמְרוּ לוֹ. לְךָ וּלְךָ.

לְךָ כִּי לְךָ. לְךָ אַף לְךָ.

לְךָ יְיָ הַמַּמְלָכָה: כִּי לוֹ נָאֶה. כִּי לוֹ יָאֶה:

מָרוֹם בִּמְלוּכָה.

נוֹרָא כַּהֲלָכָה.

סְבִיבָיו יֹאמְרוּ לוֹ. לְךָ וּלְךָ.

לְךָ כִּי לְךָ. לְךָ אַף לְךָ.

לְךָ יְיָ הַמַּמְלָכָה: כִּי לוֹ נָאֶה. כִּי לוֹ יָאֶה:

דָּגוּל בִּמְלוּכָה.

הָדוּר כַּהֲלָכָה.

וָתִיקָיו יֹאמְרוּ לוֹ. לְךָ וּלְךָ.

לְךָ כִּי לְךָ. לְךָ אַף לְךָ.

לְךָ יְיָ הַמַּמְלָכָה: כִּי לוֹ נָאֶה. כִּי לוֹ יָאֶה:

עָנָיו בִּמְלוּכָה.

פּוֹדֶה כַּהֲלָכָה.

צַדִּיקָיו יֹאמְרוּ לוֹ. לְךָ וּלְךָ.

לְךָ כִּי לְךָ. לְךָ אַף לְךָ.

לְךָ יְיָ הַמַּמְלָכָה: כִּי לוֹ נָאֶה. כִּי לוֹ יָאֶה:

זַכַּאי בִּמְלוּכָה.

חָסִין כַּהֲלָכָה.

טַפְסְרָיו יֹאמְרוּ לוֹ. לְךָ וּלְךָ.

לְךָ כִּי לְךָ. לְךָ אַף לְךָ.

לְךָ יְיָ הַמַּמְלָכָה: כִּי לוֹ נָאֶה. כִּי לוֹ יָאֶה:

קָדוֹשׁ בִּמְלוּכָה.

רַחוּם כַּהֲלָכָה.

שִׁנְאַנָּיו יֹאמְרוּ לוֹ. לְךָ וּלְךָ.

לְךָ כִּי לְךָ. לְךָ אַף לְךָ.

לְךָ יְיָ הַמַּמְלָכָה: כִּי לוֹ נָאֶה. כִּי לוֹ יָאֶה:

יָחִיד בִּמְלוּכָה.

כַּבִּיר כַּהֲלָכָה.

לִמּוּדָיו יֹאמְרוּ לוֹ. לְךָ וּלְךָ.

לְךָ כִּי לְךָ. לְךָ אַף לְךָ.

לְךָ יְיָ הַמַּמְלָכָה: כִּי לוֹ נָאֶה. כִּי לוֹ יָאֶה:

תַּקִּיף בִּמְלוּכָה.

תּוֹמֵךְ כַּהֲלָכָה.

תְּמִימָיו יֹאמְרוּ לוֹ. לְךָ וּלְךָ.

לְךָ כִּי לְךָ. לְךָ אַף לְךָ.

לְךָ יְיָ הַמַּמְלָכָה: כִּי לוֹ נָאֶה. כִּי לוֹ יָאֶה:

'On Passover Day in the Morning'

(A free version of the second night's song. In the first stanza, the reference is to Abraham.)

He saw three strangers standing by,
  Passover Eve, Passover Eve,
Fed them a lamb, and they did cry:
'We're Angels sent by God on high,
  For Passover Day in the morning.'

When Pharaoh cried: 'O woe is me!',
  Passover Eve, Passover Eve,
God passed our doors, so all could see
His firm resolve to set us free
  On Passover Day in the morning.

The walls of Jericho fell down,
  Passover Eve, Passover Eve,
And Gideon received the crown
Of victory over Midian's town
  On Passover Day in the morning.

When Esther called us to a Fast
  Passover Eve, Passover Eve,
The gallows stood there like a mast,
But Haman came to hang at last,
Deliverance as in the past
  On Passover Day in the morning.

(As in the first song, the marvels are all celebrated alphabetically and so add up to the same twenty-two. A literal translation of the first verses would read:)
And ye shall say: It is the sacrifice of the Passover.
Thou didst work powerful miracles on Passover; to the first of all festivals Thou didst raise Passover; Thou didst reveal Thyself to the 'Ezrahite' (*Abraham*) on Passover . . .
Thou didst knock on his door in the heat of the day on Passover; he fed the shining ones (*the angels*) unleavened bread on Passover, and to the herd he ran in memory of the Ox (*the Scriptural reading*) on Passover . . .
The Sodomites felt your anger and were burnt by fire on Passover; Lot escaped from them and baked unleavened bread at the end on Passover; Thou didst sweep away the land of Moph and Noph (*Egypt*) when Thou didst pass through on Passover . . .

(To be sung on the second Seder night)

וּבְכֵן וַאֲמַרְתֶּם זֶבַח פֶּסַח:

אֹמֶץ גְּבוּרוֹתֶיךָ הִפְלֵאתָ בַּפֶּסַח:
בְּרֹאשׁ כָּל מוֹעֲדוֹת נִשֵּׂאתָ פֶּסַח:
גִּלִּיתָ לְאֶזְרָחִי חֲצוֹת לֵיל פֶּסַח: **וַאֲמַרְתֶּם זֶבַח פֶּסַח:**

דְּלָתָיו דָּפַקְתָּ כְּחוֹם הַיּוֹם בַּפֶּסַח:
הִסְעִיד נוֹצְצִים עֻגוֹת מַצּוֹת בַּפֶּסַח:
וְאֶל הַבָּקָר רָץ זֵכֶר לְשׁוֹר עֵרֶךְ פֶּסַח: **וַאֲמַרְתֶּם זֶבַח פֶּסַח:**

זוֹעֲמוּ סְדוֹמִים וְלוֹהֲטוּ בָּאֵשׁ פֶּסַח:
חֻלַּץ לוֹט מֵהֶם וּמַצּוֹת אָפָה בְּקֵץ פֶּסַח:
טִאטֵאתָ אַדְמַת מוֹף וְנוֹף בְּעָבְרְךָ בַּפֶּסַח: **וַאֲמַרְתֶּם זֶבַח פֶּסַח:**

יָהּ רֹאשׁ כָּל אוֹן מָחַצְתָּ בְּלֵיל שִׁמּוּר פֶּסַח:
כַּבִּיר עַל בֵּן בְּכוֹר פָּסַחְתָּ בְּדַם פֶּסַח:
לְבִלְתִּי תֵּת מַשְׁחִית לָבֹא בִּפְתָחַי בַּפֶּסַח: **וַאֲמַרְתֶּם זֶבַח פֶּסַח:**

מְסֻגֶּרֶת סֻגָּרָה בְּעִתּוֹתֵי פֶּסַח:
נִשְׁמְדָה מִדְיָן בִּצְלִיל שְׂעוֹרֵי עֹמֶר פֶּסַח:
שׂוֹרְפוּ מִשְׁמַנֵּי פּוּל וְלוּד בִּיקַד יְקוֹד פֶּסַח: **וַאֲמַרְתֶּם זֶבַח פֶּסַח:**

עוֹד הַיּוֹם בְּנֹב לַעֲמוֹד עַד גָּעָה עוֹנַת פֶּסַח:
פַּס יַד כָּתְבָה לְקַעֲקֵעַ צוּל בַּפֶּסַח:
צָפֹה הַצָּפִית עָרוֹךְ הַשֻּׁלְחָן בַּפֶּסַח: **וַאֲמַרְתֶּם זֶבַח פֶּסַח:**

קָהָל כִּנְּסָה הֲדַסָּה לְשַׁלֵּשׁ צוֹם בַּפֶּסַח:
רֹאשׁ מִבֵּית רָשָׁע מָחַצְתָּ בְּעֵץ חֲמִשִּׁים בַּפֶּסַח:
שְׁתֵּי אֵלֶּה רֶגַע תָּבִיא לְעוּצִית בַּפֶּסַח:
תָּעֹז יָדְךָ תָּרוּם יְמִינְךָ כְּלֵיל הִתְקַדֵּשׁ חַג פֶּסַח: **וַאֲמַרְתֶּם זֶבַח פֶּסַח:**

'At Midnight'

(A free version of 'And It Happened at Midnight' on page 84)

'Twas midnight when each mighty act
  Showed how firm God's wonder stands:
Old Father Abram made his pact
  And saved his wife from strangers' hands   AT MIDNIGHT

'Twas midnight when the Angel fought
  With Jacob but could do no harm.
Laban's evil came to nought
  And Sisera fell to Deborah's charm   AT MIDNIGHT

'Twas midnight when the mournful knell
  Of Egypt rose: 'Alas! Alack!'
Haroshet was a town that fell
  To General Barak's bold attack   AT MIDNIGHT

'Twas midnight when Belshazzar woke,
  He was to die with all his men;
Of God's great power Daniel spoke,
  It saved him from the lion's den   AT MIDNIGHT

'Watchman'—our prayer says to thee—
  'What of the night?': the answer's clear:
Eternal care spells victory,
  And we can feel that God is near   AT MIDNIGHT

(This song, like the song for the second night, builds on the fanciful idea that everything important in Jewish history happened at Passover. In all, twenty-two 'marvels' are celebrated each beginning with a successive letter of the alphabet. The style is very elliptical. A literal translation of the first verses would read:)

And so it came to pass at midnight. Thou didst work many miracles at night. At the beginning of the watches on this night thou gavest victory to the holy convert (*Abraham*) when divided was the night—and it was midnight.

Thou didst sentence the King of Gerar in a dream at night; thou didst terrorize the Syrian (*Laban*) on the yesternight, and Israel fought with an angel and overcame him at night . . .

Thou didst crush the firstborn seed of Pathros (*Egypt*) at night, they found their strength gone at night, the Lord of Haroshet's (*Sisera*) host was defeated by the stars at night . . . etc.

opposite 'Chad Gadya', a living version of the old folk song

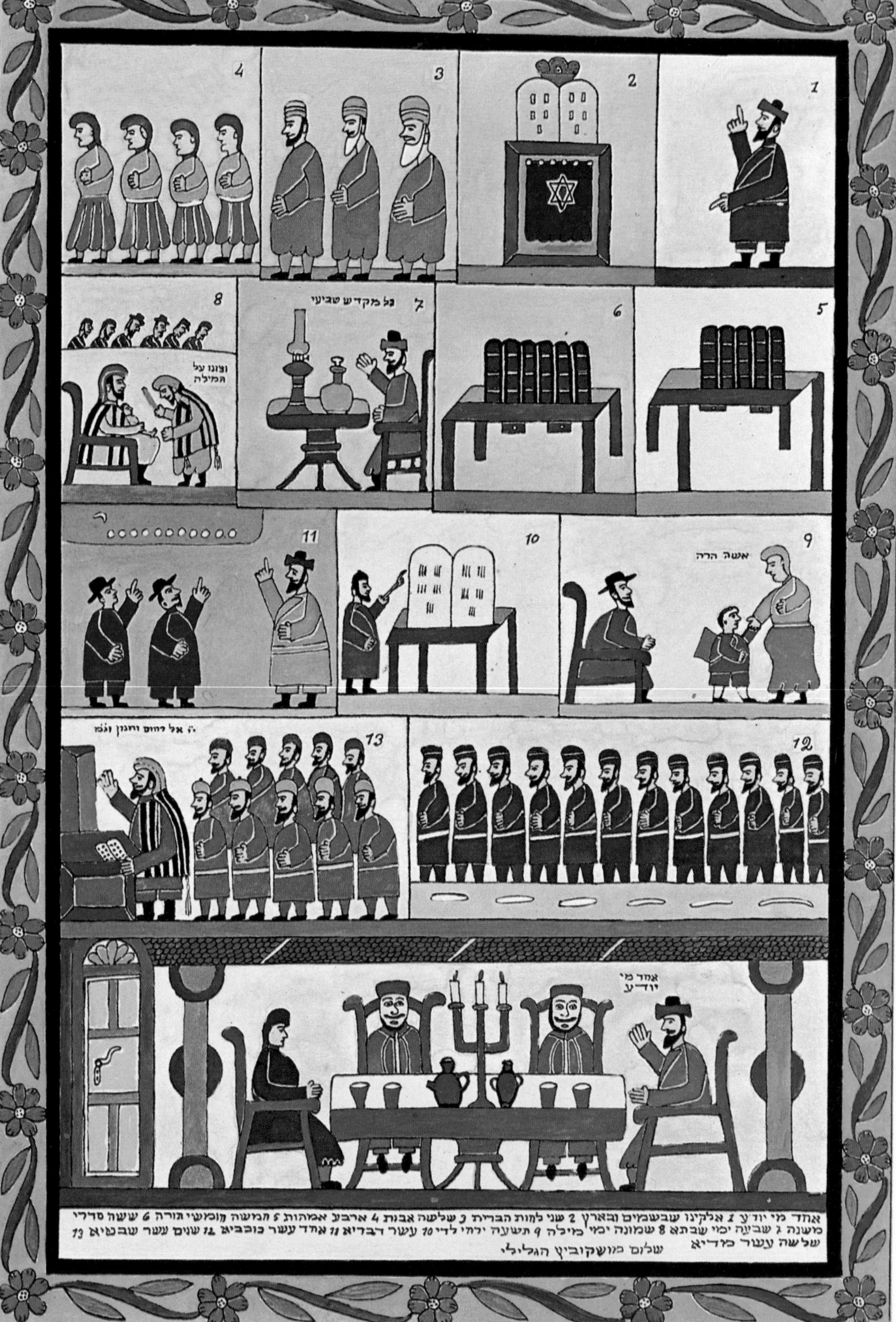

1
2
3
4
5
6
7
מקדש שביעי
8
וצונו על המילה
9
אשה הרה
10
11
12
13
אל רחום וחנון וגו'
אחד מי יודע
אחד מי יודע 1 אלקינו שבשמים ובארץ 2 שני לחות הברית 3 שלשה אבות 4 ארבע אמהות 5 חמשה חומשי תורה 6 ששה סדרי
משנה 7 שבעה ימי שבתא 8 שמונה ימי מילה 9 תשעה ירחי לידה 10 עשר דבריא 11 אחד עשר כוכביא 12 שנים עשר שבטיא 13
שלשה עשר מדיא
שלום מושקוביץ הגלילי

וּבְכֵן וַיְהִי בַּחֲצִי הַלַּיְלָה: *(To be sung on the first Seder night)*

אָז רוֹב נִסִּים הִפְלֵאתָ בַּלַּיְלָה:
בְּרֹאשׁ אַשְׁמוּרוֹת זֶה הַלַּיְלָה:
גֵּר צֶדֶק נִצַּחְתּוֹ כְּנֶחֱלַק לוֹ לַיְלָה: וַיְהִי בַּחֲצִי הַלַּיְלָה:

דַּנְתָּ מֶלֶךְ גְּרָר בַּחֲלוֹם הַלַּיְלָה:
הִפְחַדְתָּ אֲרַמִּי בְּאֶמֶשׁ לַיְלָה:
וְיִשְׂרָאֵל יָשַׁר לַמַּלְאָךְ וַיּוּכַל לוֹ לַיְלָה: וַיְהִי בַּחֲצִי הַלַּיְלָה:

זֶרַע בְּכוֹרֵי פַתְרוֹס מָחַצְתָּ בַּחֲצִי הַלַּיְלָה:
חֵילָם לֹא מָצְאוּ בְּקוּמָם בַּלַּיְלָה:
טִסַּת נְגִיד חֲרֹשֶׁת סִלִּיתָ בְּכוֹכְבֵי לַיְלָה: וַיְהִי בַּחֲצִי הַלַּיְלָה:

יָעַץ מְחָרֵף לְנוֹפֵף אִוּוּי. הוֹבַשְׁתָּ פְגָרָיו בַּלַּיְלָה:
כָּרַע בֵּל וּמַצִּיבוֹ בְּאִישׁוֹן לַיְלָה:
לְאִישׁ חֲמוּדוֹת נִגְלָה רָז חֲזוֹת לַיְלָה: וַיְהִי בַּחֲצִי הַלַּיְלָה:

מִשְׁתַּכֵּר בִּכְלֵי קֹדֶשׁ נֶהֱרַג בּוֹ בַּלַּיְלָה:
נוֹשַׁע מִבּוֹר אֲרָיוֹת פּוֹתֵר בִּעֲתוּתֵי לַיְלָה:
שִׂנְאָה נָטַר אֲגָגִי וְכָתַב סְפָרִים בַּלַּיְלָה: וַיְהִי בַּחֲצִי הַלַּיְלָה:

עוֹרַרְתָּ נִצְחֲךָ עָלָיו בְּנֶדֶד שְׁנַת לַיְלָה:
פּוּרָה תִדְרוֹךְ לְשׁוֹמֵר מַה מִלַּיְלָה:
צָרַח כַּשּׁוֹמֵר וְשָׂח אָתָא בֹקֶר וְגַם לַיְלָה: וַיְהִי בַּחֲצִי הַלַּיְלָה:

קָרֵב יוֹם אֲשֶׁר הוּא לֹא יוֹם וְלֹא לַיְלָה:
רָם הוֹדַע כִּי לְךָ יוֹם אַף לְךָ לַיְלָה:
שׁוֹמְרִים הַפְקֵד לְעִירְךָ כָּל הַיּוֹם וְכָל הַלַּיְלָה:
תָּאִיר כְּאוֹר יוֹם חֶשְׁכַת לַיְלָה: וַיְהִי בַּחֲצִי הַלַּיְלָה:

opposite A popular Seder song, 'Who Knows One?', as depicted by the primitive painter Shalom of Safed

The Songs

The rest of the Seder is song.
Different communities have their own selection. Those that have now taken firm root in the Ashkenazi Haggadah are:

'Midnight' (sixth century CE Palestinian)	וַיְהִי בַּחֲצִי הַלַּיְלָה
'Passover' (seventh century (?) Palestinian)	וּבְכֵן וַאֲמַרְתֶּם זֶבַח פֶּסַח
'Good and Proper' (Anon: time unknown)	כִּי לוֹ נָאֶה. כִּי לוֹ יָאֶה
'Mighty He!' (fourteenth century (?) German)	אַדִּיר הוּא
'Who Knows One?' (fifteenth century (?) German)	אֶחָד מִי יוֹדֵעַ
'Only One Kid' (fifteenth century (?) German)	חַד גַּדְיָא

The first four of the songs listed above are all alphabetical acrostics.
They contain a mass of biblical and Talmudic allusions, difficult to convey without detailed commentary. 'Who Knows One?' is easier to follow in style. 'Only One Kid' is *The House that Jack Built*, but taken to be also allegorical, with Israel as 'the kid'. The English versions presented here are an attempt to catch the spirit—in which a lively rhythm is as important as the fancy-free content.

Counting the Omer

Observant Jews go through a brief ritual of 'counting the *Omer*' at the Seder on the second night after the song **אדיר הוא** ('Mighty He!'), unless they have already said the prayer in synagogue. The *omer* is the sheaf of barley of the new crop which began to be 'offered' after *Pesach* had begun, continuing as a ritual for forty-nine days and ending therefore at Shavuot (the Feast of Weeks). Each night of the forty-nine is enumerated as it passes, and there are other customs of 'restraint' in joyful celebrations linked to this period. The ritual calls for this blessing:

בָּרוּךְ אַתָּה יְיָ אֱלֹהֵינוּ מֶלֶךְ הָעוֹלָם אֲשֶׁר קִדְּשָׁנוּ בְּמִצְוֹתָיו וְצִוָּנוּ עַל סְפִירַת הָעֹמֶר: הַיּוֹם יוֹם אֶחָד לָעֹמֶר:

BLESSED BE GOD WHO LED US TO HOLINESS WITH HIS *MITZVOT* AND MADE IT A *MITZVAH* TO COUNT THE *OMER*. TODAY IS THE FIRST DAY OF THE *OMER*.

Let us bless God—for the vine and its fruit: for all the produce of the field, and for the delights of the land which is the inheritance of our fathers to enjoy and love. Have compassion, O God, on thy people Israel and build Jerusalem, the Holy City, speedily in our days.
BLESSED BE GOD FOR THE LAND AND ITS FRUITS.

Envoi

נִרְצָה

Seder's over, as of yore,	חֲסַל סִדּוּר פֶּסַח כְּהִלְכָתוֹ.
Full of ordinance and lore:	כְּכָל מִשְׁפָּטוֹ וְחֻקָּתוֹ:
If next year to meet once more	כַּאֲשֶׁר זָכִינוּ לְסַדֵּר אוֹתוֹ.
Let our actions speak to Thee.	כֵּן נִזְכֶּה לַעֲשׂוֹתוֹ:
Thou, so pure, who dwell'st on high,	זָךְ שׁוֹכֵן מְעוֹנָה.
Count 'the countless', bring us nigh,	קוֹמֵם קְהַל מִי מָנָה:
End Thy people's endless cry,	קָרֵב נַהֵל נִטְעֵי כַנָּה.
Joyful and in Zion free.	פְּדוּיִם לְצִיּוֹן בְּרִנָּה:
NEXT YEAR IN JERUSALEM	**לַשָּׁנָה הַבָּאָה בִּירוּשָׁלָיִם**
In Israel, the words are:	לַשָּׁנָה הַבָּאָה בִּירוּשָׁלַיִם הַבְּנוּיָה:

'Next year in Jerusalem Rebuilt'

An early 20th-century, Venetian-style Seder plate of pewter

'Let Us Adore Thee...' יִשְׁתַּבַּח

שִׁמְךָ לָעַד מַלְכֵּנוּ הָאֵל הַמֶּלֶךְ הַגָּדוֹל וְהַקָּדוֹשׁ בַּשָּׁמַיִם וּבָאָרֶץ. כִּי לְךָ נָאֶה יְיָ אֱלֹהֵינוּ וֵאלֹהֵי אֲבוֹתֵינוּ שִׁיר וּשְׁבָחָה הַלֵּל וְזִמְרָה עֹז וּמֶמְשָׁלָה נֶצַח גְּדֻלָּה וּגְבוּרָה תְּהִלָּה וְתִפְאֶרֶת קְדֻשָּׁה וּמַלְכוּת. בְּרָכוֹת וְהוֹדָאוֹת מֵעַתָּה וְעַד עוֹלָם: בָּרוּךְ אַתָּה יְיָ אֵל מֶלֶךְ גָּדוֹל בַּתִּשְׁבָּחוֹת אֵל הַהוֹדָאוֹת אֲדוֹן הַנִּפְלָאוֹת הַבּוֹחֵר בְּשִׁירֵי זִמְרָה מֶלֶךְ אֵל חֵי הָעוֹלָמִים:

Let us adore thy Name—praise and song, strength and dominion are thine—blessing and thanks from now to eternity.
Blessed art Thou—great in praise—God of thanksgiving—Lord of wonders—King, God, Eternal.

(The toast—'To Jerusalem!'—works up to full expression on the next page.)

The fourth cup: 'To Jerusalem!'

בָּרוּךְ אַתָּה יְיָ אֱלֹהֵינוּ מֶלֶךְ הָעוֹלָם בּוֹרֵא פְּרִי הַגָּפֶן:

BLESSED IS OUR LORD, GOD, KING OF THE UNIVERSE, WHO CREATES THE FRUIT OF THE VINE.

The cup is drunk

בָּרוּךְ אַתָּה יְיָ אֱלֹהֵינוּ מֶלֶךְ הָעוֹלָם עַל הַגֶּפֶן וְעַל פְּרִי הַגֶּפֶן וְעַל תְּנוּבַת הַשָּׂדֶה וְעַל אֶרֶץ חֶמְדָּה טוֹבָה וּרְחָבָה שֶׁרָצִיתָ וְהִנְחַלְתָּ לַאֲבוֹתֵינוּ לֶאֱכוֹל מִפִּרְיָהּ וְלִשְׂבּוֹעַ מִטּוּבָהּ. רַחֵם יְיָ אֱלֹהֵינוּ עַל יִשְׂרָאֵל עַמֶּךָ. וְעַל יְרוּשָׁלַיִם עִירֶךָ. וְעַל צִיּוֹן מִשְׁכַּן כְּבוֹדֶךָ. וְעַל מִזְבְּחֶךָ. וְעַל הֵיכָלֶךָ. וּבְנֵה יְרוּשָׁלַיִם עִיר הַקֹּדֶשׁ בִּמְהֵרָה בְיָמֵינוּ וְהַעֲלֵנוּ לְתוֹכָהּ. וְשַׂמְּחֵנוּ בְּבִנְיָנָהּ. וְנֹאכַל מִפִּרְיָהּ. וְנִשְׂבַּע מִטּוּבָהּ. וּנְבָרֶכְךָ עָלֶיהָ בִּקְדֻשָּׁה וּבְטָהֳרָה (וּרְצֵה וְהַחֲלִיצֵנוּ בְּיוֹם הַשַּׁבָּת הַזֶּה) וְשַׂמְּחֵנוּ בְּיוֹם חַג הַמַּצּוֹת הַזֶּה. כִּי אַתָּה יְיָ טוֹב וּמֵטִיב לַכֹּל. וְנוֹדֶה לְּךָ עַל הָאָרֶץ וְעַל פְּרִי הַגָּפֶן:

בָּרוּךְ אַתָּה יְיָ עַל הָאָרֶץ וְעַל פְּרִי הַגָּפֶן:

opposite For the Fourth Cup, a 20th-century *Kiddush* cup from Israel, showing the words '*Yom Tov*' (festival)

ויום
טוב

forsaken us. Therefore the limbs which Thou hast formed in us and the spirit and breath which Thou hast breathed into our nostrils and the tongue which thou hast put into our mouth shall praise, bless and glorify Thy name. As David said: 'Bless the Lord, O my soul, and all within me His holy Name' (*Psalm* CIII, 1).

'Enthroned on High...'

הָאֵל בְּתַעֲצֻמוֹת עֻזֶּךָ: הַגָּדוֹל בִּכְבוֹד שְׁמֶךָ הַגִּבּוֹר לָנֶצַח וְהַנּוֹרָא
בְּנוֹרְאוֹתֶיךָ: הַמֶּלֶךְ הַיּוֹשֵׁב עַל כִּסֵּא רָם וְנִשָּׂא: שׁוֹכֵן עַד מָרוֹם וְקָדוֹשׁ
שְׁמוֹ. וְכָתוּב רַנְּנוּ צַדִּיקִים בַּיְיָ לַיְשָׁרִים נָאוָה תְהִלָּה: בְּפִי יְשָׁרִים
תִּתְרוֹמָם. וּבְשִׂפְתֵי צַדִּיקִים תִּתְבָּרַךְ. וּבִלְשׁוֹן חֲסִידִים תִּתְקַדָּשׁ.
וּבְקֶרֶב קְדוֹשִׁים תִּתְהַלָּל:

וּבְמַקְהֲלוֹת רִבְבוֹת עַמְּךָ בֵּית יִשְׂרָאֵל בְּרִנָּה יִתְפָּאַר שִׁמְךָ מַלְכֵּנוּ
בְּכָל דּוֹר וָדוֹר. שֶׁכֵּן חוֹבַת כָּל־הַיְצוּרִים לְפָנֶיךָ יְיָ אֱלֹהֵינוּ וֵאלֹהֵי
אֲבוֹתֵינוּ לְהוֹדוֹת לְהַלֵּל לְשַׁבֵּחַ לְפָאֵר לְרוֹמֵם לְהַדֵּר לְבָרֵךְ לְעַלֵּה
וּלְקַלֵּס עַל כָּל־דִּבְרֵי שִׁירוֹת וְתִשְׁבְּחוֹת דָּוִד בֶּן־יִשַׁי עַבְדְּךָ מְשִׁיחֶךָ:

God in the might of his power: the King enthroned on high: Thy Being—high and holy—is for eternity.

By the mouth of the upright shalt Thou be praised, with the words of the righteous shalt Thou be blessed, and in the midst of the saints shalt Thou be sanctified.

In the assemblies of the myriads of thy people Israel, thy name, O our King, shall be glorified with joyful cry. For such is the duty of all creatures—to praise and bless Thee, even beyond all the words and songs of David, the son of Jesse, thy anointed.

above 'Temple de Jerusalem', a 17th-century etching based on the Temple reconstruction of Alie Leone Templo (1603–1675)
opposite 'Beyond all the words and songs of David . . .' David and his lyre as seen by an Armenian illuminator of the Bible of Erzican (1269–70)

‘If Our Mouths Were Filled with Song...’

(A panegyric of praise and prayer, as the Seder moves to its conclusion)

אִלּוּ פִינוּ מָלֵא שִׁירָה כַּיָּם וּלְשׁוֹנֵנוּ רִנָּה כַּהֲמוֹן גַּלָּיו וְשִׂפְתוֹתֵינוּ שֶׁבַח
כְּמֶרְחֲבֵי רָקִיעַ. וְעֵינֵינוּ מְאִירוֹת כַּשֶּׁמֶשׁ וְכַיָּרֵחַ. וְיָדֵינוּ פְרוּשׂוֹת כְּנִשְׁרֵי
שָׁמָיִם. וְרַגְלֵינוּ קַלּוֹת כָּאַיָּלוֹת. אֵין אֲנַחְנוּ מַסְפִּיקִים לְהוֹדוֹת לְךָ יְיָ
אֱלֹהֵינוּ וֵאלֹהֵי אֲבוֹתֵינוּ. וּלְבָרֵךְ אֶת־שְׁמֶךָ. עַל־אַחַת מֵאָלֶף אֶלֶף
אַלְפֵי אֲלָפִים וְרִבֵּי רְבָבוֹת פְּעָמִים הַטּוֹבוֹת שֶׁעָשִׂיתָ עִם־אֲבוֹתֵינוּ
וְעִמָּנוּ: מִמִּצְרַיִם גְּאַלְתָּנוּ יְיָ אֱלֹהֵינוּ וּמִבֵּית עֲבָדִים פְּדִיתָנוּ. בְּרָעָב
זַנְתָּנוּ. וּבְשָׂבָע כִּלְכַּלְתָּנוּ. מֵחֶרֶב הִצַּלְתָּנוּ. וּמִדֶּבֶר מִלַּטְתָּנוּ וּמֵחֳלָיִם
רָעִים וְנֶאֱמָנִים דִּלִּיתָנוּ: עַד־הֵנָּה עֲזָרוּנוּ רַחֲמֶיךָ. וְלֹא־עֲזָבוּנוּ חֲסָדֶיךָ.
וְאַל־תִּטְּשֵׁנוּ יְיָ אֱלֹהֵינוּ לָנֶצַח: עַל־כֵּן אֵבָרִים שֶׁפִּלַּגְתָּ בָּנוּ. וְרוּחַ וּנְשָׁמָה
שֶׁנָּפַחְתָּ בְּאַפֵּינוּ וְלָשׁוֹן אֲשֶׁר שַׂמְתָּ בְּפִינוּ. הֵן הֵם יוֹדוּ וִיבָרְכוּ וִישַׁבְּחוּ
וִיפָאֲרוּ וִירוֹמְמוּ וְיַעֲרִיצוּ וְיַקְדִּישׁוּ וְיַמְלִיכוּ אֶת־שִׁמְךָ מַלְכֵּנוּ: כִּי כָל־
פֶּה לְךָ יוֹדֶה. וְכָל לָשׁוֹן לְךָ תִשָּׁבַע וְכָל־בֶּרֶךְ לְךָ תִכְרַע. וְכָל־קוֹמָה
לְפָנֶיךָ תִשְׁתַּחֲוֶה: וְכָל־הַלְּבָבוֹת יִירָאוּךָ. וְכָל־קֶרֶב וּכְלָיוֹת יְזַמְּרוּ
לִשְׁמֶךָ. כַּדָּבָר שֶׁכָּתוּב כָּל עַצְמוֹתַי תֹּאמַרְנָה יְיָ מִי־כָמוֹךָ. מַצִּיל
עָנִי מֵחָזָק מִמֶּנּוּ וְעָנִי וְאֶבְיוֹן מִגֹּזְלוֹ: מִי יִדְמֶה־לָּךְ וּמִי יִשְׁוֶה־לָּךְ וּמִי
יַעֲרָךְ־לָךְ הָאֵל הַגָּדוֹל הַגִּבּוֹר וְהַנּוֹרָא אֵל עֶלְיוֹן קֹנֵה שָׁמַיִם וָאָרֶץ: נְהַלֶּלְךָ
וּנְשַׁבֵּחֲךָ וּנְפָאֶרְךָ וּנְבָרֵךְ אֶת־שֵׁם קָדְשֶׁךָ. כָּאָמוּר לְדָוִד בָּרְכִי נַפְשִׁי
אֶת־יְיָ וְכָל־קְרָבַי אֶת־שֵׁם קָדְשׁוֹ:

If our mouths were filled with song like the sea, and our tongues with shouts of joy like the crash of its waves—if our lips could speak like the endless sky and our eyes shine like the sun and the moon—if our arms could reach out like eagles' wings and our feet were light as hinds'—we would be feeble still to praise the God of our fathers and bless thy Name for even one of the myriad benefits that Thou didst grant to our fathers and us.

Thou didst redeem us from Egypt and deliver us from the house of bondage: in hunger Thou didst feed us and sustain us in plenty: Thou didst deliver us from the sword and preserve us from pestilence . . .

Hitherto thy mercies have helped us and thy kindness has not

opposite A 19th-century Syrian Seder dish inscribed in Hebrew and Arabic with scenes from the Passover story and the names of the Twelve Tribes

ואין למו מכשול יהי שלום בחילך

שלוה בארמנותיך. למען אחי ורעי אדברה נא

שלום בך: למען בית יי' אלהינו אבקשה טוב לך: יי'

עוז לעמו יתן יי' יברך את עמו בשלום:

קדיש יתום

נשמת

כל חי תברך את שמך יי' אלהינו ורוח כל בשר תפאר ותרומם זכרך

מלכנו תמיד. מן העולם ועד העולם אתה אל ומבלעדיך אין לנו

מלך גואל ומושיע פודה ומציל ומפרנס ומרחם בכל עת צרה וצ

וצוקה אין לנו מלך אלא אתה. אלהי הראשונים והאחרונים

born—And brought out Israel from among them—With a strong hand and outstretched arm—Who parted the Red Sea asunder—And made Israel to pass through its midst—But overthrew Pharaoh and his host in the Red Sea—Who led his people through the wilderness—Who smote great kings—And slew mighty kings—Sihon, King of the Amorites—And Og, King of Bashan—And gave their land for a heritage—A heritage to Israel his servant—Who remembered us in our low estate—And released us from our enemies—Who giveth food to all mankind—

(The Great Hallel concluded)

GIVE THANKS TO THE GOD OF HEAVEN	—FOR HIS KINDNESS ENDURETH FOREVER!

'The Breath of Life' נִשְׁמַת

(In these final prayers, the emphasis moves from history to God, the source of life.)

נִשְׁמַת כָּל־חַי תְּבָרֵךְ אֶת־שִׁמְךָ יְיָ אֱלֹהֵינוּ. וְרוּחַ כָּל־בָּשָׂר תְּפָאֵר וּתְרוֹמֵם זִכְרְךָ מַלְכֵּנוּ תָּמִיד. מִן־הָעוֹלָם וְעַד־הָעוֹלָם אַתָּה אֵל. וּמִבַּלְעָדֶיךָ אֵין לָנוּ מֶלֶךְ גּוֹאֵל וּמוֹשִׁיעַ פּוֹדֶה וּמַצִּיל וּמְפַרְנֵס וּמְרַחֵם בְּכָל־עֵת צָרָה וְצוּקָה. אֵין לָנוּ מֶלֶךְ אֶלָּא אָתָּה: אֱלֹהֵי הָרִאשׁוֹנִים וְהָאַחֲרוֹנִים. אֱלוֹהַּ כָּל־בְּרִיּוֹת אֲדוֹן כָּל־תּוֹלָדוֹת הַמְהֻלָּל בְּרֹב הַתִּשְׁבָּחוֹת הַמְנַהֵג עוֹלָמוֹ בְּחֶסֶד וּבְרִיּוֹתָיו בְּרַחֲמִים. וַיְיָ לֹא־יָנוּם וְלֹא־יִישָׁן. הַמְעוֹרֵר יְשֵׁנִים וְהַמֵּקִיץ נִרְדָּמִים. וְהַמֵּשִׂיחַ אִלְּמִים. וְהַמַּתִּיר אֲסוּרִים. וְהַסּוֹמֵךְ נוֹפְלִים וְהַזּוֹקֵף כְּפוּפִים. לְךָ לְבַדְּךָ אֲנַחְנוּ מוֹדִים.

The breath of every living thing shall bless thy name, O Lord: the spirit in all flesh is constant witness to thy glory, O our King. From everlasting to everlasting, Thou art God. Without Thee, we would have no Power to redeem and save us, to sustain us and have mercy in every time of trouble and distress. God of the first things and the last things, God of all creatures, Master of all generations, showing compassion to all His creatures. 'He neither slumbers nor sleeps': He wakens the sleeping and rouses the slumbering: gives speech to the dumb and releases the bound: lifts up those burdened, supports those who fall. Let us thank God—and God alone.

opposite The 'Breath of Life' page from the Haggadah in the Rothschild Miscellany, carrying out the spirit of the prayer with great feeling

לְמַכֵּה מִצְרַיִם בִּבְכוֹרֵיהֶם	כִּי לְעוֹלָם חַסְדּוֹ:
וַיּוֹצֵא יִשְׂרָאֵל מִתּוֹכָם	כִּי לְעוֹלָם חַסְדּוֹ:
בְּיָד חֲזָקָה וּבִזְרוֹעַ נְטוּיָה	כִּי לְעוֹלָם חַסְדּוֹ:
לְגֹזֵר יַם־סוּף לִגְזָרִים	כִּי לְעוֹלָם חַסְדּוֹ:
וְהֶעֱבִיר יִשְׂרָאֵל בְּתוֹכוֹ	כִּי לְעוֹלָם חַסְדּוֹ:
וְנִעֵר פַּרְעֹה וְחֵילוֹ בְיַם־סוּף	כִּי לְעוֹלָם חַסְדּוֹ:
לְמוֹלִיךְ עַמּוֹ בַּמִּדְבָּר	כִּי לְעוֹלָם חַסְדּוֹ:
לְמַכֵּה מְלָכִים גְּדֹלִים	כִּי לְעוֹלָם חַסְדּוֹ:
וַיַּהֲרֹג מְלָכִים אַדִּירִים	כִּי לְעוֹלָם חַסְדּוֹ:
לְסִיחוֹן מֶלֶךְ הָאֱמֹרִי	כִּי לְעוֹלָם חַסְדּוֹ:
וּלְעוֹג מֶלֶךְ הַבָּשָׁן	כִּי לְעוֹלָם חַסְדּוֹ:
וְנָתַן אַרְצָם לְנַחֲלָה	כִּי לְעוֹלָם חַסְדּוֹ:
נַחֲלָה לְיִשְׂרָאֵל עַבְדּוֹ	כִּי לְעוֹלָם חַסְדּוֹ:
שֶׁבְּשִׁפְלֵנוּ זָכַר לָנוּ	כִּי לְעוֹלָם חַסְדּוֹ:
וַיִּפְרְקֵנוּ מִצָּרֵינוּ	כִּי לְעוֹלָם חַסְדּוֹ:
נוֹתֵן לֶחֶם לְכָל בָּשָׂר	כִּי לְעוֹלָם חַסְדּוֹ:
הוֹדוּ לְאֵל הַשָּׁמָיִם	כִּי לְעוֹלָם חַסְדּוֹ:

O GIVE THANKS TO THE LORD FOR HE IS GOOD —FOR HIS KINDNESS ENDURETH FOREVER!
GIVE THANKS TO THE GOD OF GODS —FOR HIS KINDNESS ENDURETH FOREVER!
GIVE THANKS TO THE LORD OF LORDS —FOR HIS KINDNESS ENDURETH FOREVER!

To Him who alone doeth great wonders—Who by wisdom made the Heavens—Who stretched out the earth above the waters—Who made great lights—The sun to rule by day—The moon and stars to rule by night—Who smote the Egyptians in their first-

Psalm CXVIII, 25–29 (These verses are clearly a chant from Temple times, leading to the Great Hallel, Psalm CXXXVI, which follows.)

אָנָּא יְיָ הוֹשִׁיעָה נָּא: אָנָּא יְיָ הוֹשִׁיעָה נָּא:

אָנָּא יְיָ הַצְלִיחָה נָא: אָנָּא יְיָ הַצְלִיחָה נָא:

בָּרוּךְ הַבָּא בְּשֵׁם יְיָ בֵּרַכְנוּכֶם מִבֵּית יְיָ:

אֵל יְיָ וַיָּאֶר לָנוּ אִסְרוּ־חַג בַּעֲבֹתִים עַד־קַרְנוֹת הַמִּזְבֵּחַ:

אֵלִי אַתָּה וְאוֹדֶךָּ אֱלֹהַי אֲרוֹמְמֶךָּ: הוֹדוּ לַיְיָ כִּי־טוֹב כִּי לְעוֹלָם חַסְדּוֹ:

O LORD, LET US BE SAVED! O LORD, LET US PROSPER!

Blessed who comes in the name of the Lord: be blessed in the house of the Lord. The Lord is God who has shown us light: order the festival with boughs, even to the horns of the altar. Thou art my God, I will thank thee: my God—I will exalt thee. O give thanks to the Lord, for He is good: his kindness endureth forever.

(A short prayer before the Great Hallel)

יְהַלְלוּךָ יְיָ אֱלֹהֵינוּ עַל כָּל־מַעֲשֶׂיךָ וַחֲסִידֶיךָ צַדִּיקִים עוֹשֵׂי רְצוֹנֶךָ. וְכָל עַמְּךָ בֵּית יִשְׂרָאֵל בְּרִנָּה יוֹדוּ וִיבָרְכוּ וִישַׁבְּחוּ וִיפָאֲרוּ וִירוֹמְמוּ וְיַעֲרִיצוּ וְיַקְדִּישׁוּ וְיַמְלִיכוּ אֶת־שִׁמְךָ מַלְכֵּנוּ תָּמִיד. כִּי לְךָ טוֹב לְהוֹדוֹת וּלְשִׁמְךָ נָאֶה לְזַמֵּר. כִּי מֵעוֹלָם וְעַד עוֹלָם אַתָּה אֵל:

All Thy works sing *Hallel* (*praise*) to thee! Those who are touched with grace and righteousness, and all thy people, the House of Israel, give thanks, and bless, and revere, and sanctify thy name, O our King! It is good to give thanks to thee—to burst into song. For thou art God, from eternity to eternity.

The Great Hallel Psalm CXXXVI. (To each event recalled from history, the Temple throng gave its antiphonal response, as we do.)

הוֹדוּ לַיְיָ כִּי טוֹב כִּי לְעוֹלָם חַסְדּוֹ:

הוֹדוּ לֵאלֹהֵי הָאֱלֹהִים כִּי לְעוֹלָם חַסְדּוֹ:

הוֹדוּ לַאֲדֹנֵי הָאֲדֹנִים כִּי לְעוֹלָם חַסְדּוֹ:

לְעֹשֵׂה נִפְלָאוֹת גְּדֹלוֹת לְבַדּוֹ כִּי לְעוֹלָם חַסְדּוֹ:

לְעֹשֵׂה הַשָּׁמַיִם בִּתְבוּנָה כִּי לְעוֹלָם חַסְדּוֹ:

לְרֹקַע הָאָרֶץ עַל הַמָּיִם כִּי לְעוֹלָם חַסְדּוֹ:

לְעֹשֵׂה אוֹרִים גְּדֹלִים כִּי לְעוֹלָם חַסְדּוֹ:

אֶת־הַשֶּׁמֶשׁ לְמֶמְשֶׁלֶת בַּיּוֹם כִּי לְעוֹלָם חַסְדּוֹ:

אֶת־הַיָּרֵחַ וְכוֹכָבִים לְמֶמְשְׁלוֹת בַּלָּיְלָה כִּי לְעוֹלָם חַסְדּוֹ:

Psalm CXVIII, 5–20

Out of the straits I called to God: God answered and set me at large. The Lord is for me, I will not fear: what can man do to me? The Lord is for me among them that help me; therefore shall I see my desire upon them that hate me.

It is better to trust in the Lord than to put confidence in man. It is better to trust in the Lord than to put confidence in princes. All nations compassed me about: in the name of the Lord will I destroy them. They compassed me about: yea, they compassed me about; in the name of the Lord will I destroy them. They compassed me about like bees: they are quenched as a fire of thorns: in the name of the Lord I will destroy them.

Thou didst thrust sore at me that I might fall: but the Lord helped me. The Lord is my strength and song, and is become my salvation. The voice of rejoicing and salvation is in the tabernacles of the righteous: the right hand of the Lord doeth valiantly. The right hand of the Lord is exalted: the right hand of the Lord doeth valiantly.

I shall not die, but live, and declare the works of the Lord. The Lord hath chastened me sore, but he hath not given me over unto death.

Open to me the gates of righteousness: I will go into them and give thanks unto the Lord. This is the gate of the Lord: the righteous may enter into it.

‘The Stone which the Builders Rejected…’

(Psalm CXVIII, 21–24. These verses are usually sung by the company, each verse being sung twice.)

אוֹדְךָ כִּי עֲנִיתָנִי וַתְּהִי־לִי לִישׁוּעָה:
אֶבֶן מָאֲסוּ הַבּוֹנִים הָיְתָה לְרֹאשׁ פִּנָּה:
מֵאֵת יְיָ הָיְתָה זֹּאת הִיא נִפְלָאת בְּעֵינֵינוּ:
זֶה־הַיּוֹם עָשָׂה יְיָ נָגִילָה וְנִשְׂמְחָה בוֹ:

I thank Thee for Thou hast heard me and become my salvation.
The stone which the builders rejected has become the corner stone.
This is the Lord’s doing: it is marvellous in our eyes.
This is the day which the Lord has made: let us rejoice and be happy on it.

Psalm CXVII

הַלְלוּ אֶת־יְיָ כָּל־גּוֹיִם שַׁבְּחוּהוּ כָּל־הָאֻמִּים: כִּי גָבַר עָלֵינוּ חַסְדּוֹ
וֶאֱמֶת־יְיָ לְעוֹלָם הַלְלוּיָהּ:

O praise the Lord, all ye nations: extol him, all ye peoples. For his loving kindness is strong to us and the truth of the Lord endureth for ever.

Repeat each of these four lines:

Psalm CXVIII, 1–4

הוֹדוּ לַייָ כִּי־טוֹב — כִּי לְעוֹלָם חַסְדּוֹ:
יֹאמַר־נָא יִשְׂרָאֵל — כִּי לְעוֹלָם חַסְדּוֹ:
יֹאמְרוּ נָא בֵית־אַהֲרֹן — כִּי לְעוֹלָם חַסְדּוֹ:
יֹאמְרוּ נָא יִרְאֵי יְיָ — כִּי לְעוֹלָם חַסְדּוֹ:

O give thanks to the Lord for He is good	—For his kindness endureth forever.
O let Israel say	—His kindness endureth forever.
O let the house of Aaron say	—His kindness endureth forever.
Let those that fear the Lord say	—His kindness endureth forever.

‘I Shall Not Die, but Live…’

Psalm CXVIII, 5–20

מִן־הַמֵּצַר קָרָאתִי יָּהּ עָנָנִי בַמֶּרְחַבְיָה: יְיָ לִי לֹא אִירָא מַה־יַּעֲשֶׂה לִי
אָדָם: יְיָ לִי בְּעֹזְרָי וַאֲנִי אֶרְאֶה בְשֹׂנְאָי: טוֹב לַחֲסוֹת בַּייָ מִבְּטֹחַ בָּאָדָם:
טוֹב לַחֲסוֹת בַּייָ מִבְּטֹחַ בִּנְדִיבִים: כָּל־גּוֹיִם סְבָבוּנִי בְּשֵׁם יְיָ כִּי אֲמִילַם:
סַבּוּנִי גַם־סְבָבוּנִי בְּשֵׁם יְיָ כִּי אֲמִילַם: סַבּוּנִי כִדְבֹרִים דֹּעֲכוּ כְּאֵשׁ קוֹצִים
בְּשֵׁם יְיָ כִּי אֲמִילַם: דָּחֹה דְחִיתַנִי לִנְפֹּל וַייָ עֲזָרָנִי: עָזִּי וְזִמְרָת יָהּ וַיְהִי־
לִי לִישׁוּעָה: קוֹל רִנָּה וִישׁוּעָה בְּאָהֳלֵי צַדִּיקִים יְמִין יְיָ עֹשָׂה חָיִל: יְמִין
יְיָ רוֹמֵמָה יְמִין יְיָ עֹשָׂה חָיִל: לֹא־אָמוּת כִּי־אֶחְיֶה וַאֲסַפֵּר מַעֲשֵׂי יָהּ:
יַסֹּר יִסְּרַנִּי יָּהּ וְלַמָּוֶת לֹא נְתָנָנִי: פִּתְחוּ־לִי שַׁעֲרֵי־צֶדֶק אָבֹא־בָם
אוֹדֶה יָהּ: זֶה־הַשַּׁעַר לַייָ צַדִּיקִים יָבֹאוּ בוֹ:

Psalm CXVI

אָהַבְתִּי כִּי־יִשְׁמַע יְיָ אֶת־קוֹלִי תַּחֲנוּנָי: כִּי־הִטָּה אָזְנוֹ לִי וּבְיָמַי אֶקְרָא:
אֲפָפוּנִי חֶבְלֵי־מָוֶת וּמְצָרֵי שְׁאוֹל מְצָאוּנִי צָרָה וְיָגוֹן אֶמְצָא: וּבְשֵׁם
יְיָ אֶקְרָא אָנָּה יְיָ מַלְּטָה נַפְשִׁי: חַנּוּן יְיָ וְצַדִּיק וֵאלֹהֵינוּ מְרַחֵם: שֹׁמֵר
פְּתָאיִם יְיָ דַּלֹּתִי וְלִי יְהוֹשִׁיעַ: שׁוּבִי נַפְשִׁי לִמְנוּחָיְכִי כִּי יְיָ גָּמַל עָלָיְכִי:
כִּי חִלַּצְתָּ נַפְשִׁי מִמָּוֶת אֶת־עֵינִי מִן־דִּמְעָה אֶת־רַגְלִי מִדֶּחִי: אֶתְהַלֵּךְ
לִפְנֵי יְיָ בְּאַרְצוֹת הַחַיִּים: הֶאֱמַנְתִּי כִּי אֲדַבֵּר אֲנִי עָנִיתִי מְאֹד אֲנִי אָמַרְתִּי
בְחָפְזִי כָּל־הָאָדָם כֹּזֵב: מָה־אָשִׁיב לַייָ כָּל־תַּגְמוּלוֹהִי עָלָי: כּוֹס־
יְשׁוּעוֹת אֶשָּׂא וּבְשֵׁם יְיָ אֶקְרָא: נְדָרַי לַייָ אֲשַׁלֵּם נֶגְדָה־נָּא לְכָל־עַמּוֹ:
יָקָר בְּעֵינֵי יְיָ הַמָּוְתָה לַחֲסִידָיו: אָנָּה יְיָ כִּי־אֲנִי עַבְדֶּךָ אֲנִי עַבְדְּךָ בֶּן־
אֲמָתֶךָ פִּתַּחְתָּ לְמוֹסֵרָי: לְךָ־אֶזְבַּח זֶבַח תּוֹדָה וּבְשֵׁם יְיָ אֶקְרָא: נְדָרַי
לַייָ אֲשַׁלֵּם נֶגְדָה־נָּא לְכָל־עַמּוֹ: בְּחַצְרוֹת בֵּית יְיָ בְּתוֹכֵכִי יְרוּשָׁלָםִ
הַלְלוּיָהּ:

I love the Lord because He heareth my voice and my supplications. Because He hath inclined his ear unto me, therefore will I call upon Him as long as I live. The cords of death compassed me, and the straits of the grave had come upon me: I found trouble and sorrow. Then called I upon the name of the Lord: O Lord, I beseech Thee, deliver my soul.

Gracious is the Lord and righteous: yea, our God is merciful. The Lord guardeth the simple: I was brought low, and He saved me. Return unto thy rest, O my soul, for the Lord hath dealt bountifully with thee. For Thou hast delivered my soul from death, mine eyes from tears, my feet from falling. I will walk before the Lord in the land of the living. I had faith even when I said I am sorely afflicted—when I said in my haste every man deceiveth.

What can I render unto the Lord for all his benefits to me? I will lift the cup of salvation and call on the name of the Lord. I will pay my vows unto the Lord in the presence of all his people. Precious in the sight of the Lord is the faith, in death, of his loving ones. O Lord, truly I am thy servant: I am thy servant, the son of thy handmaid: Thou hast loosed my bonds. I will offer to Thee the sacrifice of thanksgiving, and will call upon the name of the Lord. I will pay my vows unto the Lord in the presence of all his people. In the courts of the Lord's house, in the midst of thee, O Jerusalem: Praise ye the Lord.

הַלֵּל

Psalm CXV

לֹא לָנוּ יְיָ לֹא לָנוּ כִּי לְשִׁמְךָ תֵּן כָּבוֹד עַל־חַסְדְּךָ עַל־אֲמִתֶּךָ: לָמָּה
יֹאמְרוּ הַגּוֹיִם אַיֵּה־נָא אֱלֹהֵיהֶם: וֵאלֹהֵינוּ בַשָּׁמָיִם כֹּל אֲשֶׁר־חָפֵץ
עָשָׂה: עֲצַבֵּיהֶם כֶּסֶף וְזָהָב מַעֲשֵׂה יְדֵי אָדָם: פֶּה־לָהֶם וְלֹא יְדַבֵּרוּ עֵינַיִם
לָהֶם וְלֹא יִרְאוּ: אָזְנַיִם לָהֶם וְלֹא יִשְׁמָעוּ אַף לָהֶם וְלֹא יְרִיחוּן: יְדֵיהֶם
וְלֹא יְמִישׁוּן רַגְלֵיהֶם וְלֹא יְהַלֵּכוּ לֹא־יֶהְגּוּ בִּגְרוֹנָם: כְּמוֹהֶם יִהְיוּ עֹשֵׂיהֶם
כֹּל אֲשֶׁר־בֹּטֵחַ בָּהֶם: יִשְׂרָאֵל בְּטַח בַּייָ עֶזְרָם וּמָגִנָּם הוּא: בֵּית אַהֲרֹן
בִּטְחוּ בַייָ עֶזְרָם וּמָגִנָּם הוּא: יִרְאֵי יְיָ בִּטְחוּ בַייָ עֶזְרָם וּמָגִנָּם הוּא:
יְיָ זְכָרָנוּ יְבָרֵךְ יְבָרֵךְ אֶת־בֵּית יִשְׂרָאֵל יְבָרֵךְ אֶת־בֵּית אַהֲרֹן: יְבָרֵךְ
יִרְאֵי יְיָ הַקְּטַנִּים עִם־הַגְּדֹלִים: יֹסֵף יְיָ עֲלֵיכֶם עֲלֵיכֶם וְעַל־בְּנֵיכֶם:
בְּרוּכִים אַתֶּם לַייָ עֹשֵׂה שָׁמַיִם וָאָרֶץ: הַשָּׁמַיִם שָׁמַיִם לַייָ וְהָאָרֶץ נָתַן
לִבְנֵי־אָדָם: לֹא־הַמֵּתִים יְהַלְלוּ־יָהּ וְלֹא כָּל־יֹרְדֵי דוּמָה: וַאֲנַחְנוּ נְבָרֵךְ
יָהּ מֵעַתָּה וְעַד־עוֹלָם הַלְלוּיָהּ:

Not unto us, O Lord, not unto us, but unto thy name give glory, for thy lovingkindness and truth. Wherefore should the heathen say, Where is now their God? Our God is in the heavens: he hath done whatsoever he hath pleased.

Their idols are silver and gold, the work of men's hands. They have mouths, but they speak not: eyes have they but they see not. They have ears, but they hear not: noses have they, but they smell not. They have hands, but they handle not: feet have they but they walk not: they give no sound through their throat. They that make them are like unto them; so is everyone that trusteth in them. O Israel, trust thou in the Lord—He is their help and shield. O House of Aaron, trust in the Lord—He is their help and shield. Ye that fear the Lord, trust in the Lord—He is their help and shield. The Lord has been mindful of us—He will bless us. He will bless the house of Israel. He will bless the house of Aaron. He will bless them that fear the Lord, both small and great. The Lord shall increase you more and more, you and your children. Blessed are ye of the Lord, who made heaven and earth. The heavens are the heavens of the Lord, but the earth hath He given to the children of men. The dead praise not the Lord, neither any that go down into silence; but we will bless the Lord from this time forth and for ever more. Praise ye the Lord.

Waiting for Elijah

(We refill the cups, open the door 'for Elijah', and recite a brief passage calling for confusion on our enemies. What lies behind this?

Elijah was looked upon (following Malachi III, 23) as the precursor of the Messiah. He is one of the most vivid figures in Jewish folk-pride and legend. He was fearless as a champion of the true God; he defeated the prophets of Baal; and as his end approached, he was carried off to heaven in a fiery chariot. He wanders unceasingly through the world. At every circumcision a chair is set aside for him—'Elijah's Chair'—occupied by the sandek *who holds the child.*

As the fourth cup of wine is being poured, an extra goblet of wine is provided for Elijah, and the door is opened to greet him.

We might have expected a short prayer for this ceremony. Instead there are four biblical verses reflecting the terror which often hovered in the air among the Jews at Passover time because of the monstrous 'blood libel' and pogroms.

No one knows why these verses were chosen. One scholar suggests that 'Pour out Thy anger', was merely an echo of 'pouring out' the wine, and that the other verses were added by association with the thought.

It seems more likely that the opening of the door for Elijah broke the spell for a moment of the happy gathering, reminding the participants of the fearful world outside. Through the open door, the Jew expresses a kind of bravado—sheltering, as it were, behind the unseen presence of Elijah).

שְׁפֹךְ חֲמָתְךָ אֶל־הַגּוֹיִם אֲשֶׁר לֹא־יְדָעוּךָ וְעַל־מַמְלָכוֹת אֲשֶׁר בְּשִׁמְךָ
לֹא קָרָאוּ: כִּי־אָכַל אֶת־יַעֲקֹב וְאֶת־נָוֵהוּ הֵשַׁמּוּ: שְׁפָךְ־עֲלֵיהֶם זַעְמֶךָ
וַחֲרוֹן אַפְּךָ יַשִּׂיגֵם: תִּרְדֹּף בְּאַף וְתַשְׁמִידֵם מִתַּחַת שְׁמֵי יְיָ:

opposite A double 'Elijah chair' for the circumcision rite from Drambach, Germany (1768). When the chair was a double one, the *sandek* sat in one seat, with the other left for the prophet Elijah

'Pour out thy wrath upon the heathen that have not known Thee, and upon the kingdoms that have not called upon thy name. For they have devoured Jacob and laid waste his dwelling-place' (*Psalm* LXXIX, 6–7). 'Pour out thine indignation upon them, and let thy wrathful anger take hold of them' (*Psalm* LXIX, 25). 'Pursue them with wrath and destroy them from under the heavens of the Lord (*Lamentations* III, 66).

כוס
של אליה

(The third cup will be drunk after the biblical verses and the blessing.)

To Peace!

opposite For the Third Cup, an engraved wine bottle by Meir Austerlitz Levi of Austria (1740) and an early 19th-century glass from Bohemia bearing the words 'Elijah's cup'

יְראוּ אֶת יְיָ קְדשָׁיו כִּי אֵין מַחְסוֹר לִירֵאָיו: כְּפִירִים רָשׁוּ וְרָעֵבוּ וְדֹרְשֵׁי
יְיָ לֹא יַחְסְרוּ כָל־טוֹב: הוֹדוּ לַייָ כִּי טוֹב כִּי לְעוֹלָם חַסְדּוֹ: פּוֹתֵחַ אֶת־
יָדֶךָ וּמַשְׂבִּיעַ לְכָל־חַי רָצוֹן: בָּרוּךְ הַגֶּבֶר אֲשֶׁר יִבְטַח בַּייָ וְהָיָה יְיָ מִבְטַחוֹ:

'O fear the Lord, ye his holy ones, for there is no want to them that fear him. The young lions do lack and suffer, but they that seek the Lord do not want any good thing' (*Psalm* XXXIV, 10–11).
'Give thanks to the Lord for He is good: his kindness endureth forever' (*Psalm CXVIII*, 1).
'Thou openest Thy hand and satisfiest every living thing with favour' (*Psalm CXXXXV*, 16).
'Blessed is the man who trusteth in the Lord and the Lord shall be his trust' (*Jeremiah* XVII, 7).

נַעַר הָיִיתִי גַם־זָקַנְתִּי וְלֹא־רָאִיתִי צַדִּיק נֶעֱזָב וְזַרְעוֹ מְבַקֶּשׁ־לָחֶם:

'I have been young and now am old, yet have I not seen the righteous forsaken, nor his seed begging bread' (*Psalm* XXXVII, 25).

יְיָ עֹז לְעַמּוֹ יִתֵּן יְיָ יְבָרֵךְ אֶת־עַמּוֹ בַשָּׁלוֹם:

THE LORD WILL GIVE STRENGTH TO HIS PEOPLE; THE LORD WILL BLESS HIS PEOPLE WITH PEACE (*Psalm* XXIX, 11).

Lift the cup and recite:

בָּרוּךְ אַתָּה יְיָ אֱלֹהֵינוּ מֶלֶךְ הָעוֹלָם בּוֹרֵא פְּרִי הַגָּפֶן:

BLESSED IS OUR LORD, GOD, KING OF THE UNIVERSE, WHO CREATES THE FRUIT OF THE VINE.

The third cup is now drunk: 'TO PEACE!'

A 20th-century Spode Seder plate from England
opposite A Bokharian Seder showing colourful traditional gowns, headdresses and wall hangings

זַרְעִי וְאֶת כָּל אֲשֶׁר לִי וְכָל הַמְּסֻבִּין כָּאן אוֹתָנוּ וְאֶת כָּל אֲשֶׁר לָנוּ כְּמוֹ שֶׁנִּתְבָּרְכוּ אֲבֹתֵינוּ אַבְרָהָם יִצְחָק וְיַעֲקֹב בַּכֹּל מִכֹּל כֹּל כֵּן יְבָרֵךְ אוֹתָנוּ כֻּלָּנוּ יַחַד בִּבְרָכָה שְׁלֵמָה וְנֹאמַר אָמֵן: בַּמָּרוֹם יְלַמְּדוּ עֲלֵיהֶם וְעָלֵינוּ זְכוּת שֶׁתְּהִי לְמִשְׁמֶרֶת שָׁלוֹם וְנִשָּׂא בְרָכָה מֵאֵת יְיָ וּצְדָקָה מֵאֱלֹהֵי יִשְׁעֵנוּ: וְנִמְצָא חֵן וְשֵׂכֶל טוֹב בְּעֵינֵי אֱלֹהִים וְאָדָם:

On Sabbath:

(הָרַחֲמָן הוּא יַנְחִילֵנוּ יוֹם שֶׁכֻּלּוֹ שַׁבָּת וּמְנוּחָה לְחַיֵּי הָעוֹלָמִים):

הָרַחֲמָן הוּא יַנְחִילֵנוּ יוֹם שֶׁכֻּלּוֹ טוֹב: הָרַחֲמָן הוּא יְזַכֵּנוּ לִימוֹת הַמָּשִׁיחַ וּלְחַיֵּי הָעוֹלָם הַבָּא:

מִגְדּוֹל יְשׁוּעוֹת מַלְכּוֹ וְעֹשֶׂה חֶסֶד לִמְשִׁיחוֹ לְדָוִד וּלְזַרְעוֹ עַד עוֹלָם: עֹשֶׂה שָׁלוֹם בִּמְרוֹמָיו הוּא יַעֲשֶׂה שָׁלוֹם עָלֵינוּ וְעַל כָּל יִשְׂרָאֵל וְאִמְרוּ אָמֵן:

May the Merciful One rule us forever and ever! May the Merciful One be blessed in Heaven and Earth! May the Merciful One sustain us in honour! May the Merciful One break the yoke from our neck and lead us upright to our Land! May the Merciful One bless this house, and this table from which we have eaten! May the Merciful One send Elijah the Prophet to us, to bring us good tidings of comfort and salvation!

To be said silently: May the Merciful One bless (my father) the master of this house, (my mother) the mistress of this house, and all their children and household (my wife) (my husband) (and all our children) and all who are at this table. As our fathers, Abraham, Isaac and Jacob were blessed in all, so bless Thou us with a perfect blessing.

On Sabbath: May the Merciful One let us inherit that day which is all Sabbath and repose, in the everlasting life.

HE IS A TOWER OF SALVATION FOR HIS KING AND SHOWETH MERCY TO HIS ANOINTED, UNTO DAVID AND HIS SEED FOR EVERMORE (II *Samuel* XXII, 51). MAY HE WHO MAKES PEACE IN HIS HIGH PLACES MAKE PEACE FOR US AND FOR ALL ISRAEL: AND LET US SAY AMEN.

וּבְנֵה יְרוּשָׁלַיִם עִיר הַקֹּדֶשׁ בִּמְהֵרָה בְיָמֵינוּ. בָּרוּךְ אַתָּה
יְיָ בּוֹנֵה בְרַחֲמָיו יְרוּשָׁלָיִם. אָמֵן:

בָּרוּךְ אַתָּה יְיָ אֱלֹהֵינוּ מֶלֶךְ הָעוֹלָם הָאֵל אָבִינוּ מַלְכֵּנוּ אַדִּירֵנוּ בּוֹרְאֵנוּ גֹּאֲלֵנוּ יוֹצְרֵנוּ קְדוֹשֵׁנוּ קְדוֹשׁ יַעֲקֹב רוֹעֵנוּ רוֹעֵה יִשְׂרָאֵל הַמֶּלֶךְ הַטּוֹב וְהַמֵּטִיב לַכֹּל שֶׁבְּכָל יוֹם וָיוֹם הוּא הֵטִיב הוּא מֵטִיב הוּא יֵטִיב לָנוּ. הוּא גְמָלָנוּ הוּא גוֹמְלֵנוּ הוּא יִגְמְלֵנוּ לָעַד לְחֵן וּלְחֶסֶד וּלְרַחֲמִים וּלְרֶוַח הַצָּלָה וְהַצְלָחָה בְּרָכָה וִישׁוּעָה נֶחָמָה פַּרְנָסָה וְכַלְכָּלָה וְרַחֲמִים וְחַיִּים וְשָׁלוֹם וְכָל טוֹב וּמִכָּל טוּב לְעוֹלָם אַל יְחַסְּרֵנוּ:

May the thoughts and memories of this day ascend and reach Thee: the memory of our fathers, the memory of the Messiah, son of David thy servant, the memory of Jerusalem thy holy city, the memory of thy people, the house of Israel. May it all be remembered on this Passover day, for life and peace. Our eyes are turned to Thee, for thou art a God of grace and compassion.

O BUILD JERUSALEM, THE HOLY CITY, SPEEDILY IN OUR DAYS. BLESSED BE GOD, WHO IN HIS MERCY BUILDS JERUSALEM. AMEN.

Blessed be God, our Father and King, our Creator—our Shepherd, the Shepherd of Israel. He has been, He is, and He ever will be good to us. Blessing, salvation and comfort are from Him. Life, peace and all good things—may they never lack!

הָרַחֲמָן

הוּא יִמְלוֹךְ עָלֵינוּ לְעוֹלָם וָעֶד: הָרַחֲמָן הוּא יִתְבָּרֵךְ בַּשָּׁמַיִם וּבָאָרֶץ: הָרַחֲמָן הוּא יִשְׁתַּבַּח לְדוֹר דּוֹרִים וְיִתְפָּאַר בָּנוּ לָנֶצַח נְצָחִים וְיִתְהַדַּר בָּנוּ לָעַד וּלְעוֹלְמֵי עוֹלָמִים: הָרַחֲמָן הוּא יְפַרְנְסֵנוּ בְּכָבוֹד: הָרַחֲמָן הוּא יִשְׁבּוֹר עֻלֵּנוּ מֵעַל צַוָּארֵנוּ וְהוּא יוֹלִיכֵנוּ קוֹמְמִיּוּת לְאַרְצֵנוּ: הָרַחֲמָן הוּא יִשְׁלַח בְּרָכָה מְרֻבָּה בַּבַּיִת הַזֶּה וְעַל שֻׁלְחָן זֶה שֶׁאָכַלְנוּ עָלָיו: הָרַחֲמָן הוּא יִשְׁלַח לָנוּ אֶת אֵלִיָּהוּ הַנָּבִיא זָכוּר לַטּוֹב וִיבַשֶּׂר־לָנוּ בְּשׂוֹרוֹת טוֹבוֹת יְשׁוּעוֹת וְנֶחָמוֹת: הָרַחֲמָן הוּא יְבָרֵךְ אֶת אָבִי מוֹרִי בַּעַל הַבַּיִת הַזֶּה, וְאֶת אִמִּי מוֹרָתִי בַּעֲלַת הַבַּיִת הַזֶּה אוֹתָם וְאֶת בֵּיתָם וְאֶת זַרְעָם וְאֶת כָּל אֲשֶׁר לָהֶם (ואם הוא נשוי אומר) אוֹתִי וְאֶת אִשְׁתִּי וְאֶת

opposite View of Jerusalem from the Mount of Olives

Blessed be God who, in his goodness, feeds the whole world with grace, lovingkindness and compassion. Through his great goodness, food has never failed us—and may it never fail us—as witness to his great Name. For he feeds and sustains everyone, and is bountiful to all, with food for all his creatures. Blessed be God, who feeds us all.

Let us thank God that He caused our fathers to inherit a broad and goodly land; that He brought us out of slavery in Egypt, and gave us his Torah and statutes. Let us thank him for a life of grace and kindness, and for our sustenance every day and hour.

For all this, we thank and bless God. May his name be a blessing in the mouth of all living continually for evermore. As it is written: 'When thou hast eaten and art satisfied, then thou shalt bless the Lord thy God for the good land which He hath given thee' (*Deuteronomy* XIII, 10). Blessed be God, for the Land, and the food.

Be merciful, O God, to thy people Israel, to thy city Jerusalem, to Zion, the seat of thy glory, to the kingdom of the House of David, thy anointed, and to the great and holy Temple which is called by thy name. O God, our Father, feed us, nourish and sustain us, and free us speedily from all our troubles. Let us not stand in need of the benefactions of men of flesh and blood, but look to thy open and generous hand, so that we may not be shamed or confounded ever more.

On Sabbath, this is added:

May it be thy will to strengthen us through obedience to thy *mitzvot*, and the *mitzvah* of the Seventh Day—this great and holy Sabbath, when we rest and are refreshed in love, in accordance with thy will. O that we may see the consolation of Zion, and the rebuilding of Jerusalem, thy holy city. Salvation and comfort are from God.

אֱלֹהֵינוּ וֵאלֹהֵי אֲבוֹתֵינוּ יַעֲלֶה וְיָבֹא וְיַגִּיעַ וְיֵרָאֶה וְיֵרָצֶה וְיִשָּׁמַע וְיִפָּקֵד
וְיִזָּכֵר זִכְרוֹנֵנוּ וּפִקְדוֹנֵנוּ וְזִכְרוֹן אֲבוֹתֵינוּ. וְזִכְרוֹן מָשִׁיחַ בֶּן דָּוִד עַבְדֶּךָ.
וְזִכְרוֹן יְרוּשָׁלַיִם עִיר קָדְשֶׁךָ. וְזִכְרוֹן כָּל עַמְּךָ בֵּית יִשְׂרָאֵל לְפָנֶיךָ.
לִפְלֵטָה לְטוֹבָה לְחֵן וּלְחֶסֶד וּלְרַחֲמִים לְחַיִּים וּלְשָׁלוֹם בְּיוֹם חַג הַמַּצּוֹת
הַזֶּה. זָכְרֵנוּ יְיָ אֱלֹהֵינוּ בּוֹ לְטוֹבָה. וּפָקְדֵנוּ בוֹ לִבְרָכָה. וְהוֹשִׁיעֵנוּ בוֹ לְחַיִּים
טוֹבִים. וּבִדְבַר יְשׁוּעָה וְרַחֲמִים חוּס וְחָנֵּנוּ וְרַחֵם עָלֵינוּ וְהוֹשִׁיעֵנוּ כִּי
אֵלֶיךָ עֵינֵינוּ כִּי אֵל חַנּוּן וְרַחוּם אָתָּה:

Grace after the Meal

בָּרוּךְ אַתָּה יְיָ אֱלֹהֵינוּ מֶלֶךְ הָעוֹלָם הַזָּן אֶת הָעוֹלָם כֻּלּוֹ בְּטוּבוֹ בְּחֵן בְּחֶסֶד וּבְרַחֲמִים הוּא נוֹתֵן לֶחֶם לְכָל בָּשָׂר כִּי לְעוֹלָם חַסְדּוֹ: וּבְטוּבוֹ הַגָּדוֹל תָּמִיד לֹא חָסַר לָנוּ וְאַל יֶחְסַר לָנוּ מָזוֹן לְעוֹלָם וָעֶד. בַּעֲבוּר שְׁמוֹ הַגָּדוֹל כִּי הוּא אֵל זָן וּמְפַרְנֵס לַכֹּל וּמֵטִיב לַכֹּל וּמֵכִין מָזוֹן לְכָל בְּרִיּוֹתָיו אֲשֶׁר בָּרָא. בָּרוּךְ אַתָּה יְיָ הַזָּן אֶת הַכֹּל: **נוֹדֶה לְּךָ** יְיָ אֱלֹהֵינוּ עַל שֶׁהִנְחַלְתָּ לַאֲבוֹתֵינוּ אֶרֶץ חֶמְדָּה טוֹבָה וּרְחָבָה וְעַל שֶׁהוֹצֵאתָנוּ יְיָ אֱלֹהֵינוּ מֵאֶרֶץ מִצְרַיִם וּפְדִיתָנוּ מִבֵּית עֲבָדִים וְעַל בְּרִיתְךָ שֶׁחָתַמְתָּ בִּבְשָׂרֵנוּ וְעַל תּוֹרָתְךָ שֶׁלִּמַּדְתָּנוּ וְעַל חֻקֶּיךָ שֶׁהוֹדַעְתָּנוּ וְעַל חַיִּים חֵן וָחֶסֶד שֶׁחוֹנַנְתָּנוּ וְעַל אֲכִילַת מָזוֹן שָׁאַתָּה זָן וּמְפַרְנֵס אוֹתָנוּ תָּמִיד בְּכָל יוֹם וּבְכָל עֵת וּבְכָל שָׁעָה: **וְעַל הַכֹּל** יְיָ אֱלֹהֵינוּ אֲנַחְנוּ מוֹדִים לָךְ וּמְבָרְכִים אוֹתָךְ יִתְבָּרַךְ שִׁמְךָ בְּפִי כָּל חַי תָּמִיד לְעוֹלָם וָעֶד. כַּכָּתוּב. וְאָכַלְתָּ וְשָׂבָעְתָּ וּבֵרַכְתָּ אֶת־יְיָ אֱלֹהֶיךָ עַל־הָאָרֶץ הַטֹּבָה אֲשֶׁר נָתַן־לָךְ. בָּרוּךְ אַתָּה יְיָ עַל הָאָרֶץ וְעַל הַמָּזוֹן: **רַחֵם נָא** יְיָ אֱלֹהֵינוּ עַל יִשְׂרָאֵל עַמֶּךָ וְעַל יְרוּשָׁלַיִם עִירֶךָ וְעַל צִיּוֹן מִשְׁכַּן כְּבוֹדֶךָ וְעַל מַלְכוּת בֵּית דָּוִד מְשִׁיחֶךָ וְעַל הַבַּיִת הַגָּדוֹל וְהַקָּדוֹשׁ שֶׁנִּקְרָא שִׁמְךָ עָלָיו: אֱלֹהֵינוּ אָבִינוּ רְעֵנוּ זוּנֵנוּ פַּרְנְסֵנוּ וְכַלְכְּלֵנוּ וְהַרְוִיחֵנוּ וְהַרְוַח לָנוּ יְיָ אֱלֹהֵינוּ מְהֵרָה מִכָּל צָרוֹתֵינוּ: וְנָא אַל תַּצְרִיכֵנוּ יְיָ אֱלֹהֵינוּ לֹא לִידֵי מַתְּנַת בָּשָׂר וָדָם וְלֹא לִידֵי הַלְוָאָתָם כִּי אִם לְיָדְךָ הַמְּלֵאָה הַפְּתוּחָה הַקְּדוֹשָׁה וְהָרְחָבָה שֶׁלֹּא נֵבוֹשׁ וְלֹא נִכָּלֵם לְעוֹלָם וָעֶד:

On Sabbath, this is added:

רְצֵה וְהַחֲלִיצֵנוּ יְיָ אֱלֹהֵינוּ בְּמִצְוֹתֶיךָ וּבְמִצְוַת יוֹם הַשְּׁבִיעִי הַשַּׁבָּת הַגָּדוֹל וְהַקָּדוֹשׁ הַזֶּה כִּי יוֹם זֶה גָּדוֹל וְקָדוֹשׁ הוּא לְפָנֶיךָ לִשְׁבָּת־בּוֹ וְלָנוּחַ בּוֹ בְּאַהֲבָה כְּמִצְוַת רְצוֹנֶךָ. בִּרְצוֹנְךָ הָנִיחַ לָנוּ יְיָ אֱלֹהֵינוּ שֶׁלֹּא תְהִי צָרָה וְיָגוֹן וַאֲנָחָה בְּיוֹם מְנוּחָתֵנוּ וְהַרְאֵנוּ יְיָ אֱלֹהֵינוּ בְּנֶחָמַת צִיּוֹן עִירֶךָ וּבְבִנְיַן יְרוּשָׁלַיִם עִיר קָדְשֶׁךָ כִּי אַתָּה בַּעַל הַיְשׁוּעוֹת וּבַעַל הַנֶּחָמוֹת:

'Hide and seek'

(*The 'hidden'* (tsafun) matzah *has been purloined by a young member of the company, who produces it—if it is not discovered—in the hope of a* quid pro quo.

The formal name for this matzah *is* afikoman, *from the Greek* epikomion. *It came to mean 'dessert' or 'savoury' and is a specific reminder of the Paschal sacrifice. Everyone must therefore eat a little of it—'at least the size of an olive'. The meal is then officially over.)*

בָּרֵךְ:

(The Grace after the Meal, preceded by a Psalm (126) *to be sung to any favourite tune)*

שִׁיר הַמַּעֲלוֹת בְּשׁוּב יְיָ אֶת־שִׁיבַת צִיּוֹן הָיִינוּ כְּחֹלְמִים: אָז יִמָּלֵא
שְׂחוֹק פִּינוּ וּלְשׁוֹנֵנוּ רִנָּה אָז יֹאמְרוּ בַגּוֹיִם הִגְדִּיל יְיָ לַעֲשׂוֹת עִם־אֵלֶּה:
הִגְדִּיל יְיָ לַעֲשׂוֹת עִמָּנוּ הָיִינוּ שְׂמֵחִים: שׁוּבָה יְיָ אֶת־שְׁבִיתֵנוּ
כַּאֲפִיקִים בַּנֶּגֶב: הַזֹּרְעִים בְּדִמְעָה בְּרִנָּה יִקְצֹרוּ: הָלוֹךְ יֵלֵךְ וּבָכֹה נֹשֵׂא
מֶשֶׁךְ־הַזָּרַע בֹּא־יָבֹא בְרִנָּה נֹשֵׂא אֲלֻמֹּתָיו:

A pilgrim song for the ascents (to Jerusalem).
When the Lord returned the captivity of Zion, we were like those that dream. Then was our mouth filled with laughter and our tongue with singing. Then said they among the heathen: 'the Lord hath done great things for them'. The Lord hath done great things for us, whereof we are glad. Transform our captivity, O Lord, like the streams in the south. They that sow in tears shall reap in joy. He that goeth forth weeping, bearing precious seed, shall come again with rejoicing, bearing his sheaves.

The cups are filled for the third time, to be drunk after the Grace.

If three or more males are present, this formal introduction precedes the Grace

The host: רַבּוֹתַי נְבָרֵךְ:
Gentlemen, let us say Grace.

The company: יְהִי שֵׁם יְיָ מְבֹרָךְ מֵעַתָּה וְעַד־עוֹלָם:
May the name of the Lord be blessed from now to eternity.

The host: בִּרְשׁוּת רַבּוֹתַי נְבָרֵךְ (אֱלֹהֵינוּ) שֶׁאָכַלְנוּ מִשֶּׁלּוֹ:
If it please you, let us bless Him (our God) of whose bounty we have eaten.

The company: בָּרוּךְ (אֱלֹהֵינוּ) שֶׁאָכַלְנוּ מִשֶּׁלּוֹ וּבְטוּבוֹ חָיִינוּ:
Blessed be He (our God) of whose bounty we have eaten and by whose goodness we live.

The host repeats after them: בָּרוּךְ (אֱלֹהֵינוּ) שֶׁאָכַלְנוּ מִשֶּׁלּוֹ וּבְטוּבוֹ חָיִינוּ:

The company: בָּרוּךְ הוּא וּבָרוּךְ שְׁמוֹ:
Blessed be He and blessed be His name.

opposite Late 19th-century table-cloth from Persia embroidered in the traditional style, with a passage from the Haggadah and the *Kiddush* blessing

רָחְצָה

(*Wash the hands with a blessing*)

בָּרוּךְ אַתָּה יְיָ אֱלֹהֵינוּ מֶלֶךְ הָעוֹלָם. אֲשֶׁר קִדְּשָׁנוּ בְּמִצְוֹתָיו וְצִוָּנוּ עַל נְטִילַת יָדָיִם:

Blessed be God, who made each *mitzvah* (commandment) bring us holiness and laid on us the washing of hands before food.

מוֹצִיא מַצָּה

(*Two blessings, first one on 'bread', and then a special one for* matzah)

בָּרוּךְ אַתָּה יְיָ אֱלֹהֵינוּ מֶלֶךְ הָעוֹלָם. הַמּוֹצִיא לֶחֶם מִן הָאָרֶץ:
בָּרוּךְ אַתָּה יְיָ אֱלֹהֵינוּ מֶלֶךְ הָעוֹלָם. אֲשֶׁר קִדְּשָׁנוּ בְּמִצְוֹתָיו וְצִוָּנוּ עַל אֲכִילַת מַצָּה:

Blessed be God, who brings food out of the earth.
Blessed be God, who made each *mitzvah* bring us holiness, and laid on us the eating of *matzah.*

A piece of the top matzah *and the middle (broken)* matzah *is given to—and eaten by—each person present.*

מָרוֹר

*A little of the bitter herb is dipped into—or mixed with—*haroset, *for each guest to eat, preceded, of course, by a blessing:*

בָּרוּךְ אַתָּה יְיָ אֱלֹהֵינוּ מֶלֶךְ הָעוֹלָם. אֲשֶׁר קִדְּשָׁנוּ בְּמִצְוֹתָיו וְצִוָּנוּ עַל אֲכִילַת מָרוֹר:

Blessed be God, who made each *mitzvah* bring us holiness and laid on us the eating of *maror.*

כּוֹרֵךְ:

Now break the bottom matzah *and put some of the bitter herb between two pieces for each participant, in memory of Hillel's custom.*

זֵכֶר לְמִקְדָּשׁ כְּהִלֵּל: כֵּן עָשָׂה הִלֵּל בִּזְמַן שֶׁבֵּית הַמִּקְדָּשׁ קַיָּם. הָיָה כּוֹרֵךְ (פֶּסַח) מַצָּה וּמָרוֹר וְאוֹכֵל בְּיַחַד. לְקַיֵּם מַה שֶּׁנֶּאֱמַר. עַל מַצּוֹת וּמְרֹרִים יֹאכְלֻהוּ:

To remind us of the Temple: a custom of Hillel. This is what Hillel—living in Temple times—used to do. He used to make a sandwich of *matzah* and *maror,* to fulfil the verse: 'They shall eat it with *matzah* and *maror*' (*Numbers* IV, 2).

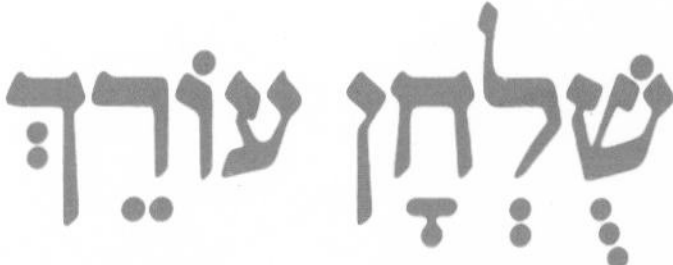

The Seder dish is removed, and now Dinner is served!

הֶהָרִים תִּרְקְדוּ כְאֵילִים גְּבָעוֹת כִּבְנֵי־צֹאן: מִלִּפְנֵי אָדוֹן חוּלִי אָרֶץ
מִלִּפְנֵי אֱלוֹהַּ יַעֲקֹב: הַהֹפְכִי הַצּוּר אֲגַם־מָיִם חַלָּמִישׁ לְמַעְיְנוֹ־מָיִם:

When Israel went forth from Egypt, the house of Jacob from a people of strange tongue, Judah became his sanctuary, Israel his dominion.

The sea looked and fled, Jordan was driven backward. The mountains skipped like rams, the hills like young sheep.

What aileth thee, O sea, that thou didst flee, Jordan that thou wast driven back? Ye mountains that ye skipped like rams, ye hills like young sheep?

Tremble, O earth, in the presence of the God of Jacob, who turned the rock into a pool of water, the flinty rock into a fountain.

(*We prepare for the second toast*) ## 'To Freedom'

Lift up the cup of wine and say:

בָּרוּךְ אַתָּה יְיָ אֱלֹהֵינוּ מֶלֶךְ הָעוֹלָם. אֲשֶׁר גְּאָלָנוּ וְגָאַל אֶת־אֲבוֹתֵינוּ
מִמִּצְרַיִם. וְהִגִּיעָנוּ לַלַּיְלָה הַזֶּה לֶאֱכָל־בּוֹ מַצָּה וּמָרוֹר: כֵּן יְיָ אֱלֹהֵינוּ
וֵאלֹהֵי אֲבוֹתֵינוּ הַגִּיעֵנוּ לְמוֹעֲדִים וְלִרְגָלִים אֲחֵרִים הַבָּאִים לִקְרָאתֵנוּ
לְשָׁלוֹם שְׂמֵחִים בְּבִנְיַן עִירֶךְ וְשָׂשִׂים בַּעֲבוֹדָתֶךְ. וְנֹאכַל שָׁם מִן הַזְּבָחִים
וּמִן הַפְּסָחִים אֲשֶׁר יַגִּיעַ דָּמָם עַל קִיר מִזְבַּחֲךְ לְרָצוֹן. וְנוֹדֶה לְּךְ שִׁיר
חָדָשׁ עַל גְּאֻלָּתֵנוּ וְעַל פְּדוּת נַפְשֵׁנוּ: בָּרוּךְ אַתָּה יְיָ גָּאַל יִשְׂרָאֵל:

Blessed be God, King of the Universe, who has redeemed us, as He redeemed our ancestors from Egypt, and has brought us to this night on which we eat *matzah* and bitter herb.

Let us pray to God, the God of our Fathers, that He bring us to other festivals and holy days that will come to us in peace—joyful in building God's City, and happy in His service.

Let us sing a new song of thanks to God for our salvation and freedom. Blessings to God who has saved Israel!

בָּרוּךְ אַתָּה יְיָ אֱלֹהֵינוּ מֶלֶךְ הָעוֹלָם. בּוֹרֵא פְּרִי הַגָּפֶן:

BLESSED IS OUR LORD, GOD, KING OF THE UNIVERSE, WHO CREATES THE FRUIT OF THE VINE.

The second cup of wine is drunk

opposite For the Second Cup, a 17th-century ivory Seder goblet from southern Germany showing Moses before Pharaoh. Part of the inscription around the rim, '*Shalach et ami*' ('let my people go'), is visible. The cup is signed in Hebrew, 'the work of Yosef ben Yitzchak'

אלא את אותנו גאל עמהם
שנ׳ ואותנו הוציא משם
למען הביא אותנו אל הארץ
אשר נשבע לאבותינו :

כל אחד יגביה

לפיכך

אנחנו חייבים להודות להלל

כל אחד יגביה [illegible]

Lift up the cup of wine and say:

לְפִיכָךְ אֲנַחְנוּ חַיָּבִים לְהוֹדוֹת לְהַלֵּל לְשַׁבֵּחַ לְפָאֵר לְרוֹמֵם לְהַדֵּר
וּלְקַלֵּס לְמִי שֶׁעָשָׂה לַאֲבוֹתֵינוּ וְלָנוּ אֶת כָּל הַנִּסִּים הָאֵלּוּ וְהוֹצִיאָנוּ
מֵעַבְדוּת לְחֵרוּת מִיָּגוֹן לְשִׂמְחָה מֵאֵבֶל לְיוֹם טוֹב וּמֵאֲפֵלָה לְאוֹר
גָּדוֹל וּמִשִּׁעְבּוּד לִגְאֻלָּה וְנֹאמַר לְפָנָיו שִׁירָה חֲדָשָׁה **הַלְלוּיָהּ:**

At this moment, then, we thank God: we praise, glorify, exalt and bless the Power that did all these miracles for our ancestors and us. He brought us from slavery to freedom, from sorrow to joy, from mourning to holiday, from darkness to a great light, from servitude to redemption. Let us then sing a new song: HALLELUYAH.

Psalm CXIII

הַלְלוּיָהּ

הַלְלוּ עַבְדֵי יְיָ הַלְלוּ אֶת־שֵׁם יְיָ: יְהִי שֵׁם יְיָ מְבֹרָךְ מֵעַתָּה וְעַד־עוֹלָם:
מִמִּזְרַח־שֶׁמֶשׁ עַד־מְבוֹאוֹ מְהֻלָּל שֵׁם יְיָ: רָם עַל־כָּל־גּוֹיִם יְיָ עַל־
הַשָּׁמַיִם כְּבוֹדוֹ: מִי כַּייָ אֱלֹהֵינוּ הַמַּגְבִּיהִי לָשָׁבֶת: הַמַּשְׁפִּילִי לִרְאוֹת
בַּשָּׁמַיִם וּבָאָרֶץ: מְקִימִי מֵעָפָר דָּל מֵאַשְׁפֹּת יָרִים אֶבְיוֹן: לְהוֹשִׁיבִי
עִם־נְדִיבִים עִם נְדִיבֵי עַמּוֹ: מוֹשִׁיבִי עֲקֶרֶת הַבַּיִת אֵם־הַבָּנִים שְׂמֵחָה
הַלְלוּיָהּ:

Praise ye the Lord! O ye servants of the Lord, praise the name of the Lord. Blessed be the name of the Lord now and for evermore.

From the rising of the sun unto its setting, praised be the name of the Lord. High above all nations is the Lord, above the heavens his glory.

Who is like unto the Lord, our God who dwells on high yet looketh down upon the heavens and the earth. He raiseth the weak man from the dust, the poor man from the dunghill, to seat him with princes, with the princes of His people. He maketh the barren woman to live as a joyful mother of children. Halleluyah!

Psalm CXIV

בְּצֵאת יִשְׂרָאֵל מִמִּצְרָיִם בֵּית יַעֲקֹב מֵעַם לֹעֵז: הָיְתָה יְהוּדָה לְקָדְשׁוֹ
יִשְׂרָאֵל מַמְשְׁלוֹתָיו: הַיָּם רָאָה וַיָּנֹס הַיַּרְדֵּן יִסֹּב לְאָחוֹר: הֶהָרִים רָקְדוּ
כְאֵילִים גְּבָעוֹת כִּבְנֵי־צֹאן: מַה־לְּךָ הַיָּם כִּי תָנוּס הַיַּרְדֵּן תִּסֹּב לְאָחוֹר:

opposite 'Lefichach . . .', the affirmation at the head of this page, illustrated with a Seder scene in the Yahuda Haggadah (southern German, mid-15th century)

3. Maror מָרוֹר

זֶה שֶׁאָנוּ אוֹכְלִים עַל שׁוּם מָה. עַל שׁוּם שֶׁמֵּרְרוּ הַמִּצְרִים אֶת חַיֵּי אֲבוֹתֵינוּ בְּמִצְרַיִם. שֶׁנֶּאֱמַר: וַיְמָרְרוּ אֶת־חַיֵּיהֶם בַּעֲבֹדָה קָשָׁה בְּחֹמֶר וּבִלְבֵנִים וּבְכָל־עֲבֹדָה בַּשָּׂדֶה אֵת כָּל־עֲבֹדָתָם אֲשֶׁר־עָבְדוּ בָהֶם בְּפָרֶךְ:

Why do we eat this bitter herb? Because the Egyptians embittered the lives of our ancestors in Egypt; as it says: 'They made their lives bitter with hard labour, in mortar and in brick, and all manner of hard work in the fields. In all their work, they made them slave with rigour' (*Exodus* I, 14).

'In Every Generation...'

בְּכָל דּוֹר וָדוֹר חַיָּב אָדָם לִרְאוֹת אֶת עַצְמוֹ כְּאִלּוּ הוּא יָצָא מִמִּצְרַיִם.

שֶׁנֶּאֱמַר וְהִגַּדְתָּ לְבִנְךָ בַּיּוֹם הַהוּא לֵאמֹר בַּעֲבוּר זֶה עָשָׂה יְיָ לִי בְּצֵאתִי מִמִּצְרָיִם:

שֶׁלֹּא אֶת אֲבוֹתֵינוּ בִּלְבַד גָּאַל הַקָּדוֹשׁ בָּרוּךְ הוּא. אֶלָּא אַף אוֹתָנוּ גָּאַל עִמָּהֶם.

שֶׁנֶּאֱמַר וְאוֹתָנוּ הוֹצִיא מִשָּׁם לְמַעַן הָבִיא אֹתָנוּ לָתֶת לָנוּ אֶת־הָאָרֶץ אֲשֶׁר נִשְׁבַּע לַאֲבֹתֵינוּ:

IN EVERY GENERATION, EVERY JEW MUST FEEL AS IF HE HIMSELF CAME OUT OF EGYPT.

As the Bible says: 'And thou shalt tell thy son in that day saying: It is because of what God did for me when I came out of Egypt' (*Exodus* XIII, 8).

GOD DID NOT ONLY REDEEM OUR ANCESTORS BUT HE REDEEMED US WITH THEM.

As it says: 'And He took us out from there, to bring us to the land which he had promised to our ancestors' (*Deuteronomy* VI, 23).

The Three Essentials

רַבָּן גַּמְלִיאֵל הָיָה אוֹמֵר. כָּל שֶׁלֹּא אָמַר שְׁלשָׁה דְּבָרִים אֵלּוּ בַּפֶּסַח לֹא יָצָא יְדֵי חוֹבָתוֹ. וְאֵלּוּ הֵן. **פֶּסַח. מַצָּה. וּמָרוֹר:**

Rabban Gamaliel used to say: 'To fulfil your obligation on Passover, you must declare these three central words:
PESACH, MATZAH, MAROR.'

1. Pesach פֶּסַח

שֶׁהָיוּ אֲבוֹתֵינוּ אוֹכְלִים בִּזְמַן שֶׁבֵּית הַמִּקְדָּשׁ קַיָּם. עַל שׁוּם מָה. עַל שׁוּם שֶׁפָּסַח הַקָּדוֹשׁ בָּרוּךְ הוּא עַל בָּתֵּי אֲבוֹתֵינוּ בְּמִצְרַיִם. שֶׁנֶּאֱמַר וַאֲמַרְתֶּם זֶבַח־פֶּסַח הוּא לַייָ אֲשֶׁר פָּסַח עַל־בָּתֵּי בְנֵי־יִשְׂרָאֵל בְּמִצְרַיִם בְּנָגְפּוֹ אֶת־מִצְרַיִם וְאֶת־בָּתֵּינוּ הִצִּיל וַיִּקֹּד הָעָם וַיִּשְׁתַּחֲווּ:

Why did our ancestors eat the Passover sacrifice when the Temple still stood? Because God had 'passed over' the houses of our ancestors in Egypt (*during the slaying of the first-born*); as it says: 'It is the sacrifice of God's Passover, in that he passed over the houses of the children of Israel in Egypt' (*Exodus* XII, 27).

2. Matzah מַצָּה

זוֹ שֶׁאָנוּ אוֹכְלִים עַל שׁוּם מָה. עַל שׁוּם שֶׁלֹּא הִסְפִּיק בְּצֵקָם שֶׁל אֲבוֹתֵינוּ לְהַחֲמִיץ עַד שֶׁנִּגְלָה עֲלֵיהֶם מֶלֶךְ מַלְכֵי הַמְּלָכִים הַקָּדוֹשׁ בָּרוּךְ הוּא וּגְאָלָם שֶׁנֶּאֱמַר וַיֹּאפוּ אֶת־הַבָּצֵק אֲשֶׁר הוֹצִיאוּ מִמִּצְרַיִם עֻגֹת מַצּוֹת כִּי לֹא חָמֵץ כִּי־גֹרְשׁוּ מִמִּצְרַיִם וְלֹא יָכְלוּ לְהִתְמַהְמֵהַּ וְגַם־צֵדָה לֹא־עָשׂוּ לָהֶם:

Why do we eat this *matzah?* Because when our ancestors in Egypt were trying to escape, God revealed himself to them and saved them before the bread they were baking had time to rise; as it says: 'And they baked unleavened wafers of the dough which they brought out of Egypt' (*Exodus* XII, 39).

Page from the Sarajevo Haggadah showing a decorated *matzah* and tools for decorating *matzah* from Eastern Europe (19th century)

'We'd Have Been Satisfied'

HOW MANY WONDERFUL THINGS WE HAVE TO THANK GOD FOR!

If He'd saved us from Egypt, but left them still armed—ENOUGH!

If their might had been smashed, but their gods left unharmed —ENOUGH!

If He'd dealt with their gods, with first-born still healthy— —ENOUGH!

If He'd slain all their first-born, with Egypt still wealthy— ENOUGH!

If He'd given us their wealth, but not split the sea —ENOUGH!

If the waves had been split, but no dry path free —ENOUGH!

If He'd brought us across, but they'd not been drowned —ENOUGH!

If Pharoah had perished, but no food we'd found —ENOUGH!

If He'd met all our needs, but manna'd been missing —ENOUGH!

If He'd given us manna, but no Sabbath blessing —ENOUGH!

If He'd given us the Sabbath, but no Torah to teach —ENOUGH!

If He'd given us the Torah, but no Land to reach —ENOUGH!

If He'd brought us to Israel without our own shrine—but stay!

He built us the Temple—the house of His choosing—HURRAY!

HOW GREAT—DOUBLED AND RE-DOUBLED—HAS GOD'S BOUNTY BEEN TO US!

He brought us out of Egypt, dealt rightly with the Egyptians and their gods, gave us their wealth, slew their first-born, divided the sea for us, brought us through on dry land but sank our enemy in its depths, met our needs in the wilderness for forty years, fed us with manna, gave us the Sabbath, brought us to Mount Sinai, gave us the Torah, brought us into the Land of Israel and built for us His chosen house, to let us atone for all our sins.

כַּמָּה מַעֲלוֹת טוֹבוֹת לַמָּקוֹם עָלֵינוּ:

אִלּוּ הוֹצִיאָנוּ מִמִּצְרַיִם. וְלֹא עָשָׂה בָהֶם שְׁפָטִים דַּיֵּנוּ:

אִלּוּ עָשָׂה בָהֶם שְׁפָטִים. וְלֹא עָשָׂה בֵאלֹהֵיהֶם דַּיֵּנוּ:

אִלּוּ עָשָׂה בֵאלֹהֵיהֶם. וְלֹא הָרַג בְּכוֹרֵיהֶם דַּיֵּנוּ:

אִלּוּ הָרַג בְּכוֹרֵיהֶם. וְלֹא נָתַן לָנוּ אֶת מָמוֹנָם דַּיֵּנוּ:

אִלּוּ נָתַן לָנוּ אֶת מָמוֹנָם. וְלֹא קָרַע לָנוּ אֶת הַיָּם דַּיֵּנוּ:

אִלּוּ קָרַע לָנוּ אֶת הַיָּם. וְלֹא הֶעֱבִירָנוּ בְתוֹכוֹ בֶּחָרָבָה דַּיֵּנוּ:

אִלּוּ הֶעֱבִירָנוּ בְתוֹכוֹ בֶּחָרָבָה. וְלֹא שִׁקַּע צָרֵינוּ בְּתוֹכוֹ דַּיֵּנוּ:

אִלּוּ שִׁקַּע צָרֵינוּ בְּתוֹכוֹ. וְלֹא סִפֵּק צָרְכֵּנוּ בַּמִּדְבָּר אַרְבָּעִים שָׁנָה דַּיֵּנוּ:

אִלּוּ סִפֵּק צָרְכֵּנוּ בַּמִּדְבָּר אַרְבָּעִים שָׁנָה. וְלֹא הֶאֱכִילָנוּ אֶת־הַמָּן דַּיֵּנוּ:

אִלּוּ הֶאֱכִילָנוּ אֶת־הַמָּן. וְלֹא נָתַן לָנוּ אֶת־הַשַּׁבָּת דַּיֵּנוּ:

אִלּוּ נָתַן לָנוּ אֶת־הַשַּׁבָּת. וְלֹא קֵרְבָנוּ לִפְנֵי הַר סִינַי דַּיֵּנוּ:

אִלּוּ קֵרְבָנוּ לִפְנֵי הַר סִינַי. וְלֹא נָתַן לָנוּ אֶת־הַתּוֹרָה דַּיֵּנוּ:

אִלּוּ נָתַן לָנוּ אֶת הַתּוֹרָה. וְלֹא הִכְנִיסָנוּ לְאֶרֶץ יִשְׂרָאֵל דַּיֵּנוּ:

אִלּוּ הִכְנִיסָנוּ לְאֶרֶץ יִשְׂרָאֵל. וְלֹא בָנָה לָנוּ אֶת־בֵּית הַבְּחִירָה דַּיֵּנוּ:

עַל אַחַת כַּמָּה וְכַמָּה טוֹבָה כְפוּלָה וּמְכֻפֶּלֶת לַמָּקוֹם עָלֵינוּ. שֶׁהוֹצִיאָנוּ מִמִּצְרַיִם.

וְעָשָׂה בָהֶם שְׁפָטִים. וְעָשָׂה בֵאלֹהֵיהֶם. וְהָרַג בְּכוֹרֵיהֶם. וְנָתַן לָנוּ אֶת מָמוֹנָם. וְקָרַע לָנוּ אֶת הַיָּם. וְהֶעֱבִירָנוּ בְתוֹכוֹ בֶּחָרָבָה. וְשִׁקַּע צָרֵינוּ בְּתוֹכוֹ. וְסִפֵּק צָרְכֵּנוּ בַּמִּדְבָּר אַרְבָּעִים שָׁנָה. וְהֶאֱכִילָנוּ אֶת הַמָּן. וְנָתַן לָנוּ אֶת הַשַּׁבָּת. וְקֵרְבָנוּ לִפְנֵי הַר סִינַי. וְנָתַן לָנוּ אֶת הַתּוֹרָה. וְהִכְנִיסָנוּ לְאֶרֶץ יִשְׂרָאֵל. וּבָנָה לָנוּ אֶת בֵּית הַבְּחִירָה לְכַפֵּר עַל כָּל עֲוֹנוֹתֵינוּ:

Even more, if you spin out the verses…

רַבִּי אֱלִיעֶזֶר אוֹמֵר. מִנַּיִן שֶׁכָּל מַכָּה וּמַכָּה שֶׁהֵבִיא הַקָּדוֹשׁ בָּרוּךְ הוּא
עַל הַמִּצְרִים בְּמִצְרַיִם הָיְתָה שֶׁל אַרְבַּע מַכּוֹת. שֶׁנֶּאֱמַר: יְשַׁלַּח־בָּם
חֲרוֹן אַפּוֹ עֶבְרָה וָזַעַם וְצָרָה מִשְׁלַחַת מַלְאֲכֵי רָעִים: עֶבְרָה אַחַת.
וָזַעַם שְׁתַּיִם. וְצָרָה שָׁלֹשׁ. מִשְׁלַחַת מַלְאֲכֵי רָעִים אַרְבַּע. אֱמוֹר מֵעַתָּה
בְּמִצְרַיִם לָקוּ אַרְבָּעִים מַכּוֹת. וְעַל הַיָּם לָקוּ מָאתַיִם מַכּוֹת:

Rabbi Eliezer said: 'How do we know that each of the ten plagues that God brought on the Egyptians was the same as *four* plagues? From the verse: "He sent upon them his fierce anger—wrath, indignation and trouble, a visitation of messengers of harm" (*Psalms* LXXVIII, 49). Wrath is one; indignation makes two; trouble, three; the visitation, four. So you see that there were forty plagues in Egypt, which would make two hundred at the Red Sea.'

רַבִּי עֲקִיבָא אוֹמֵר. מִנַּיִן שֶׁכָּל מַכָּה וּמַכָּה שֶׁהֵבִיא הַקָּדוֹשׁ בָּרוּךְ הוּא
עַל הַמִּצְרִים בְּמִצְרַיִם הָיְתָה שֶׁל חָמֵשׁ מַכּוֹת. שֶׁנֶּאֱמַר: יְשַׁלַּח־בָּם
חֲרוֹן אַפּוֹ עֶבְרָה וָזַעַם וְצָרָה מִשְׁלַחַת מַלְאֲכֵי רָעִים. חֲרוֹן אַפּוֹ אַחַת.
עֶבְרָה שְׁתַּיִם. וָזַעַם שָׁלֹשׁ. וְצָרָה אַרְבַּע. מִשְׁלַחַת מַלְאֲכֵי רָעִים חָמֵשׁ.
אֱמוֹר מֵעַתָּה בְּמִצְרַיִם לָקוּ חֲמִשִּׁים מַכּוֹת. וְעַל הַיָּם לָקוּ חֲמִשִּׁים
וּמָאתַיִם מַכּוֹת:

Rabbi Akiva said: 'How do we know that each of the ten plagues that God brought on the Egyptians was the same as *five* plagues? From the same verse quoted by Rabbi Eliezer, but adding the general phrase "fierce anger" to the other four. So there were *fifty* plagues in Egypt, which would yield two hundred and fifty at the Red Sea.'

(*Akiva, quoted here in a light-hearted* reductio ad absurdum, *was one of the most interesting, humane and brilliant of the rabbis, active in public affairs and a powerful figure with the authorities. He is thought of as a supporter of the rebel leader Bar Kokhba, and it is this—and his martyr's death around* 134 CE—*that put the seal on a rich life, documented in detail, but also powerful in legend.*)

The Ten Plagues

דָּבָר אַחֵר. בְּיָד חֲזָקָה שְׁתַּיִם. וּבִזְרֹעַ נְטוּיָה שְׁתַּיִם. וּבְמֹרָא גָּדֹל שְׁתַּיִם. וּבְאֹתוֹת שְׁתַּיִם. וּבְמֹפְתִים שְׁתַּיִם. אֵלּוּ עֶשֶׂר מַכּוֹת שֶׁהֵבִיא הַקָּדוֹשׁ בָּרוּךְ הוּא עַל הַמִּצְרִים בְּמִצְרַיִם. וְאֵלּוּ הֵן. **דָּם. צְפַרְדֵּעַ. כִּנִּים. עָרוֹב. דֶּבֶר. שְׁחִין. בָּרָד. אַרְבֶּה. חֹשֶׁךְ. מַכַּת בְּכוֹרוֹת:**

Another way to treat the verse is to add up the words:
'Mighty hand'—that's two words. 'Outstretched arm'—two. 'Great terror'—two. 'Signs'—plural, so at least two. 'Wonders'—same thing—two.
Add them up and you have ten: the Ten Plagues that God brought on the Egyptians. Here they are:

1. BLOOD 2. FROGS 3. LICE 4. BEASTS 5. BLIGHT 6. BOILS 7. HAIL 8. LOCUSTS 9. DARKNESS 10. SLAYING OF THE FIRST-BORN.

רַבִּי יְהוּדָה הָיָה נוֹתֵן בָּהֶם סִמָּנִים. דְּצַךְ עֲדַשׁ בְּאַחַב:

Rabbi Judah took the first letter of each Hebrew word and made a mnemonic:
D'tzach, Adash, B'ahav

רַבִּי יוֹסֵי הַגְּלִילִי אוֹמֵר. מִנַּיִן אַתָּה אוֹמֵר שֶׁלָּקוּ הַמִּצְרִים בְּמִצְרַיִם עֶשֶׂר מַכּוֹת. וְעַל הַיָּם לָקוּ חֲמִשִּׁים מַכּוֹת. בְּמִצְרַיִם מַה הוּא אוֹמֵר וַיֹּאמְרוּ הַחַרְטֻמִּם אֶל־פַּרְעֹה אֶצְבַּע אֱלֹהִים הִוא: וְעַל הַיָּם מַה הוּא אוֹמֵר. וַיַּרְא יִשְׂרָאֵל אֶת־הַיָּד הַגְּדֹלָה אֲשֶׁר עָשָׂה יְיָ בְּמִצְרַיִם וַיִּירְאוּ הָעָם אֶת־יְיָ וַיַּאֲמִינוּ בַּייָ וּבְמֹשֶׁה עַבְדּוֹ: כַּמָּה לָקוּ בְּאֶצְבַּע עֶשֶׂר מַכּוֹת. אֱמוֹר מֵעַתָּה בְּמִצְרַיִם לָקוּ עֶשֶׂר מַכּוֹת. וְעַל הַיָּם לָקוּ חֲמִשִּׁים מַכּוֹת:

Rabbi Yose of Galilee said: 'How can we establish that if the Egyptians were smitten with ten plagues in Egypt, they got another fifty at the Red Sea? On Egypt, the verse says: "Then the magicians said: This is the finger of God" (*Exodus* VIII, 19). But on the Red Sea, it says: "and Israel saw the great hand which the Lord laid on the Egyptians" (*Exodus* XIV, 31). With "one finger" they were smitten with ten plagues; "a hand", at the Red Sea, must have produced another fifty plagues.'

The plague of frogs. Detail from the Basle Haggadah (1815–6)

opposite, top The locust plague, represented here by an attack on wheat
opposite, below An imaginary reconstruction of the plague from the Schocken Haggadah

בְּיָד חֲזָקָה. זוֹ הַדֶּבֶר. כְּמָה שֶׁנֶּאֱמַר הִנֵּה יַד־יְיָ הוֹיָה בְּמִקְנְךָ אֲשֶׁר בַּשָּׂדֶה
בַּסּוּסִים בַּחֲמֹרִים בַּגְּמַלִּים בַּבָּקָר וּבַצֹּאן דֶּבֶר כָּבֵד מְאֹד: **וּבִזְרֹעַ נְטוּיָה.**
זוֹ הַחֶרֶב. כְּמָה שֶׁנֶּאֱמַר וְחַרְבּוֹ שְׁלוּפָה בְּיָדוֹ נְטוּיָה עַל־יְרוּשָׁלָםִ:
וּבְמֹרָא גָּדֹל. זֶה גִּלּוּי שְׁכִינָה. כְּמָה שֶׁנֶּאֱמַר אוֹ הֲנִסָּה אֱלֹהִים לָבוֹא
לָקַחַת לוֹ גוֹי מִקֶּרֶב גּוֹי בְּמַסֹּת בְּאֹתֹת וּבְמוֹפְתִים וּבְמִלְחָמָה וּבְיָד
חֲזָקָה וּבִזְרוֹעַ נְטוּיָה וּבְמוֹרָאִים גְּדֹלִים כְּכֹל אֲשֶׁר־עָשָׂה לָכֶם יְיָ אֱלֹהֵיכֶם
בְּמִצְרַיִם לְעֵינֶיךָ: **וּבְאֹתוֹת.** זֶה הַמַּטֶּה. כְּמָה שֶׁנֶּאֱמַר וְאֶת־הַמַּטֶּה
הַזֶּה תִּקַּח בְּיָדֶךָ אֲשֶׁר תַּעֲשֶׂה־בּוֹ אֶת־הָאֹתֹת: **וּבְמֹפְתִים.** זֶה הַדָּם.
כְּמָה שֶׁנֶּאֱמַר וְנָתַתִּי מוֹפְתִים בַּשָּׁמַיִם וּבָאָרֶץ

דָּם וָאֵשׁ וְתִימְרוֹת עָשָׁן:

'And the Lord brought us out of Egypt'—not through an angel, and not through a seraph, and not through an intermediary, but the Holy One, blessed be He, in His glory and with His own Being, as it is said: 'I will pass through the land of Egypt on this night, and will kill every first-born of man and beast, and I will execute judgments against all the gods of Egypt: I am the Lord' (*Exodus XII*, 12):

'I will pass through the land of Egypt . . .'—I and no angel; 'I will kill every first-born . . .'—I and no seraph; 'I will execute judgments . . .'—I and no intermediary; 'I am the Lord'—it is I and no other.

'With a mighty hand'—this was the pestilence; 'with outstretched arm'—this was the sword; 'with great terror!': for *mora* (terror) read *mareh* (appearance)—the Revelation of the Presence; 'with signs'—the rod of Moses; 'with wonders'—the plague of blood. As the verse says: 'I will show wonders in the heavens and in the earth—

BLOOD, FIRE AND PILLARS OF SMOKE' (*Joel* III, 3).

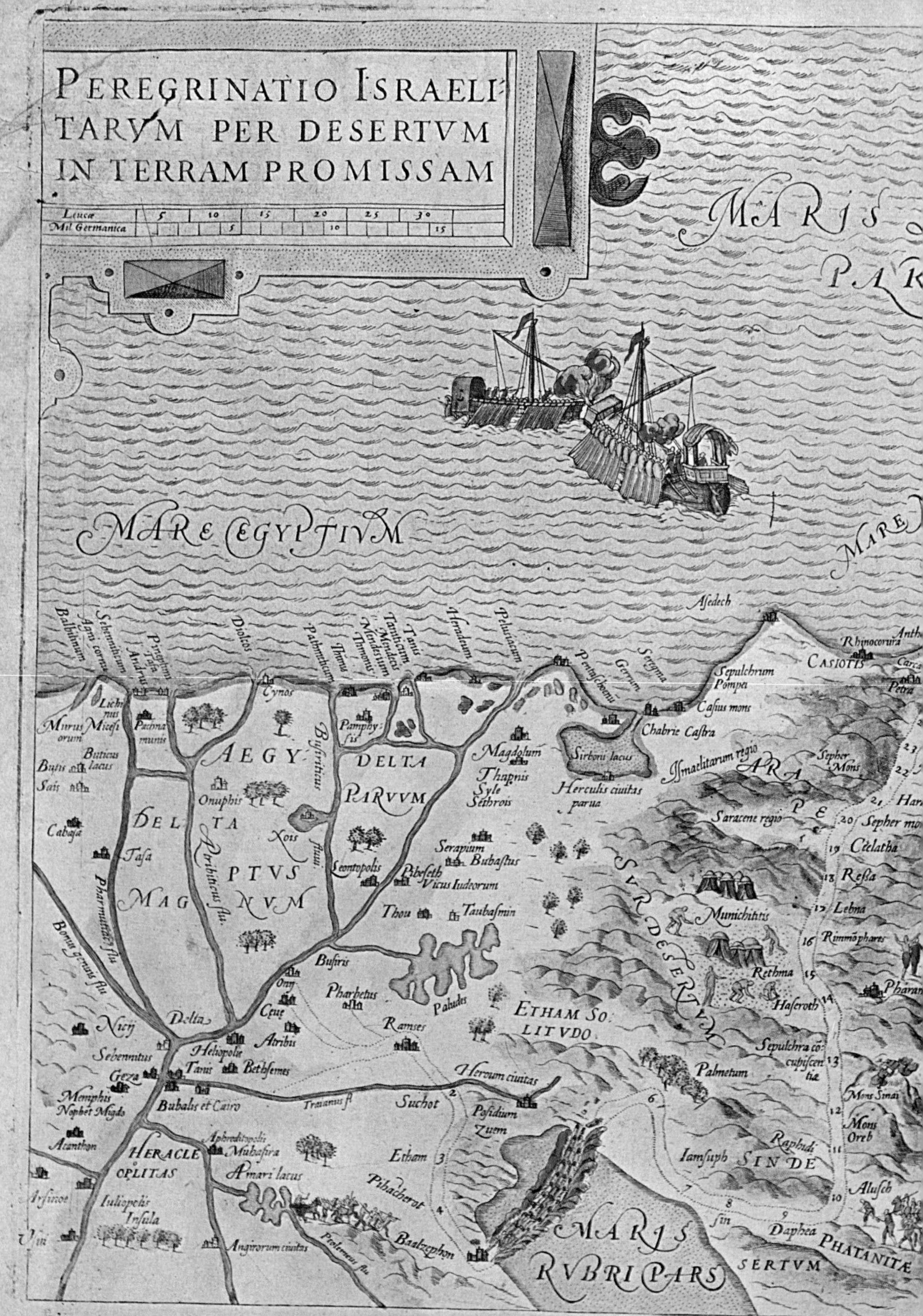
PEREGRINATIO ISRAELITARUM PER DESERTUM IN TERRAM PROMISSAM
Leucæ 5 10 15 20 25 30
Mil Germanica 5 10 15
MARE ÆGYPTIUM
MARIS
PAR
MARE
Asedech
Rhinocorura
CASIOTIS
Petra
Sepulchrum Pompei
Casius mons
Chabrie Castra
Sirbonis lacus
Herculis ciuitas parua
Ismaelitarum regio
ARA
PE
Saracene regio
Sepher Mons
Sepher mo
Celatha
Resa
Lebna
Rimmophares
Munichthis
Rethma
Haseroth
Pharan
SUR DESERTUM
ETHAM SOLITUDO
Sepulchra concupiscentiæ
Palmetum
Mons Sinai
Mons Oreb
Raphidi
Iamsuph
SINDE
Alusch
Daphea
PHATANITÆ
SERTUM
MARIS RUBRI PARS
Baalzephon
Pihachierot
Etham
Suchot
Posidium
Zuem
Herowm ciuitas
Ramses
Paludes
Pharbetus
Busiris
Thou
Taubasmin
Serapium
Bubastus
Pibeseth
Vicus Iudeorum
Leontopolis
Magdolum
Thapnis
Syle
Sethrois
DELTA PARUUM
AEGYPTUS
DELTA MAGNUM
Onuphis
Xois
Tasa
Cabasa
Sais
Butis
Buticus lacus
Pathmunis
Cynos
Diolcos
Heracleum
Pelusiacum
Delta
Heliopolis
Tanis
Bethsemes
Atribis
Sebennitus
Geza
Memphis Noph et Migdo
Bubalis et Cairo
Traianus fl
Acanthon
HERACLEOPLITAS
Aphroditopolis
Amari lacus
Arsinoe
Iuliopolis Insula
Angirorum ciuitas
Ptolemeus flu
Pharmuticus flu
Bonus genius flu
Busiriticus fluu
Athribiticus flu
Delta

MARE SYRIUM
Beritus
Leontopolis
Lycus flu.
TRIPOLIS regio
Libanus
Sidon
Sarepta
Cana maior
Auium
Tyrus
Zor. Tyrus antiqua
Ecduppa
Album promont.
SYROPHOENICIA
HEVEI
Chammat
Sedad
Salcha
Gabala
Amorei
Antilibanus
Maghedon
Sandalium
Achzib
Ptolomais
Acon
ASER
Cesaria Philippi
Basan Regio
ITURALA
Damascus
Naphtalis
NAPTALIM
Carmelum promo.
Magdiel
Dora
Megiddo
Caesarea
Michmetat
Cana mont
Nazaret
Tabor mont.
INFERIOR
Ribba
Hanaton
Gaulon
Seleucia
SAMACHONITET LACUS
Rimmon
Capernaum
Betsaida
Magdala
Naim
Sunem
Taanach
Galboa mont
Gazer
Sichem
Tiberias
Tarichee
Ennon
Horozaim
Astarot
Argat
Iulias
Ephron
Iabis
Philadelphia
Pella
Neue
Capitolias
Aere
COELE
SAMARIA
Salem
Arom
Geba
Remmon
Naorata
Betehoro
Galgulis
Antipatris
EPHRAIM
IOSEPH
Iordanus fl.
Peuel
Labox flu.
Laazertes
AMMONITARUM regio uel PHILADELPHIA
RUBEN
SYRIAE PARS
Diospolis Lidda
Ioppe
Azotus
Modin
Rama
Luza
Gibon
Aialon
Eleutheros
BENIAMIN
HIERUSALEM
Ierus
Bosor
Aroer
Arnen
Nathahel
Telemannu
Ebron
Machanaim
Lachis
Iebusei
Herodium
Engedi
Medaba
Abarim
DELPHIA
Hippus mons
IUDA
AMOREI
IUDAEA
SIMEI
EDOM
Segor
Gemela regio
Akraboim
Abarim montes
LACUS ASPHALTITES
MARE MORTUUM aut SALSUM
40 Almonidiblathaim
MOABITARUM
Seir montes
Cades barnea
Lucit
Disabad
Cacachrysea
Theman
Idumea
Dedan
Dodanim
Colchiel
Zered flu.
39 Dibon Gad
REGIO
38 Leabarim
ARABIAE DESERTAE PARS
Meseroth
Gebalene regio
BIA
TREA
ZIN uel CADES
37 Oboth
36 Phunon
Petra Sela
Arachen
Recem
Arabia
Nabathea
Nabath
35 Sal mons
Gidgad mons
DESERTUM
34 Hor mons
SEPTENT.
OCCID.
ORIE
MERID
Satebatha
Maria
33 Zin uel Cades desertum
Ebrona
Aziongaber
NEHTALI
ASER
DAN
IUDAS
EPHRAIM
MERARITAE
ISACHAR
GERSONITAE
TABERNACULUM
MOSES
ARON
MANASSE
ZEBULON
CHAATITAE
BENIAMIN
GAD
SIMEON
IUDAS
Michele van lochom graueur du Roy

ויוציאנו
יי ממצרים ביד
חזקה ובזרוע נט

אֱלֹהִים אֶת־נַאֲקָתָם וַיִּזְכֹּר אֱלֹהִים אֶת־בְּרִיתוֹ אֶת־אַבְרָהָם אֶת־
יִצְחָק וְאֶת־יַעֲקֹב: וַיַּרְא אֶת־עָנְיֵנוּ. זוֹ פְּרִישׁוּת דֶּרֶךְ אֶרֶץ. כְּמָה שֶׁנֶּאֱמַר
וַיַּרְא אֱלֹהִים אֶת־בְּנֵי יִשְׂרָאֵל וַיֵּדַע אֱלֹהִים: וְאֶת־עֲמָלֵנוּ. אֵלּוּ הַבָּנִים.
כְּמָה שֶׁנֶּאֱמַר כָּל־הַבֵּן הַיִּלּוֹד הַיְאֹרָה תַּשְׁלִיכֻהוּ וְכָל־הַבַּת תְּחַיּוּן:
וְאֶת־לַחֲצֵנוּ. זֶה הַדְּחַק. כְּמָה שֶׁנֶּאֱמַר וְגַם־רָאִיתִי אֶת־הַלַּחַץ אֲשֶׁר
מִצְרַיִם לֹחֲצִים אֹתָם:

'We cried'—as in the verse: 'And the children of Israel sighed by reason of their bondage'; 'he heard our voice', remembering 'his covenant with Abraham, Isaac and Jacob'; 'our affliction'—this was the breaking up of family life, an explanation of the verse: 'and God looked upon the children of Israel and God had respect for them' (*Exodus* II, 25); 'our labour'—meaning our children, of whom Pharaoh said: 'every son that is born ye shall cast into the Nile, and every daughter ye shall save alive'; 'our oppression'—as in the verse: 'I have seen the oppression, wherewith the Egyptians oppress them' (*Exodus* III, 9).

'With Signs and Wonders...'

וַיּוֹצִאֵנוּ יְיָ מִמִּצְרַיִם בְּיָד חֲזָקָה וּבִזְרֹעַ נְטוּיָה וּבְמֹרָא גָּדֹל
וּבְאֹתוֹת וּבְמֹפְתִים:

AND THE LORD BROUGHT US OUT OF EGYPT WITH A MIGHTY HAND AND OUTSTRETCHED ARM, WITH GREAT TERROR, AND WITH SIGNS AND WONDERS (*Deuteronomy* XXVI, 8).

וַיּוֹצִאֵנוּ יְיָ מִמִּצְרַיִם. לֹא עַל יְדֵי מַלְאָךְ. וְלֹא עַל יְדֵי שָׂרָף. וְלֹא עַל יְדֵי
שָׁלִיחַ. אֶלָּא הַקָּדוֹשׁ בָּרוּךְ הוּא בִּכְבוֹדוֹ וּבְעַצְמוֹ. שֶׁנֶּאֱמַר וְעָבַרְתִּי
בְאֶרֶץ מִצְרַיִם בַּלַּיְלָה הַזֶּה וְהִכֵּיתִי כָל־בְּכוֹר בְּאֶרֶץ מִצְרַיִם מֵאָדָם
וְעַד־בְּהֵמָה וּבְכָל־אֱלֹהֵי מִצְרַיִם אֶעֱשֶׂה שְׁפָטִים אֲנִי יְיָ:

וְעָבַרְתִּי בְאֶרֶץ־מִצְרַיִם. אֲנִי וְלֹא מַלְאָךְ. וְהִכֵּיתִי כָל־בְּכוֹר בְּאֶרֶץ
מִצְרַיִם. אֲנִי וְלֹא שָׂרָף. וּבְכָל־אֱלֹהֵי מִצְרַיִם אֶעֱשֶׂה שְׁפָטִים. אֲנִי וְלֹא
הַשָּׁלִיחַ. אֲנִי יְיָ. אֲנִי הוּא וְלֹא אַחֵר:

opposite 'And He brought us forth', a page from the Sassoon Haggadah (Franco-Spanish, 14th century). The arms of the liberated Jews are raised as if to reflect the familiar phrase '*bizroa netuyah*' ('with outstretched arms').
overleaf A map engraved by Michael Lochom (Paris, 1641) showing the route of the Israelites through the desert to the Promised Land

'He went down to Egypt'—impelled by Divine decree; 'And sojourned there'—not to settle permanently; 'Few in number'—not more than 'three score and ten'; 'great, mighty and populous'—as in the verse: 'I caused thee to multiply as the bud of the field . . .' (*Ezekiel* XVI, 7).

Hard Bondage…

וַיָּרֵעוּ אֹתָנוּ הַמִּצְרִים וַיְעַנּוּנוּ וַיִּתְּנוּ עָלֵינוּ עֲבֹדָה קָשָׁה:

AND THE EGYPTIANS ILL-TREATED, HUMILIATED AND IMPOSED HARD BONDAGE UPON US (*Deuteronomy* XXVI, 6).

וַיָּרֵעוּ אֹתָנוּ הַמִּצְרִים. כְּמָה שֶׁנֶּאֱמַר הָבָה נִתְחַכְּמָה לוֹ פֶּן־יִרְבֶּה וְהָיָה כִּי־תִקְרֶאנָה מִלְחָמָה וְנוֹסַף גַּם־הוּא עַל שֹׂנְאֵינוּ וְנִלְחַם־בָּנוּ וְעָלָה מִן־הָאָרֶץ: **וַיְעַנּוּנוּ.** כְּמָה שֶׁנֶּאֱמַר וַיָּשִׂימוּ עָלָיו שָׂרֵי מִסִּים לְמַעַן עַנֹּתוֹ בְּסִבְלֹתָם וַיִּבֶן עָרֵי מִסְכְּנוֹת לְפַרְעֹה אֶת־פִּתֹם וְאֶת־רַעַמְסֵס: **וַיִּתְּנוּ עָלֵינוּ עֲבֹדָה קָשָׁה.** כְּמָה שֶׁנֶּאֱמַר וַיַּעֲבִדוּ מִצְרַיִם אֶת בְּנֵי יִשְׂרָאֵל בְּפָרֶךְ:

'Ill-treated us', as it is said: 'Let us deal cleverly with them, lest they multiply . . . and join our enemies'; 'afflicted us'—with task-masters, to build Pithom and Raamses; 'hard bondage'—enslaving the children of Israel 'with rigour' *(Exodus* I, 13*)*.

'He Heard Our Voice…'

וַנִּצְעַק אֶל־יְיָ אֱלֹהֵי אֲבֹתֵינוּ וַיִּשְׁמַע יְיָ אֶת־קֹלֵנוּ וַיַּרְא אֶת־עָנְיֵנוּ וְאֶת־עֲמָלֵנוּ וְאֶת־לַחֲצֵנוּ:

AND WE CRIED UNTO THE LORD, THE GOD OF OUR FATHERS, AND THE LORD HEARD OUR VOICE, AND SAW OUR AFFLICTION AND OUR LABOUR AND OUR OPPRESSION (*Deuteronomy* XXVI, 7).

וַנִּצְעַק אֶל יְיָ אֱלֹהֵי אֲבֹתֵינוּ. כְּמָה שֶׁנֶּאֱמַר וַיְהִי בַיָּמִים הָרַבִּים הָהֵם וַיָּמָת מֶלֶךְ מִצְרַיִם וַיֵּאָנְחוּ בְנֵי־יִשְׂרָאֵל מִן־הָעֲבֹדָה וַיִּזְעָקוּ וַתַּעַל שַׁוְעָתָם אֶל־הָאֱלֹהִים מִן־הָעֲבֹדָה: **וַיִּשְׁמַע יְיָ אֶת־קֹלֵנוּ.** כְּמָה שֶׁנֶּאֱמַר וַיִּשְׁמַע

opposite The building of Pithom and Raamses from the Barcelona Haggadah (14th century)

כמה שנאמר וישימו עליו
שרי מסים למען ענתו
בסבלתם ויבן ערי מסכנות
לפרעה את פיתום ואת
רעמסס

ויתנו

The Miracles Spelt Out…

(*A homily on Deuteronomy XXVI*, 5–8. *The translation is shortened, until we come to the Plagues.*)

צֵא וּלְמַד מַה בִּקֵּשׁ לָבָן הָאֲרַמִּי לַעֲשׂוֹת לְיַעֲקֹב אָבִינוּ. שֶׁפַּרְעֹה לֹא גָזַר אֶלָּא עַל הַזְּכָרִים וְלָבָן בִּקֵּשׁ לַעֲקוֹר אֶת־הַכֹּל. שֶׁנֶּאֱמַר

אֲרַמִּי אֹבֵד אָבִי וַיֵּרֶד מִצְרַיְמָה וַיָּגָר שָׁם בִּמְתֵי מְעָט וַיְהִי־שָׁם לְגוֹי גָּדוֹל עָצוּם וָרָב:

Look what Laban the Syrian tried to do to our father Jacob! Pharaoh issued a decree only against the males, but Laban tried to uproot all! (*The verse 'A wandering Syrian was my father' can be read: 'A Syrian would have destroyed my father.')* Here, then, is the Bible verse to be expounded:

A SYRIAN WOULD HAVE DESTROYED MY FATHER: HE WENT DOWN TO EGYPT AND SOJOURNED THERE, FEW IN NUMBER; AND HE BECAME THERE A GREAT, MIGHTY AND POPULOUS NATION (*Deuteronomy* XXVI, 5):

וַיֵּרֶד מִצְרַיְמָה. אָנוּס עַל־פִּי הַדִּבּוּר: **וַיָּגָר שָׁם.** מְלַמֵּד שֶׁלֹּא יָרַד יַעֲקֹב אָבִינוּ לְהִשְׁתַּקֵּעַ בְּמִצְרַיִם אֶלָּא לָגוּר שָׁם. שֶׁנֶּאֱמַר וַיֹּאמְרוּ אֶל פַּרְעֹה לָגוּר בָּאָרֶץ בָּאנוּ כִּי אֵין מִרְעֶה לַצֹּאן אֲשֶׁר לַעֲבָדֶיךָ כִּי כָבֵד הָרָעָב בְּאֶרֶץ כְּנָעַן וְעַתָּה יֵשְׁבוּ נָא עֲבָדֶיךָ בְּאֶרֶץ גֹּשֶׁן: **בִּמְתֵי מְעָט.** כְּמָה שֶׁנֶּאֱמַר בְּשִׁבְעִים נֶפֶשׁ יָרְדוּ אֲבֹתֶיךָ מִצְרָיְמָה וְעַתָּה שָׂמְךָ יְיָ אֱלֹהֶיךָ כְּכוֹכְבֵי הַשָּׁמַיִם לָרֹב: **וַיְהִי שָׁם לְגוֹי.** מְלַמֵּד שֶׁהָיוּ יִשְׂרָאֵל מְצֻיָּנִים שָׁם: **גָּדוֹל עָצוּם.** כְּמָה שֶׁנֶּאֱמַר וּבְנֵי יִשְׂרָאֵל פָּרוּ וַיִּשְׁרְצוּ וַיִּרְבּוּ וַיַּעַצְמוּ בִּמְאֹד מְאֹד וַתִּמָּלֵא הָאָרֶץ אֹתָם: **וָרָב.** כְּמָה שֶׁנֶּאֱמַר רְבָבָה כְּצֶמַח הַשָּׂדֶה נְתַתִּיךְ וַתִּרְבִּי וַתִּגְדְּלִי וַתָּבֹאִי בַּעֲדִי עֲדָיִים שָׁדַיִם נָכֹנוּ וּשְׂעָרֵךְ צִמֵּחַ וְאַתְּ עֵרֹם וְעֶרְיָה:

opposite A 16th-century enamelled casket from Limoges showing scenes from the Israelites' descent into Egypt. On the lid, Joseph and his brothers; on the side, Joseph escaping from Potiphar's wife

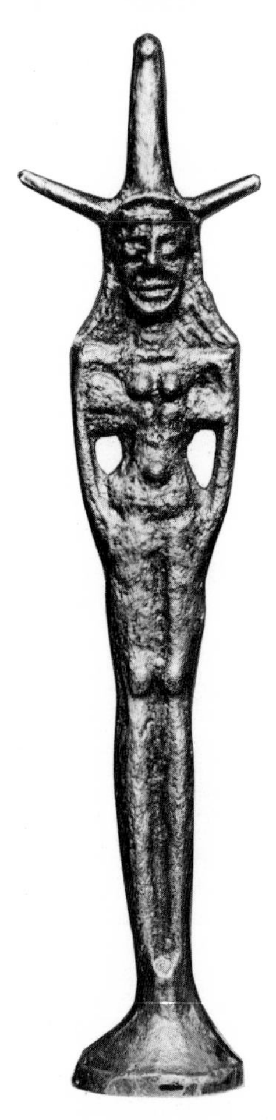

Bronze-horned Astarte figurine cast from a stone mould found in a high place in Naharia

IN THE BEGINNING, OUR ANCESTORS WERE IDOLATORS, BUT THE ALMIGHTY HAS BROUGHT US TO HIS WORSHIP. The story is in the Bible (*Joshua* XXIV, 2–4): 'And Joshua said unto all the people, thus saith the Lord, God of Israel. Your ancestors dwelt on the other side of the river—Terah, father of Abraham and Nahor—and they worshipped other gods. I took your father from the other side of the river, and settled him in the whole land of Canaan, built up his family, and gave him Isaac. To Isaac, I gave Jacob and Esau, who has Mount Seir as an inheritance.
BUT JACOB AND HIS CHILDREN WENT DOWN TO EGYPT.

The Promise Kept…

בָּרוּךְ שׁוֹמֵר הַבְטָחָתוֹ לְיִשְׂרָאֵל בָּרוּךְ הוּא.

שֶׁהַקָּדוֹשׁ בָּרוּךְ הוּא חִשֵּׁב אֶת הַקֵּץ לַעֲשׂוֹת כְּמָה שֶׁאָמַר לְאַבְרָהָם אָבִינוּ בִּבְרִית בֵּין הַבְּתָרִים שֶׁנֶּאֱמַר וַיֹּאמֶר לְאַבְרָם יָדֹעַ תֵּדַע כִּי גֵר יִהְיֶה זַרְעֲךָ בְּאֶרֶץ לֹא לָהֶם וַעֲבָדוּם וְעִנּוּ אֹתָם אַרְבַּע מֵאוֹת שָׁנָה: וְגַם אֶת הַגּוֹי אֲשֶׁר יַעֲבֹדוּ דָּן אָנֹכִי

וְאַחֲרֵי כֵן יֵצְאוּ בִּרְכֻשׁ גָּדוֹל.

BLESSED BE GOD WHO HAS KEPT HIS PROMISE TO ISRAEL. He looked ahead to the end of bondage when he said to Abraham: 'Thy seed will be strangers in a strange land, and will be afflicted for four hundred years. But I will judge the nation to whom they are enslaved:
AND THEY WILL COME OUT WITH GREAT SUBSTANCE' (*Genesis* XV, 13–14).

The cups are raised

וְהִיא שֶׁעָמְדָה לַאֲבוֹתֵינוּ וְלָנוּ. שֶׁלֹּא אֶחָד בִּלְבַד עָמַד עָלֵינוּ לְכַלּוֹתֵנוּ אֶלָּא שֶׁבְּכָל דּוֹר וָדוֹר עוֹמְדִים עָלֵינוּ לְכַלּוֹתֵנוּ. וְהַקָּדוֹשׁ בָּרוּךְ הוּא מַצִּילֵנוּ מִיָּדָם:

It is this promise which has supported our fathers and us. For it was not one man who rose against us to destroy us: in every generation there are those who seek to destroy us. But God saves us from their hands.

The intelligent one quotes the Bible to ask: 'What are the duties and statutes and principles commanded by God?' (*Deuteronomy* VI, 20). In reply you can instruct him in the detailed laws of the Passover (*as set out in the Mishnah, which ends with:*) 'After the Passover meal, one must not disperse for revelry.'

The wicked one quotes the verse: 'What mean you by this service?' (*Exodus* XII, 26). He stresses *you*, and not *him;* and because he excludes himself and thus denies God, you can reply with another verse (*Exodus* XIII, 8) to set his teeth on edge: 'It is because of what God did for me when I came out of Egypt.' For *me*, and not for *him*. If *he* had been there, he wouldn't have been redeemed.

The simple one quotes: 'What is all this?' (*Exodus* XIII, 14). You can answer him with the same verse: 'By strength of hand, God brought us out of Egypt, from the house of bondage.'

For the one who doesn't know how to ask, you must open up yourself, as it says (*Exodus* XIII, 8): 'And thou shalt tell thy son that day, saying "It is because of what God did for me when I came out of Egypt."'

יָכוֹל מֵרֹאשׁ חֹדֶשׁ. תַּלְמוּד לוֹמַר בַּיּוֹם הַהוּא. אִי בַּיּוֹם הַהוּא יָכוֹל מִבְּעוֹד יוֹם. תַּלְמוּד לוֹמַר בַּעֲבוּר זֶה. בַּעֲבוּר זֶה לֹא אָמַרְתִּי אֶלָּא בְּשָׁעָה שֶׁיֵּשׁ מַצָּה וּמָרוֹר מֻנָּחִים לְפָנֶיךָ:

On '*that day*': not, therefore, at the beginning of the month. What time of day? At evening, when *matzah* and bitter herbs are laid before us.

The Breakthrough from Idolatry

מִתְּחִלָּה עוֹבְדֵי עֲבוֹדָה זָרָה הָיוּ אֲבוֹתֵינוּ וְעַכְשָׁו קֵרְבָנוּ הַמָּקוֹם לַעֲבוֹדָתוֹ.

שֶׁנֶּאֱמַר: וַיֹּאמֶר יְהוֹשֻׁעַ אֶל־כָּל־הָעָם כֹּה־אָמַר יְיָ אֱלֹהֵי יִשְׂרָאֵל בְּעֵבֶר הַנָּהָר יָשְׁבוּ אֲבוֹתֵיכֶם מֵעוֹלָם תֶּרַח אֲבִי אַבְרָהָם וַאֲבִי נָחוֹר וַיַּעַבְדוּ אֱלֹהִים אֲחֵרִים: וָאֶקַּח אֶת־אֲבִיכֶם אֶת־אַבְרָהָם מֵעֵבֶר הַנָּהָר וָאוֹלֵךְ אוֹתוֹ בְּכָל־אֶרֶץ כְּנָעַן וָאַרְבֶּה אֶת־זַרְעוֹ וָאֶתֶּן־לוֹ אֶת־יִצְחָק: וָאֶתֵּן לְיִצְחָק אֶת־יַעֲקֹב וְאֶת־עֵשָׂו וָאֶתֵּן לְעֵשָׂו אֶת־הַר שֵׂעִיר לָרֶשֶׁת אוֹתוֹ **וְיַעֲקֹב וּבָנָיו יָרְדוּ מִצְרָיִם:**

כֹּל יְמֵי חַיֶּיךָ הַלֵּילוֹת. וַחֲכָמִים אוֹמְרִים. יְמֵי חַיֶּיךָ הָעוֹלָם הַזֶּה. כֹּל יְמֵי חַיֶּיךָ לְהָבִיא לִימוֹת הַמָּשִׁיחַ:

Rabbi Elazar ben Azariah said: 'I'm a man of seventy, but I could never find a scriptural authority for the need to talk about the Exodus *at night* until Ben Zoma drew it from the verse: "That thou mayest remember the day when thou camest forth out of the land of Egypt all the days of thy life" (*Deuteronomy* XVI, 3). If it had said: *the days of thy life*, it would have meant "the days" only; but *all the days of thy life* must indicate the nights as well. Other scholars say: *the days of thy life means:* "in *this* world", all *the days of thy life* must include the times of the Messiah.'

בָּרוּךְ הַמָּקוֹם בָּרוּךְ הוּא בָּרוּךְ שֶׁנָּתַן תּוֹרָה לְעַמּוֹ יִשְׂרָאֵל בָּרוּךְ הוּא:

BLESSED BE THE ALMIGHTY THAT HE GAVE THE TORAH TO HIS PEOPLE ISRAEL.

The Four Sons

כְּנֶגֶד אַרְבָּעָה בָנִים דִּבְּרָה תוֹרָה.

אֶחָד חָכָם. וְאֶחָד רָשָׁע. וְאֶחָד תָּם.

וְאֶחָד שֶׁאֵינוֹ יוֹדֵעַ לִשְׁאוֹל:

חָכָם מַה הוּא אוֹמֵר מָה הָעֵדֹת וְהַחֻקִּים וְהַמִּשְׁפָּטִים אֲשֶׁר צִוָּה יְיָ אֱלֹהֵינוּ אוֹתָנוּ: וְאַף אַתָּה אֱמָר־לוֹ כְּהִלְכוֹת הַפֶּסַח אֵין מַפְטִירִין אַחַר הַפֶּסַח אֲפִיקוֹמָן: **רָשָׁע** מַה הוּא אוֹמֵר מָה הָעֲבֹדָה הַזֹּאת לָכֶם: לָכֶם וְלֹא לוֹ. וּלְפִי שֶׁהוֹצִיא אֶת־עַצְמוֹ מִן הַכְּלָל וְכָפַר בָּעִקָּר. אַף אַתָּה הַקְהֵה אֶת שִׁנָּיו וֶאֱמָר־לוֹ בַּעֲבוּר זֶה עָשָׂה יְיָ לִי בְּצֵאתִי מִמִּצְרָיִם. לִי וְלֹא לוֹ. אִלּוּ הָיָה שָׁם לֹא הָיָה נִגְאָל: **תָּם** מַה הוּא אוֹמֵר מַה זֹּאת. וְאָמַרְתָּ אֵלָיו בְּחֹזֶק יָד הוֹצִיאָנוּ יְיָ מִמִּצְרַיִם מִבֵּית עֲבָדִים: **וְשֶׁאֵינוֹ יוֹדֵעַ לִשְׁאוֹל** אַתְּ פְּתַח לוֹ. שֶׁנֶּאֱמַר וְהִגַּדְתָּ לְבִנְךָ בַּיּוֹם הַהוּא לֵאמֹר בַּעֲבוּר זֶה עָשָׂה יְיָ לִי בְּצֵאתִי מִמִּצְרָיִם:

THE LANGUAGE OF THE TORAH CAN BE DRAWN ON TO DEAL WITH FOUR TYPES OF CHILDREN—AN INTELLIGENT ONE, A WICKED ONE, A SIMPLE ONE AND ONE STILL TOO YOUNG TO ASK QUESTIONS.

opposite Ancient Egyptian tools—hoe, rake, mallet, chisel and plumbline—used in construction work

below The Four Sons, a detail from an 18th-century pewter Seder plate from Germany

אפילו פעם אחת והלילה הזה שתי פעמים
שבכל הלילות אנו אוכלין חמץ או מצה
והלילה הזה כלו מצה שבכל הלילות אנו
אוכלין שאר ירקות והלילה הזה מרור
שבכל הלילות אנו אוכלין בין יושבין בין
מסובין והלילה הזה כלנו מסובין

עבדים היינו לפרעה במצרים
ויוציאנו ײ אלהינו משם
ביד חזקה ובזרוע נטויה שאלו לא הוציא
הקב״ה את אבותינו ממצרים הרי אנו בנינו
ובני בנינו משועבדים היינו לפרעה
במצרים: ואפילו כלנו חכמים כלנו
נבונים כלנו זקנים כלנו יודעים את התורה
מצוה עלינו לספר ביציאת מצרים שכל
המספר ביציאת מצרים הרי זה משובח

מעשה ברבי אליעזר ורבי יהושע
ורבי אלעזר בן עזריה

(The answer begins)

'We Were Slaves...' עֲבָדִים הָיִינוּ

לְפַרְעֹה בְּמִצְרָיִם וַיּוֹצִיאֵנוּ יְיָ אֱלֹהֵינוּ מִשָּׁם בְּיָד חֲזָקָה וּבִזְרוֹעַ נְטוּיָה. וְאִלּוּ לֹא הוֹצִיא הַקָּדוֹשׁ בָּרוּךְ הוּא אֶת אֲבוֹתֵינוּ מִמִּצְרַיִם הֲרֵי עֲדַיִן אָנוּ וּבָנֵינוּ וּבְנֵי בָנֵינוּ מְשֻׁעְבָּדִים הָיִינוּ לְפַרְעֹה בְּמִצְרָיִם. וַאֲפִלּוּ כֻּלָּנוּ חֲכָמִים כֻּלָּנוּ נְבוֹנִים כֻּלָּנוּ זְקֵנִים כֻּלָּנוּ יוֹדְעִים אֶת הַתּוֹרָה. מִצְוָה עָלֵינוּ לְסַפֵּר בִּיצִיאַת מִצְרָיִם. וְכָל הַמַּרְבֶּה לְסַפֵּר בִּיצִיאַת מִצְרַיִם הֲרֵי זֶה מְשֻׁבָּח:

OUR ANCESTORS WERE SLAVES TO PHARAOH IN EGYPT but God brought us out from there 'with a strong hand and an outstretched arm'. If the Holy One, Blessed be He, had not brought our ancestors out of Egypt, we, and our children, and our children's children would still be slaves to Pharaoh in Egypt.

So even if we were all wise and clever and old and learned in the Torah, it would still be our duty to tell the story of the Exodus from Egypt. The more one talks about the Exodus, the more praiseworthy it is.

'The More One Talks...'

מַעֲשֶׂה בְּרַבִּי אֱלִיעֶזֶר וְרַבִּי יְהוֹשֻׁעַ וְרַבִּי אֶלְעָזָר בֶּן עֲזַרְיָה וְרַבִּי עֲקִיבָא וְרַבִּי טַרְפוֹן שֶׁהָיוּ מְסֻבִּין בִּבְנֵי בְרַק וְהָיוּ מְסַפְּרִים בִּיצִיאַת מִצְרַיִם כָּל אוֹתוֹ הַלַּיְלָה עַד שֶׁבָּאוּ תַלְמִידֵיהֶם וְאָמְרוּ לָהֶם רַבּוֹתֵינוּ הִגִּיעַ זְמַן קְרִיאַת שְׁמַע שֶׁל שַׁחֲרִית:

The story is told that a number of rabbis were holding a Seder at B'nei B'rak—Rabbi Eliezer, Rabbi Joshua, Rabbi Elazar ben Azariah, Rabbi Akiva and Rabbi Tarfon—and went on talking about the Exodus all night, until their pupils arrived and said: 'Masters! It is time for the Morning Service.'

אָמַר רַבִּי אֶלְעָזָר בֶּן עֲזַרְיָה. הֲרֵי אֲנִי כְּבֶן שִׁבְעִים שָׁנָה. וְלֹא זָכִיתִי שֶׁתֵּאָמֵר יְצִיאַת מִצְרַיִם בַּלֵּילוֹת עַד שֶׁדְּרָשָׁהּ בֶּן זוֹמָא. שֶׁנֶּאֱמַר: לְמַעַן תִּזְכֹּר אֶת יוֹם צֵאתְךָ מֵאֶרֶץ מִצְרַיִם כֹּל יְמֵי חַיֶּיךָ. יְמֵי חַיֶּיךָ הַיָּמִים.

opposite 'We were slaves . . .' from the Ferrara Haggadah (northern Italy, 1515). The wine stains evoke the feeling of repeated use

The Four Questions

The youngest child present now asks:

מַה נִּשְׁתַּנָּה הַלַּיְלָה הַזֶּה מִכָּל־הַלֵּילוֹת.

1 שֶׁבְּכָל־הַלֵּילוֹת אָנוּ אוֹכְלִין חָמֵץ וּמַצָּה. הַלַּיְלָה הַזֶּה
כֻּלּוֹ מַצָּה:

2 שֶׁבְּכָל־הַלֵּילוֹת אָנוּ אוֹכְלִין שְׁאָר יְרָקוֹת. הַלַּיְלָה הַזֶּה
מָרוֹר:

3 שֶׁבְּכָל־הַלֵּילוֹת אֵין אָנוּ מַטְבִּילִין אֲפִילוּ פַּעַם אֶחָת.
הַלַּיְלָה הַזֶּה שְׁתֵּי פְעָמִים:

4 שֶׁבְּכָל־הַלֵּילוֹת אָנוּ אוֹכְלִין בֵּין יוֹשְׁבִין וּבֵין מְסֻבִּין.
הַלַּיְלָה הַזֶּה כֻּלָּנוּ מְסֻבִּין:

WHY IS THIS NIGHT DIFFERENT FROM ALL OTHER NIGHTS?

1 ON ALL OTHER NIGHTS, WE CAN EAT BREAD OR *MATZAH*: WHY, TONIGHT, ONLY *MATZAH*?

2 ON ALL OTHER NIGHTS, WE CAN EAT ANY KIND OF HERBS: WHY, TONIGHT, BITTER HERBS?

3 ON ALL OTHER NIGHTS, WE DON'T DIP THE HERBS WE EAT INTO ANYTHING: WHY, TONIGHT, DO WE DIP TWICE (*First into salt-water, and then into* Haroset)?

4 ON ALL OTHER NIGHTS, WE CAN EAT EITHER SITTING UP STRAIGHT OR RECLINING: WHY, TONIGHT, DO WE ALL RECLINE?

(*A note for the pedantic. The translation 'Why is this night different . . .' is a mistranslation!* Ma nishtana *really means: 'How different this night is . . .' The meal has already begun, and the child is expressing his surprise. But at this stage in history, with so many built-in echoes, we should let it stand: 'Why is this night different?'*)

opposite A scene paralleled throughout the world: a child asking the Four Questions

Preparing for the Afikoman

יַחַץ

The middle matzah *of the three is broken in two, and half is put away for the* afikoman. *(The* afikoman *will reappear later on page 57. The word is Greek,* epikomion, *meaning 'a festival procession'. It came to have a variety of other meanings in Talmud times, including the one here—'dessert' or 'savoury' after the meal.)*
The custom now is for the children to 'steal' the afikoman *at some point, and surrender it only in return for a present.*

'Let All Who Are Hungry…'

מַגִּיד

(This section—'The Story'—will be introduced by the Four Questions, on page 27. But first, an invitation—to all. It is written in Aramaic, the vernacular of the times, so that everyone present could understand it and join in.)
The matzahs *are uncovered, the Seder plate is lifted, and all say:*

הָא לַחְמָא עַנְיָא דִּי אֲכַלוּ אַבְהָתַנָא בְּאַרְעָא דְמִצְרָיִם. כָּל
דִּכְפִין יֵיתֵי וְיֵכֹל. כָּל דִּצְרִיךְ יֵיתֵי וְיִפְסַח. הָשַׁתָּא הָכָא.
לְשָׁנָה הַבָּאָה בְּאַרְעָא דְיִשְׂרָאֵל. הָשַׁתָּא עַבְדֵי. לְשָׁנָה
הַבָּאָה בְּנֵי חוֹרִין:

THIS IS THE BREAD OF AFFLICTION WHICH OUR ANCESTORS ATE IN THE LAND OF EGYPT. LET ALL WHO ARE HUNGRY COME AND EAT. LET ALL WHO ARE IN NEED COME AND CELEBRATE PASSOVER. THIS YEAR WE ARE HERE: NEXT YEAR, IN THE LAND OF ISRAEL! THIS YEAR WE ARE SLAVES: NEXT YEAR, FREE MEN!

The Seder plate is put down, the matzahs *are covered, and the second cup is filled.*

opposite An early 19th-century combined Seder dish and holder from Austria for the three ritual rounds of *matzah opposite* For the First Cup, a late 17th-century silver goblet from Germany showing 'the Wise Son' (all Four Sons are shown on page 91)

On Saturday nights, the following is added:

בָּרוּךְ אַתָּה יְיָ אֱלֹהֵינוּ מֶלֶךְ הָעוֹלָם בּוֹרֵא מְאוֹרֵי הָאֵשׁ: בָּרוּךְ אַתָּה
יְיָ אֱלֹהֵינוּ מֶלֶךְ הָעוֹלָם הַמַּבְדִּיל בֵּין קֹדֶשׁ לְחוֹל בֵּין אוֹר לְחֹשֶׁךְ בֵּין
יִשְׂרָאֵל לָעַמִּים. בֵּין יוֹם הַשְּׁבִיעִי לְשֵׁשֶׁת יְמֵי הַמַּעֲשֶׂה. בֵּין קְדֻשַּׁת
שַׁבָּת לִקְדֻשַּׁת יוֹם טוֹב הִבְדַּלְתָּ. וְאֶת יוֹם הַשְּׁבִיעִי מִשֵּׁשֶׁת יְמֵי הַמַּעֲשֶׂה
קִדַּשְׁתָּ. הִבְדַּלְתָּ וְקִדַּשְׁתָּ אֶת עַמְּךָ יִשְׂרָאֵל בִּקְדֻשָּׁתֶךָ. בָּרוּךְ אַתָּה
יְיָ הַמַּבְדִּיל בֵּין קֹדֶשׁ לְקֹדֶשׁ:

Blessed is God who creates the light of fire. Blessed is God who has let us see the line between sacred and profane—between light and darkness. He set the holiness of Sabbath apart from the six days of work. He set the people of Israel apart for holiness. Blessings to God who showed us the nature of holiness.

She'heheyanu!

בָּרוּךְ אַתָּה יְיָ אֱלֹהֵינוּ מֶלֶךְ הָעוֹלָם שֶׁהֶחֱיָנוּ וְקִיְּמָנוּ וְהִגִּיעָנוּ
לַזְּמַן הַזֶּה:

THANKS BE TO GOD WHO KEPT US ALIVE AND SUSTAINED US AND BROUGHT US TO THIS MOMENT.

We drink the first cup of wine

The host washes his hands in preparation for the eating of Karpas *(a plant such as celery or parsley), but without a blessing.*

The procedure is for everyone present to be given a piece of the vegetable, which is dipped into salt-water and munched, in the spirit of an hors d'oeuvres. *(Originally the meal followed immediately. But first there is a blessing.)*

בָּרוּךְ אַתָּה יְיָ אֱלֹהֵינוּ מֶלֶךְ הָעוֹלָם בּוֹרֵא פְּרִי הָאֲדָמָה.

Blessed is our Lord, God, King of the Universe, who creates the fruit of the soil.

מועדים לשמחה
שבעת ימים תאכל מצות
מצה
מצות
זרוע
ביצה
מרור
חרוסת
כרפס
חזרת
חגים וזמנים לששון

קַדֵּשׁ
Sanctification

When the first night of Passover is Friday evening, the blessing on wine starts with the following:

וַיְהִי־עֶרֶב וַיְהִי־בֹקֶר יוֹם הַשִּׁשִּׁי וַיְכֻלּוּ הַשָּׁמַיִם וְהָאָרֶץ וְכָל־צְבָאָם׃
וַיְכַל אֱלֹהִים בַּיּוֹם הַשְּׁבִיעִי מְלַאכְתּוֹ אֲשֶׁר עָשָׂה וַיִּשְׁבֹּת בַּיּוֹם הַשְּׁבִיעִי
מִכָּל־מְלַאכְתּוֹ אֲשֶׁר עָשָׂה׃ וַיְבָרֶךְ אֱלֹהִים אֶת־יוֹם הַשְּׁבִיעִי וַיְקַדֵּשׁ
אֹתוֹ כִּי בוֹ שָׁבַת מִכָּל מְלַאכְתּוֹ אֲשֶׁר־בָּרָא אֱלֹהִים לַעֲשׂוֹת׃

'And the evening and the morning were the sixth day. Thus the heavens and the earth were finished, and all the host of them. And on the seventh day God ended his work which he had made; and he rested on the seventh day from all his work which he had made. And God blessed the seventh day and sanctified it: because that in it he had rested from all his work which God created and made' (*Genesis* I, 31; II, 1–3).

בָּרוּךְ אַתָּה יְיָ אֱלֹהֵינוּ מֶלֶךְ הָעוֹלָם בּוֹרֵא פְּרִי הַגָּפֶן׃

BLESSED IS OUR LORD, GOD, KING OF THE UNIVERSE, WHO CREATES THE FRUIT OF THE VINE.

The words in brackets are added on Friday evenings.

בָּרוּךְ אַתָּה יְיָ אֱלֹהֵינוּ מֶלֶךְ הָעוֹלָם אֲשֶׁר בָּחַר בָּנוּ מִכָּל עָם וְרוֹמְמָנוּ
מִכָּל לָשׁוֹן וְקִדְּשָׁנוּ בְּמִצְוֹתָיו. וַתִּתֶּן לָנוּ יְיָ אֱלֹהֵינוּ בְּאַהֲבָה (שַׁבָּתוֹת
לִמְנוּחָה וּ) מוֹעֲדִים לְשִׂמְחָה חַגִּים וּזְמַנִּים לְשָׂשׂוֹן. אֶת־יוֹם (הַשַּׁבָּת
הַזֶּה וְאֶת יוֹם) חַג הַמַּצּוֹת הַזֶּה זְמַן חֵרוּתֵנוּ (בְּאַהֲבָה) מִקְרָא־קֹדֶשׁ
זֵכֶר לִיצִיאַת מִצְרָיִם. כִּי־בָנוּ בָחַרְתָּ וְאוֹתָנוּ קִדַּשְׁתָּ מִכָּל הָעַמִּים.
(וְשַׁבָּת) וּמוֹעֲדֵי קָדְשְׁךָ (בְּאַהֲבָה וּבְרָצוֹן) בְּשִׂמְחָה וּבְשָׂשׂוֹן הִנְחַלְתָּנוּ.
בָּרוּךְ אַתָּה יְיָ מְקַדֵּשׁ (הַשַּׁבָּת וְ) יִשְׂרָאֵל וְהַזְּמַנִּים׃

Blessed is God, who chose us among all people to seek holiness through his commandments. With love, Thou hast given us, O Lord [Sabbaths for rest] festivals for joy—[this Sabath day and] this Passover Feast—this Feast of Freedom, a holy gathering to remember the Exodus from Egypt. Thou has chosen us and given us a heritage of [Sabbath and] festivals for joy and gladness. Blessed be God who has sanctified [the Sabbath and] Israel and the festive seasons.

opposite Embroidered, 19th-century cover for the *matzah* plate from India showing items used in the Seder free to indulge in the speculative explanations and commentaries, called *midrash*. There is much of this *midrash* in the Haggadah itself, as we shall see, and we can approach it best through the ancient version, amended here and there for special reasons.

But if the Bible passages should stay 'ancient' in English, the opposite is true of the blessings, the prayers and the affirmations of the Haggadah, where we want to stay faithful to the tradition and yet speak in an English that reflects our own voice. In offering a new translation of these passages, the most obvious criterion has been to make the English clear and forceful; but by the same token we have felt obliged to make the translation briefer in some places than the original. We want to be in tune with the generations before us; but the style of the original is often so long-winded—so elaborate and repetitious—that to hear it translated word for word into English robs it of the reverence and directness that we want to express. In the present translation, therefore, these sections of the Haggadah are sometimes 'slimmed down' to convey the emotion and purpose of each such passage, rather than presenting a full, pedantically literal translation which buries the *spirit* of the passage in endless quotation or euphuism.

If we read the Haggadah in the original—which is far the best way—everything rings true. If we read it (or parts of it) in English, at the Seder, it must also ring true. On every page, the original *in full* and a new—sometimes shorter—translation are alternatives.

And what about the songs? Here, above all, some attempt has to be made to convey the mood of the original imaginatively. Each song or chant has a style of its own, which is completely lost if a literal translation is presented. For one thing, the complicated allusions don't come through. For another, the rhythm of the original disappears beneath a mound of verbosity. There is no simple solution to this problem, but we have tried a fresh approach to some of the songs and chants, as the reader will see, offering a 'free version' side by side with some indication of the literal meaning. The songs will no doubt still be sung in the original; but the new versions in English may offer some idea of the mood—cheerful as well as reverent—which first inspired them.

A NOTE ON THE PRESENTATION

In this Haggadah, words in italics are instructions for the Seder. If in round brackets, they are interpolations by the translator.

A Note on the Translation

The full Haggadah text, presented here, includes narratives, blessings, prayers, affirmations, Bible passages (especially Psalms), rabbinic arguments and songs. Though most of it is in Hebrew (the rest in Aramaic), it is Hebrew of many periods and styles. Read and understood in the original, it all harmonizes because of the 'inter-echoes' of the tradition: one period draws on another, there is endless allusion which the historic memory takes for granted. Archaism is no hindrance: it is indeed part of the appeal when one is reading the original. But how is one to convey the flavour of this for those who wish to read the Haggadah—or part of it—in an English translation?

There is no real problem for the Psalms and other Bible passages. By using the King James (or Authorized) Version as a basis, one hears 'ancient' words which have entwined themselves into English literature with something of the same mysterious, evocative power that the original Bible exercises over Hebrew literature. The King James Version, like the original Hebrew, was archaic even when it was first written down. It is full of grace, poetry and reverence, and like the original, it speaks now with a richness that has grown with the centuries. Later versions have, of course, 'corrected' the translation here and there—or suggested new answers to some difficult problems in the text. But to try to apply these 'corrections' to the biblical passages quoted in the Haggadah would destroy the mood in which they are being quoted there. It so happens that the King James Version largely drew on rabbinic ideas of what the ancient biblical words meant. By using the King James Version, therefore, we come closest to preserving the loving intimacy which the rabbis had for the original. They did not always understand what each word of the Bible meant, and it was indeed partly because the text was often full of puzzles that they felt

Each participant (including children) must have a glass for wine: four cups of wine will be drunk—though not necessarily drained to the dregs. The wine need not be fermented, but should be 'special for Passover'. Red wine is customary, but at one period in mediaeval times white wine was advised by some to counter any possible association with the monstrous blood libel.

Ceremonies

The service begins with *Kiddush* (the blessing on wine), then *hors d'oeuvres* and linked rituals, after which we come to the Four Questions, the 'story' (leading to the Ten Plagues), the *Dayyenu* chant, the eating of bitter herbs and *haroset*, and then the meal.

At an early stage in the proceedings (immediately after the *hors d'oeuvres*), the host will have put aside half of the middle piece of *matzah*, which then becomes known as the *afikoman*. During the bustle of the meal, the children purloin the *afikoman* and hide it. It is usually recovered only after the children have been promised a ransom of presents. When recovered, a little piece of it is eaten by all present, and this officially concludes the eating—but not the drinking.

Following grace after meals, there are psalms, prayers and songs. Detailed instructions are given at the relevant places in the Haggadah.

'To Freedom!'–'To Peace!'

One of the main aims of this new presentation of the Haggadah is to help the celebrants to know where they are in the Service and what is going on.

The new translation (see the note which follows) should help; but it should be achieved, also, by the listing of the ceremonies around the Four Cups of wine, as shown in the contents page. Traditionally, the Order of Service (the word *seder* means 'order' in this sense) is set out in the Haggadah under fifteen headings. We show these traditional headings, of course; but as the Four Cups are one of the most ancient features of the Haggadah, we group the old headings around them. The religious affirmation with each cup of wine is also, in effect, a toast—'To Life!' 'To Freedom!' 'To Peace!' 'To Jerusalem!' The Seder takes clear shape arranged this way: two cups before, two cups after, and in between—the banquet.

opposite Introductory page to an 18th-century Haggadah inscribed by Abraham, scribe of Ehringen, Alt Breisach, Germany, showing order of the Seder and preparations

סימן לסדר של פסח
קדש
ורחץ
כרפס
יחץ
מגיד
רחצה
מוציא
מצה
מרור
כורך
שלחן עורך
צפון
ברך

הא
לחמא עניא
THIS

opposite Table set for the Seder

1. Bitter herbs (*maror*): Some grated horse-radish, in memory of the 'bitterness' of slavery in Egypt.
2. *Haroset:* A sweet paste made of apples, nuts and cinnamon, grated fine and mixed with a little wine; the purpose is to soften the bitterness of the *maror* and also to simulate the 'mortar' used by our ancestors in building work during the slavery in Egypt.
3. A bone: The portion of a shankbone of a lamb, with a little meat on it, roasted, in memory of the ancient Temple sacrifice.
4. A baked egg: Thought to symbolize the other Temple sacrifices at Passover time, and also, perhaps, as a symbol of mourning for the lost Temple. (An egg is a familiar mourning symbol in the East, and is the 'ritual' food eaten after a funeral. This may be the origin of the custom of serving hard-boiled eggs in salt-water as the first course of the meal itself; but the egg is also, of course, a widespread symbol of fertility for the spring season, as other folk-customs for this season indicate.)
5. Lettuce or celery: It will be dipped in salt-water at an early stage in the ceremonies; in origin it was the *hors d'oeuvres* leading directly to the meal. (A small dish of salt-water should be handy, for the dipping.)

The ingredients will be arranged on two dishes in front of the head of the household.

On the first dish (it can be a basket) will be three *matzahs*, covered with a pretty cloth. On the second dish (often a specially made *k'arah* or plate), the ingredients listed above will be arranged as follows:

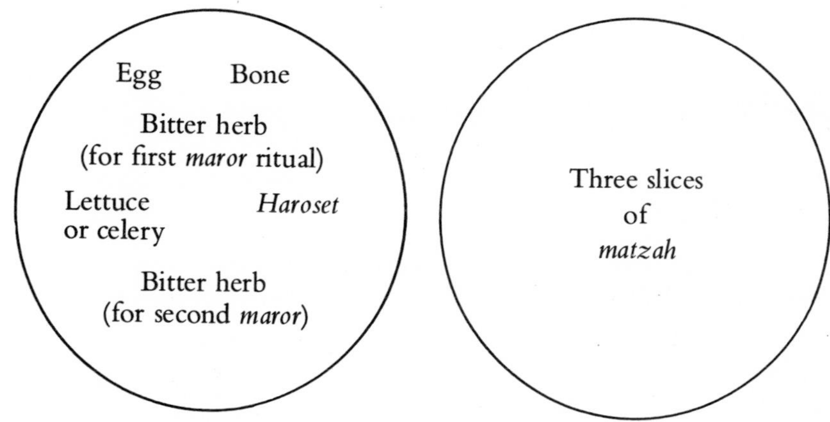

Guests for the Seder

Apart from the religious basis of the Seder, the most important ingredients are good company and good food. Both need a certain amount of advance preparation.

The company should, if at all possible, be built around the family, however scattered its members might normally be; but a Seder never achieves its full flavour unless there is also a good mixture of guests, preferably (as at any successful party) from a variety of backgrounds.

In planning the food and table-space, the hostess must always be able to accomodate unexpected last-minute guests. Part of this arises from the religious command to ensure that 'anyone who is hungry' can join the Seder. An open invitation covering this is recited in the Haggadah, before the ceremonies begin. An extra chair has to be provided also—as we shall see—for the prophet Elijah, who is expected by the tradition to appear one day as the precursor of the Messiah. But there will be other guests, too. It is very much in the spirit of the Seder to bring someone home from synagogue, or from the office, or from a chance encounter. One of the charms of the Seder is that non-Jews also often find this ceremony a heart-warming contact with Jewish life.

Festive Candles

As on Sabbath eve, the housewife will spread the table with a white cloth and light candles before the ceremonies begin. The blessing to accompany this ritual runs:

בָּרוּךְ אַתָּה יְיָ אֱלֹהֵינוּ מֶלֶךְ הָעוֹלָם אֲשֶׁר קִדְּשָׁנוּ בְּמִצְוֹתָיו
וְצִוָּנוּ לְהַדְלִיק נֵר שֶׁל [שַׁבָּת וְ] יוֹם טוֹב:

BLESSED BE GOD WHO HAS LED US TO HOLINESS THROUGH HIS COMMANDMENTS AND COMMANDED US TO KINDLE THE LIGHTS OF [SABBATH AND] FESTIVALS.

In observant households, the host makes his own contribution to the sparkle of the evening by wearing a white *kittel* (long gown), which is both 'holy' and festive.

Food

The food should be, quite literally, a banquet, as it must have been to the ancient Israelites when the menu was *one whole lamb, roasted*. There are no ritual rules about the menu today, although for many people a first course of hard-boiled eggs in salt-water has become *de rigueur*, as explained below.

Seder Table

To set the Seder Table for the ceremonies, the housewife will acquire the following, in addition to *matzah* itself:

'Searching for the *Chametz*' by Picart

in living terms it helps to generate an air of sparkling freshness on Seder night. The more specific removal of *chametz* (food and dishes) will take place on the day before Passover. In observant households there is a ritual to seal this clearing-out process. On the night before, the head of the household does a formal search by candlelight to find any stray crumbs, some of which will be deposited deliberately so that they may be found. The crumbs are swept with a feather into a little box, and on the next morning all is burnt. There is a special prayer to go with this, followed by a solemn statement: 'May all leaven in my possession, whether I have seen it or not, or whether I have removed it or not, be annulled and considered as dust of the earth.'

opposite A 19th-century ceramic Seder dish from Potylicz, Poland, a town which specialized in Passover ware

doubt for those abroad about the actual day of the new moon in the Holy Land, especially for Jews further afield in Egypt or Asia Minor. Accordingly, the rabbis ordained that the Jews in exile (the *Galut*) should have the festival extended to eight days instead of seven—from the fifteenth of Nisan to the twenty-second. This would give leeway to ensure that the exact period in the Holy Land was properly covered. In the Holy Land, only the first day and the last day of the seven were holy (with work forbidden), as laid down in the Bible. With the eight day period in the *Galut*, the first two and the last two were to be holy, with only four 'semi-holy' days in between.

Later, when astronomical calculations made it possible to know everywhere when it was new moon in the Holy Land, the rabbis nevertheless maintained the custom of having two holy days at the beginning and two at the end in the *Galut*. This meant, of course, having two 'first days' for Passover, and consequently two Seder nights.

In Israel, the old rule of one first day (and only one Seder) still operates. There are some Jews in the *Galut* who think it sensible, under modern conditions, to keep in line with practice in Israel and therefore keep only one Seder. But most prefer to follow the rabbinical ordinance, now hallowed by centuries of tradition.

To fit the lunar calendar to the solar calendar, the rabbis introduced an extra lunar month (an extra Adar) every few years, just before the Passover month of Nisan. The determining factor used to be—and still is—to ensure that by the time Passover comes, the crops will be ripe enough for the Jews to regard Passover as a spring festival. In practice it works out that the first night of Passover is always on the first full moon immediately after the spring equinox.

Prohibition of 'Leaven' *(chametz)*

The biblical command does not only point to the eating of *matzah* on Passover. In its full form, it orders the removal from the household for the duration of the festival of all leavened food (*chametz*), and all dishes and utensils that have been 'connected' with *chametz* during the rest of the year.

Chametz covers any fermented product of grain. To ensure that contact with *chametz* should not be made accidentally, virtually everything for Passover is made separately, under strict supervision; and observant households will put away all their 'normal' dishes at Passover time and use special Passover dishes.

As a basis for this, the home will be thoroughly spring-cleaned well in advance. The purpose is deeply religious in origin, but

חג
המצות

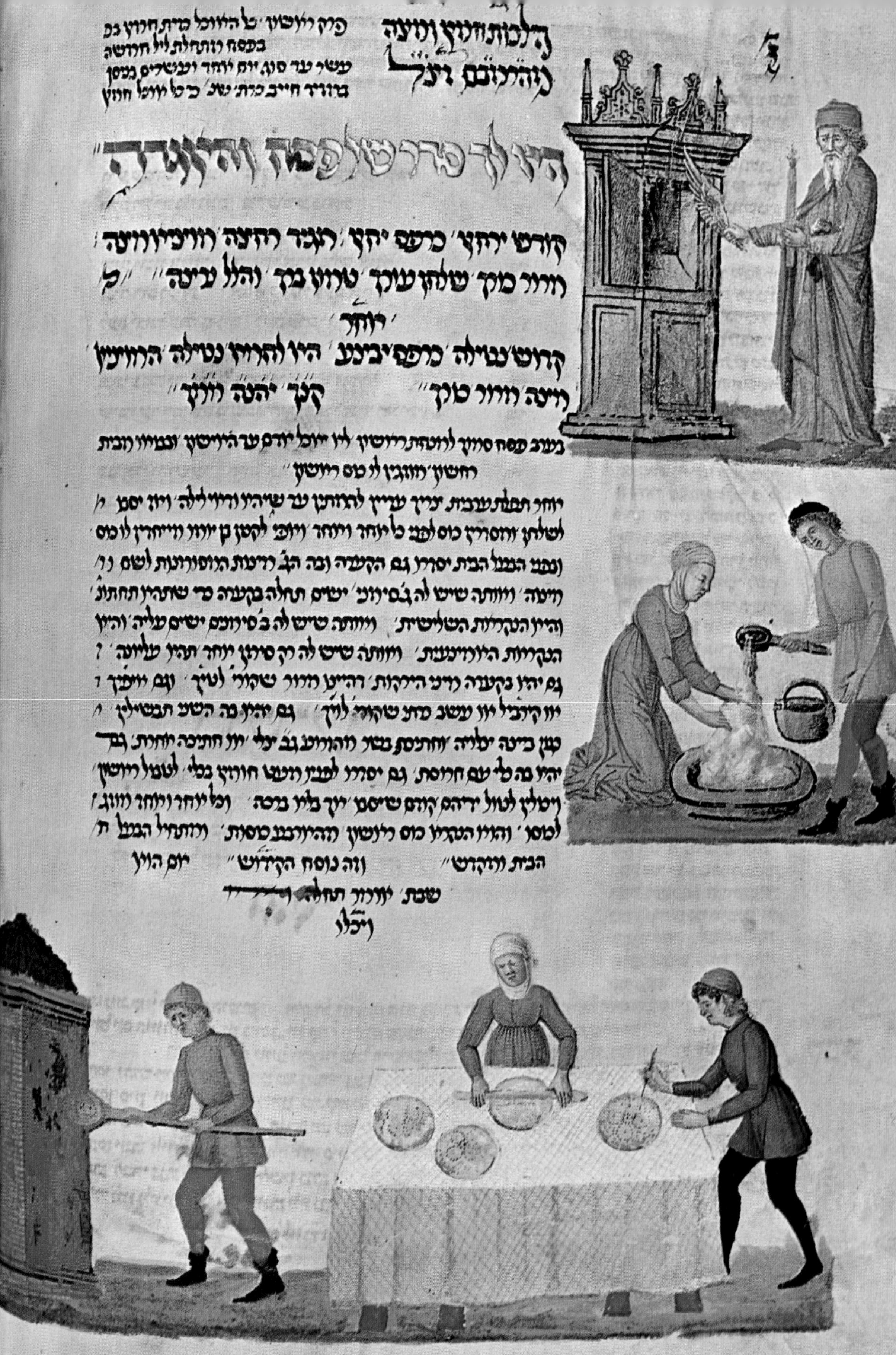

הא לך סדר של פסח והאגדה

קדש ורחץ כרפס יחץ מגיד רחצה מוציא מצה

מרור כורך שלחן עורך צפון ברך הלל נרצה

Preparations for the Seder

From time immemorial, Jews have celebrated Passover in memory of their liberation from slavery in Egypt, as described in the book of Exodus in the Bible. Throughout the festival, *matzah* (unleavened bread) is eaten instead of ordinary bread, to recall the hurried baking of *matzah* during the Exodus itself. The Bible tells us that on the last night in Egypt each Jewish household ritually slaughtered a lamb and then consumed it at a family gathering. This ritual was commemorated in Temple times by each householder in the sacrifice of a lamb at the Temple on Passover Eve. The lamb was then eaten at a festive gathering of the family or by a group of friends, who spent the evening recalling the memory of the historic deliverance with prayers and psalms. This banquet—reverent in purpose and joyful in practice—has been perpetuated through the ages in the Seder ceremony.

opposite Preparations for the Seder from the Haggadah chapter in the Rothschild Miscellany (northern Italy, *ca.* 1470)

The Haggadah is the book which gradually emerged over the centuries, fixing the rituals of the Seder. Details of the history behind the Haggadah are given in the chapters at the other end this book.

One Seder Night or Two Seder Nights

According to the Bible, Passover begins on the fifteenth day of the month of Nisan and lasts for seven days. In Jewish ceremony, a festive day (such as Sabbath or Passover) begins at sunset on the previous evening. The sacrifice and the eating of the lamb were therefore on the night of the fourteenth day of the month.

The Hebrew months are organized on a lunar basis, each beginning with the new moon, so that the evening of the fourteenth was always full moon. In early times, when the determination of the arrival of the new moon was by observation only, the authorities in Palestine went to great trouble to spread the decision on timing by messengers or fire-signals, which could quickly reach as far as their fellow-Jews in Babylonia; but there could still be some

The Seder Service

Introduction

Preparations for the Seder 8
A Note on the Translation 18

The Seder

20

1. THE FIRST CUP 'TO LIFE!'
Sanctification . . . . קַדֵּשׁ
Wash the hands . . . . וּרְחַץ
Celery or lettuce . . . . כַּרְפַּס
Divide the *matzah* . . . . יַחַץ

2. THE SECOND CUP 'TO FREEDOM!'
Four Questions and The Story . . . מַגִּיד
Wash the hands . . . . רָחְצָה
Blessings on the *matzah* . . . . מוֹצִיא מַצָּה
Bitter herb . . . . מָרוֹר
Bitter herb and *matzah* . . . . . כּוֹרֵךְ

Dinner is Served שֻׁלְחָן עוֹרֵךְ

3. THE THIRD CUP 'TO PEACE!'
Afikoman . . . . צָפוּן
Grace after the meal . . . . בָּרֵךְ

4. THE FOURTH CUP 'TO JERUSALEM!'
Psalms . . . . הַלֵּל
Envoi . . . . נִרְצָה

followed by
THE SONGS 83

A depiction of Kiddush at the Seder from *Sefer Haminhagim* (Amsterdam, 1768). Note the 'Four Sons' sitting between their parents.

הגדה של פסח

PASSOVER HAGGADAH

עם תרגום חדש מאת חיים רפאל

with a new translation by Chaim Raphael

הרג בכוריהם
ולא נתן לנו
את ממונם
נתן לנו את ממונם
ולא קרע לנו
את הים
קרע לנו את הים
ולא העבירנו
בתוכו בחרבה

opposite Seder scene from the Darmstadt Haggadah

overleaf Part of '*Dayyenu*' from the Mocatta Haggadah (Spain, 13th century) with the key words incorporated in the decorative borders: '*ilu lo*' ('if he had not') on the right and '*dayyenu*' ('it would have been sufficient') on the left

הגדה של פסח

PASSOVER HAGGADAH

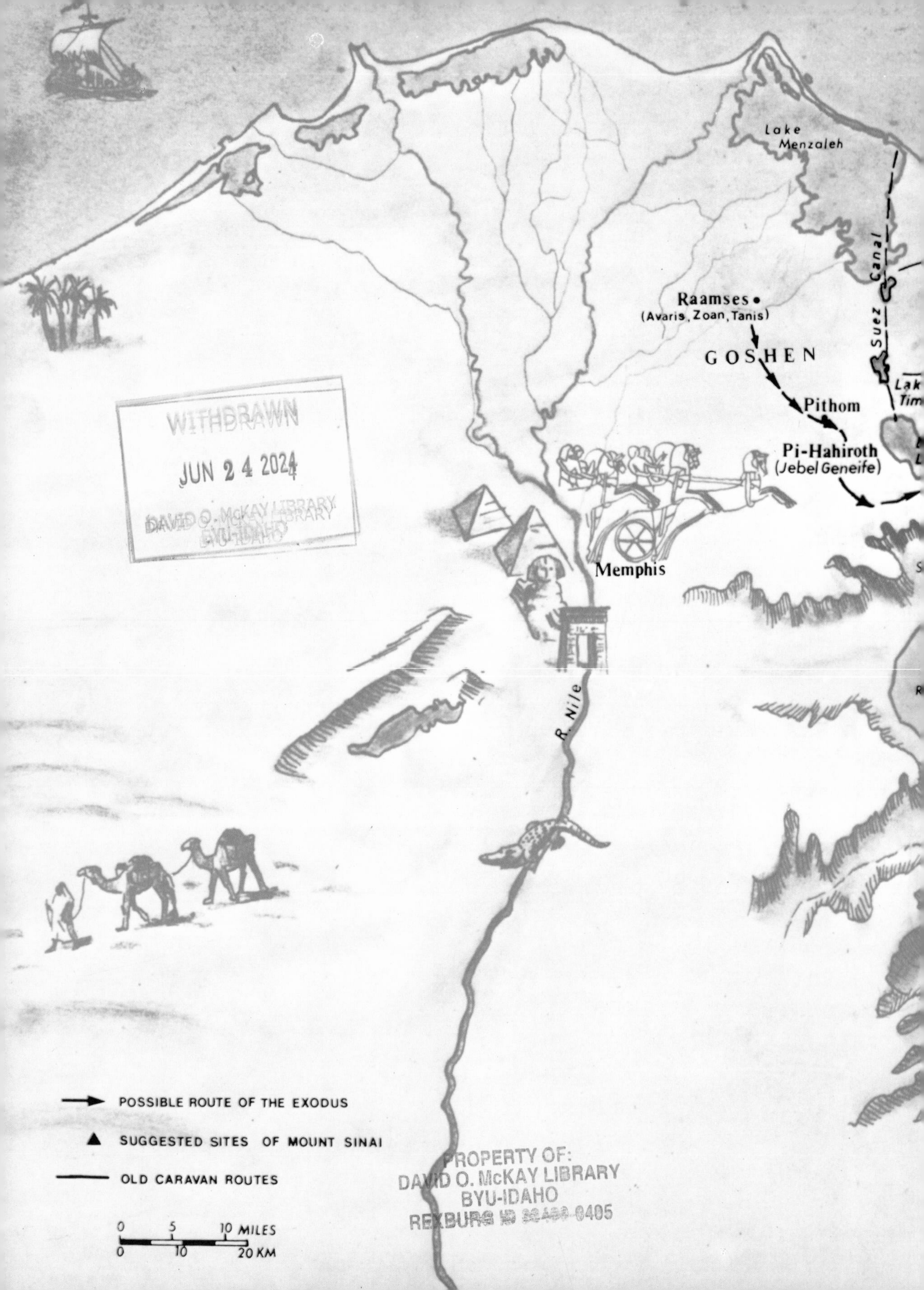

Lake Menzaleh
Suez Canal
Raamses
(Avaris, Zoan, Tanis)
GOSHEN
Pithom
Pi-Hahiroth
(Jebel Geneife)
Memphis
R. Nile
POSSIBLE ROUTE OF THE EXODUS
SUGGESTED SITES OF MOUNT SINAI
OLD CARAVAN ROUTES
0 5 10 MILES
0 10 20 KM